Advance Praise for Leigh Burgess

"Leigh is a once-in-a-lifetime leader, an extraordinary entrepreneur, and human being. In over a decade of coaching high-performing professionals, I've encountered very few people with her unique blend of brilliance, drive, and heart. She has an uncanny ability to set bold goals and bring them to life with impressive speed, creativity, and joy, what I can only describe as her 'secret sauce'.

But what truly sets Leigh apart is not just her business acumen, it's who she is: generous, grounded, and always shining her light to uplift those around her. No ask is ever too big, she leads with unmatched kindness and generosity, and the world is better for having her in it. We need more leaders like Leigh, and I'm grateful she's sharing her wisdom through her books and coaching to show us what's possible when we lead with purpose, heart, and bold vision."

—Amina AlTai, Executive Coach, Speaker,
and *USA Today* Bestselling Author

"Leigh's Bold Framework is more than a concept, it's a catalyst. Through my role at Zoom Video Communications, I lead Women in Leadership roundtables and thought leadership events, where her work has helped women identify their core values, confront what holds them back, and reflect on the bold steps they didn't take, and why. Leigh empowers you to move forward with clarity and confidence. Her insights have sparked meaningful change in our community and in me personally. Bold isn't just a trait, it's a practice. Leigh shows us how."

—Janine Moreno, CIO Advisor,
Zoom Video Communications

"Leigh has a remarkable ability to bring out the best in others by asking the right questions, offering meaningful insights, and creating a space where individuals feel seen, heard, and challenged to grow. Her coaching style is both empowering and results-driven, helping others gain clarity, build confidence, and reach their goals. Leigh's impact as a coach is profound, and those who have the opportunity to learn from her are truly fortunate."

—Ardaman Singh, CHRO,
Greater Somerset County YMCA

"Leigh has had a profound impact on both my personal and professional growth. Through the Bold Leaders Collective, multiple Bold Tables, Bold Retreats, and the Bold Summit, every interaction with Leigh has been deeply meaningful and transformative. Her leadership, coaching, and unwavering support have helped me gain clarity, build confidence, and reach goals I once only imagined. I've made lifelong connections and experienced real growth as a direct result of her influence. Her book, *Be Bold Today*, is a powerful and practical framework that continues to shape how I show up in the world. If you have the chance to work with Leigh or attend one of her events, take it. She's an extraordinary leader, mentor, and friend."

—Melissa Cohen, Owner,
MBC Consulting Solutions, LLC

"Leigh has given the world an opportunity to redefine what being 'Bold' means as we each go through our own personal journey. Through the BOLD framework in her book, as well as coaching, Bold Tables and her Bold Mastermind Program, she has inspired me to take my next bold step! Truly life changing and something I am forever grateful for!"

—Christie Burke,
Sales Executive, Zoom

"Simply put, Leigh changes the lives of everyone she works with. Experiencing a Bold Retreat, group coaching and later on becoming a member of the Bold Leaders Collective, has set me on a course that deep down I felt was out of reach for me. Leigh's approach and the network she's curating help open your mind to what's possible and give you the courage to be bold in pursuit of your professional and personal dreams."

—Mary Garrick, Owner & Chief Strategist,
Mainstay Creative

"Leigh has tapped into a need and an opportunity to empower us, especially women, to be our best selves, and to trust that we have what we need to be that boldly and without apology."

—Susan P. Landis, Executive Director,
Association of Clinical Research Professionals

"I discovered Leigh Burgess and her remarkable BOLD community. I knew that both Leigh and her community were something I needed to be a part of. What sets Leigh's BOLD community apart is its ability to foster deep connections that go beyond the superficial. I am forever grateful to have been connected to some of the best people through Leigh, forging authentic relationships with women who embody living life boldly. These are genuine connections with individuals who not only live boldly themselves but also inspire others to embrace their unique versions of boldness. I am here for the long term and eagerly anticipate continuing to build connections that unite, inspire, and elevate!"

—Kate Speer, Open to Amazing,
Kate Stefko Speer, LLC

"Leigh curates bold, a boldness releasing the greatest potential of individuals and organizations aligned with their purpose. Leigh's bold approach surfaces what you want and why you want it and then empowers you to achieve success."

—Stacy Olinger, Founder and CEO,
Caleb Healthcare Group

"The BOLD Retreat happened almost by chance, when an invite appeared right at the time of feeling professionally burnt out. Joining a true community of smart and passionate women looking to shift and step up in their lives, professionally, personally, physically, made me realize I did not need to play safe, and that the future is what I make it to be. For those sleepwalking through this one precious life, joining the community helps you wake up while there's still time to realize, I am more than enough, I am here for a purpose. Leigh models the actions that inspire, motivate, and encourage each step forward. Highly recommend all things BOLD, as life is better when you live out loud."

—Nancy Paynter, Life Science and
Digital Innovation Leader

"Leigh has a craft that is very special . . . she helps women see their value through BOLD lenses. My first interaction with Leigh was registering for her first BOLD retreat and taking advantage of a special offering for executive coaching. I had no idea what a great decision that would be! Having an outside view of your challenges helps to identify ways to approach and advance your BOLD journey!"

—Christine Chandler, COO/CCO,
M&T Realty Capital

"Leigh has a talent for inspiring and motivating others. Her positive energy is infectious, and it has the power to uplift and drive you to achieve your full potential. Whether it's through heartfelt words of encouragement or leading by example, Leigh empowers individuals to embrace their strengths and overcome any obstacles they might face."

—Nadine Lavigne, Member of the
Bold Leaders Collective

"Leigh Burgess is the epitome of *bold*. She's courageous, uplifting, and honest, and an incredible coach. She is such an inspiration and someone who I truly admire."

—Alissa Randall, All About Headshots, CEO

"Leigh is a dynamic leader who deeply cares about individuals. She has an ability to help so many people accomplish their goals and work through whatever is standing in their way."

—Amanda Slavin, Cofounder of LearningFREQUENCY
and Author of *The Seventh Level*

"Witnessing, hearing, and reading Leigh's expressions of her journey to her-self is impactful, insightful, and inspirational."

—Carolyn Carpenter, Healthcare Executive

"There's a growth mindset, and then there is the BOLD mindset. Leigh shows us how intentional focus, bravery, and the support of community creates the '*you*' you knew you always could be."

—Denise Brown, MD, Health Care
C-Level Executive and Board Member

"Leigh's guidance, methodologies, community, and curation have given me the tools, support, and accountability that I needed to level up key areas of my life. I started my engagement with Leigh on a Bold Retreat. I was able to successfully meet these goals and continue to expand. I have never been happier and contribute much to the work with Leigh."

—Sarah Owen, Chief Product Officer, One Inc.

"BOLD has been an empowering community, from the curated events that Leigh produces to the interactions with extraordinary members who care, help, and share their experiences to support your leadership journey."

—Mirna Eusebio Lithgow,
Founder and CEO, LeapView Group

"I have had the pleasure of knowing Leigh for over 10 years. My appreciation of her has deepened as the years have passed. Her ability to bring together people who can learn, grow, and laugh together has been wonderful to watch and experience."

—Tracy Gosselin, Chief Nursing Executive,
Memorial Sloan Kettering Cancer Center

"Leigh inspires me to live a bold life and take action. Life is too short to be anything less than the boldest version of ourselves!"

—Nick Hutchison, Founder of BookThinkers
and Bestselling Author of *Rise of the Reader*

THE BOLD LEADER

THE BOLD LEADER

DECIDE WHAT MATTERS AND DELIVER WHAT COUNTS

LEIGH BURGESS

Foreword by Cassandra Worthy

WILEY

Published by John Wiley & Sons, Inc., Hoboken, New Jersey.
Published simultaneously in Canada.

For general information on our other products and services or for technical support, please contact our Customer Care Department within the United States at (800) 762-2974, outside the United States at (317) 572-3993 or fax (317) 572-4002.

Wiley also publishes its books in a variety of electronic formats. Some content that appears in print may not be available in electronic formats. For more information about Wiley products, visit our web site at www.wiley.com.

Library of Congress Cataloging-in-Publication Data is Available:

ISBN 9781394343478 (Cloth)
ISBN 9781394343485 (ePub)
ISBN 9781394343492 (ePDF)

Cover Design. Leigh Burgess
Author Photo: © Mayah Burgess
Printed and bound by CPI Group (UK) Ltd, Croydon, CR0 4YY
C9781394343378_031025

This book is dedicated to bold leaders everywhere–to those who bravely step forward into the unknown, and see the power of possibility through the lens of their bold belief.

To my daughter, my boldest partner–May you always listen to your heart, trust your vision, and never doubt just how extraordinary you truly are. In so many ways, you've become my greatest teacher without even knowing it.

To my husband, my best friend and constant source of strength–Your belief, patience, quiet strength, and unwavering love have been the foundation of every bold step I've taken since we met. Life is better and bolder because of you.

To my mom and dad, sisters, and brother–Thank you for showing me what courage, resilience, and unconditional support truly look like. Your belief has given me the courage to dream bigger and live bolder.

May we all keep moving boldly, one courageous choice at a time.

Contents

Foreword

I almost quit.

It was the aftermath of a multi-billion-dollar acquisition, and the air was thick with uncertainty. I was burned out, frustrated, and refreshing a pro/con list of quitting in my mind on the daily. On paper, I had it together. Inside, the quit pros were piling up and I was unraveling.

That moment became my pivot.

Instead of walking away, inspired by a mentor, I got curious. I started listening to the emotional friction I was feeling, the discomfort, the pressure, the resistance, and I began to see it not as weakness, but as data. As signals guiding me into an opportunity to choose how I experienced the uncertainty surrounding me. Then my career catapulted. And my making that mental shift was the exact moment *Change Enthusiasm*® was born, a neuroscience-backed mindset which I'm beyond grateful has transcended into a movement helping leaders around the world meet constant change and the emotion it inspires with intention, agency, and growth.

Every leader today is facing their opportunity to choose how they will show up for themselves and those they lead. That's why this book matters.

The BOLD Leader isn't just a leadership book, it's a full-system reset. Leigh Burgess has done something rare, she's built a model that demonstrates the power of authentic leadership in the face of relentless change, emotionally, cognitively, and strategically. By weaving in how our brains actually process bold decisions, she equips leaders to move from reactive habits to intentional action, measuring what truly matters, not just what shows up on the everyday dashboard.

Leigh doesn't offer feel-good soundbites or quick fixes. She offers process, structure, and rhythm, tools that help you shift from stuck to in motion, from burnout to belief, from performance to purposeful alignment.

What I love most is that Leigh never tries to remove the hard parts. She honors them. She teaches leaders to partner with discomfort rather than push it away. She celebrates the power and importance of mindset, in fact, she breaks down why it's where true alignment and fulfillment begin. Her BOLD Framework doesn't just sit in theory, it moves. It's something you can feel and see. And her D90 Method takes what feels overwhelming and makes it tangible, actionable, and real.

But here's what sets Leigh apart, she doesn't just lead differently, she *lives* differently. She walked away from a life that checked all the boxes but cost too much of her truth. She's built a company, a movement, and a message by choosing alignment over approval, every single time. And what she's laid out in this book is the same roadmap that helped her rebuild her own operating system.

As a female founder and author, I know first-hand the intention and focus at play when one strives to bring to life the methods leaned upon to champion their own life with the hope it can help another.

That is the intention and focus powering the methods, insights, and strategies within the pages that follow.

If you've felt the inner tension that something in your leadership needs to evolve as the pace of change and uncertainty accelerate or you've sensed that your calendar is full but your energy is depleted, this book is your companion. Leigh doesn't just meet you where you are, she reminds you of where you're capable of going.

This isn't about fearless leadership.

It's about *honest* leadership.

And that kind of leadership changes everything.

So take a breath. Turn the page. The next bold chapter of your leadership journey starts right here.

Let's get it!

—Cassandra Worthy

Introduction

You did not pick up this book by chance.

You are here because you are already leading.

It is a team, a business, a vision, or it is the quiet, daily decision to show up when it would be easier to shrink back. Whatever the setting, your choices ripple outward. People look to you. Outcomes depend on you. And that weight? I know it well.

Because I have been where you are.

Not leading from a title, but from the thick of it.

When the pressure is real.

When the stakes are high.

When the answers aren't obvious and the voices around can be loud.

This book is not about the kind of leadership that rewards performance or perfection. It is not about mastering someone else's blueprint or pretending to have it all figured out.

It is about something far more powerful:

Leadership that is true to who you are.

Leadership that is fully aligned with your values.

Not fearless, but fiercely present.

Not loud, but unmistakably clear.

The world needs leaders who are willing to show up real, ready, and willing to choose courage over certainty.

If that is what you are here for, you are not just ready to lead. You are ready to lead boldly.

And that is exactly what we are going to do, together.

Everyone's leadership journey is unique and not many start at the top. My first job was mowing lawns. Later, I unloaded trucks for FedEx and UPS, often the only woman on the shift. I became the only woman promoted to lead the overnight operation, directing a crew that processed hundreds of thousands of packages nightly.

I worked my way up through schools, hospitals, and research centers, collecting every lesson, every challenge, every hard-earned win, and building a career that never fit neatly into any box.

But even as I climbed, I realized I was not following the traditional playbook. I have always felt a little outside of "the popular leader club." Different. I was open to failure, willing to try new things, move faster, and would say the unpopular thing. I stood up for what was right even when it conflicted with organizational politics. I took big swings to create better outcomes.

At times, I felt like I did not fit the mold of what was expected of me. I felt at times, I was expected to keep my head down, go along with the popular vote and fall in line when directed.

And to be honest? I am glad I did not fit in.

Because I believe that bold leadership is not about checking boxes or fitting neatly anywhere.

"Bold leadership is not a one-time act of courage, it is a muscle, built decision by decision, through insight, intention, and practice."

It is about standing strong in the messy moments and choosing to move forward anyway.

It is trusting your voice even when fear is loud.

It is building something meaningful, especially when it's hard or uncertain.

And if I have learned anything, it is this: bold leadership does not come from perfect timing, perfect plans, or perfect confidence. It comes from learning how to act with clarity, courage, and conviction, especially when fear is in the room.

Every journey that matters begins at the edge of your comfort zone. As soon as you decide that good enough, average, and mediocre will not guide you to greatness, you open yourself to powerful new possibilities.

That is exactly why I wrote this book.

It will not give you another set of rules or tell you how to look more confident on the surface. Instead, I want to give you a real, practical framework you can lean on when things get tough. I will show you how to use fear as fuel, how to keep moving forward even when you are unsure, and how to define success in your way, not by someone else's checklist.

You do not need permission.

You just need to *decide*.

Then take action.

No one can make you bold.

It is your *choice*.

What Bold Leadership Means to Me

Let me paint a picture for you.

You are sitting at the head of the table. Everyone is looking at you, not just for answers, but for direction. The room is tense. The stakes are high. And the truth is: you do not have all the answers. But you do have something more valuable.

Clarity.

You are locked in on your goals.

And you are willing to take action.

That is bold leadership.

It does not wait for all the data or depend on perfect certainty.

It steps in when others stall out.

It says, "This is what we know. Here is what we are going to do next."

Bold leadership is not about being louder. It is not about titles or always knowing what to say. It is about showing up clearly when it counts and doing the hard things others avoid.

Let me show you what that looks like in real life:

- When your team is stuck spinning in analysis, you draw a line, set a deadline, and move forward.

- When a project is unraveling, you do not double down to protect pride, you make the call to stop.

- When someone is not delivering, you step in early and have the direct conversation no one else will.

- When a new opportunity shows up and everyone hesitates, you trust your instincts and take the lead.

- And when your values and the profitable path collide, you choose alignment because long-term trust beats short-term gain.

This is leadership with weight behind it. Leadership that does not rely on noise, but on knowing.

It is not reactive. It is responsive.

It is not about constantly pushing, it is about knowing when to press and when to pause.

This is what I call operational boldness.

Less about the speech. More about the choice.

Less about being impressive. More about being intentional.

Bold leaders do not just create results.

They build trust, momentum, and a ripple effect that outlasts any one meeting, moment, or title.

That is the kind of leadership this book will help you claim.

Decision by decision.

Moment by moment.

Exactly where you are.

Why This Book Exists

This book began with one unshakable truth: Playing it safe is no longer safe.

In a world moving faster by the day, more noise, more pressure, more uncertainty, *waiting* feels like the responsible thing to do. But hesitation? It is expensive.

Not just in missed opportunities, but in clarity, momentum, and trust.

We have been sold a version of leadership that says:

Wait until you are 100% sure.

Play it safe until the room agrees.

Hold the role, even if you are crumbling inside.

That is not leadership. That is performance.

And it is exhausting.

This book is about something far more powerful.

Leadership that is rooted in truth, guided by aligned action, and brave enough to move, *even when certainty never shows up.*

Because bold leadership looks different.

It is not louder. Not tougher. Not shinier.

It is clearer.

More intentional.

More grounded in what matters most and more willing to deliver what actually counts, not just what looks good from the outside.

Let me be clear:

Bold leadership isn't about being fearless.

It's about being present with fear and still choosing to act.

It's not about having all the answers.

It's about having the courage to ask better questions, take the next step, and stay in integrity while you do it.

So how do you know if you are *actually* leading boldly?

How do you measure leadership in a way that goes beyond performance reviews, promotions, or profitability?

That is what this book is here to answer.

Because bold leadership is not just a mindset, it is a measurable, repeatable, and deeply human.

And it is the kind of leadership the world needs now.

The BOLD Leader: Decide What Matters and Deliver What Counts was born from one unshakable truth, that playing it safe is no longer safe.

"In a world of constant disruption, noise, complexity, and acceleration, hesitation will cost you far more than a bold move ever could."

And yet, so much leadership advice still clings to tired myths: Wait until you are sure. Play it safe until you have all the answers. Perform the role even if you are doubting everything inside.

You will not find that advice here.

This book is about a different kind of leadership, a leadership rooted in truth, aligned action, and the courage to move even when certainty is impossible. The traits of a bold leader are different and different for a reason (Figure 0.1). You do not need to be louder, flashier, or tougher to lead boldly. You need to be clear, aligned, committed to what matters most and brave enough to deliver what counts, not just what is expected.

Bold leadership is not about fearlessness. It is about fear presence.

It is about leading through fear, not away from it.

The ⑤ Traits of Bold Leadership

Risk Strategist
Treats uncertainty as strategic capital.

Vision Mapper
Turns bold ideas into data-driven roadmaps.

Resilience Builder
Harvests failures as engines for growth.

Network Weaver
Co-creates value through strategic alliances.

Trust Builder
Creates the safe space that fuels bold action.

Figure 0.1 The 5 Traits of Bold Leadership

But, how do you know if you are leading boldly? How do you measure growth that goes beyond traditional success metrics? What I have learned is that discomfort is not danger, it is data.

Bold Brain 101

Let us start with something simple and true.

You cannot lead boldly if you do not understand how your brain works.

Not because you are doing it wrong—but because, biologically speaking, your brain is wired to resist boldness.

Its number one job. To protect you.

Not to innovate, speak up, take a risk, or challenge the status quo.

Your brain is designed to keep you safe. To keep you alive.

That is why fear shows up before big decisions.

Why you feel tension before trying something new.

Why your mind races when you are about to say what no one else will say.

It is not a flaw in your character.

It is a feature of your biology.

Over millions of years, your brain has evolved to detect danger, avoid risk, and repeat patterns that feel familiar, even if those patterns no longer serve you. This is part of something called negativity bias: our built-in tendency to focus more on what could go wrong than what could go right.

Negativity bias once kept us alive when we lived in caves.

Today, it is what fuels imposter syndrome, overthinking, self-doubt, and the tendency to over-index on playing it safe.

But here is the bold opportunity: Your brain can change.

Thanks to neuroplasticity, we now know that the brain is adaptable. Every time you make a bold move, even a small one, you start rewiring your brain. You create new neural pathways that build your tolerance for risk, your clarity under pressure, and your confidence in the unknown.

And each time you pause to reflect on what worked, what mattered, what aligned, you strengthen the parts of your brain that drive wise, intentional leadership.

In fact, the prefrontal cortex, the brain's center for decision-making, focus, and executive function, can become more efficient through reflective practice. The more we engage with risk in meaningful ways, the more our brain learns to view challenge not as a threat, but as a growth opportunity.

Once you understand how your brain works, everything changes.

Your decisions become sharper.

Your fear loses its grip.

And boldness stops being something you try on, it becomes the way you lead.

Throughout this book, I will share practical, science-backed tools to help you recognize your brain's patterns under stress and show you how to shift them, moment by moment.

You do not need a degree in neuroscience to lead boldly.

You just need to understand how your brain works and how boldness builds it stronger.

Once you do, everything changes.

Your decisions get clearer.

Your fear gets quieter.

And boldness becomes more than a one-time act.

It becomes your way of leading.

My Bold Beginning

I did not leave my corporate career because I had a shiny plan.

I left because I could not ignore the truth anymore.

After more than 20 years climbing the ranks, many titles, earning degrees, managing multi-million-dollar initiatives, I was supposed to feel successful. From the outside, I did. I had everything the world tells you to chase: a big role, big salary, big responsibility. The boxes were checked.

But inside?

I felt disconnected. Diminished.

Done.

I could not name it at first. I just knew something was off. I would sit in meetings and feel like a stranger to my own voice. My health was slipping, my joy had gone quiet, and the definition of leadership I was living did not match the one I believed in.

And so, I did something that made no sense on paper.

I walked away.

No safety net.

No next job lined up.

Just a quiet but unshakable belief that I could build something different and more importantly, that I *had* to.

That decision became the beginning of everything.

It led to the founding of Bold Industries Group, and the creation of the BOLD Framework (Believe, Own, Learn, Design) a leadership model born not from theory, but from necessity. At first, it was just for me. A way to find my footing again. A way to recover my clarity, my health, my voice.

But it did not stay just mine for long.

Because the more I shared my story, the more I heard the same words echoed back:

"I feel that way, too."

"I've been successful, but I don't feel successful."

"I don't want to keep performing, I want to lead with purpose."

Alongside my daughter, who shares this bold vision, we built a company around the kind of leadership that does not get taught in MBA programs or corporate playbooks.

Leadership that is deeply personal. Fiercely honest.

Rooted not in fearlessness, but in presence and courage.

Along the way, I earned three master's degrees, in health services administration, educational leadership, and human and organizational systems, not to prove anything, but to understand leadership from every angle. Now, with my doctorate nearly complete, I have realized something surprising:

The best leadership wisdom does not live in textbooks.

It lives in lived experience.

In the pivots.

In the quiet decisions no one sees.

In the moments when you choose alignment over applause.

Bold leadership does not rush to impress.

It listens carefully, moves deliberately, and speaks when it counts.

It is the ability to hold tension without breaking, to navigate challenges without losing your center.

It is not about having a perfect plan.

It is about making meaningful choices in real time, with courage, with care, and with a deep understanding of what truly matters.

If you have picked up this book you are ready to lead boldly.

In a way that honors your voice, your values, and your vision— you are in the right place.

Let us walk it out together, from page one.

Why Bold Metrics Matter

A few years ago, I sat in a leadership meeting surrounded by dashboards, rows of numbers, color-coded charts, quarterly KPIs glowing on the screen.

We were hitting the marks.

Revenue was up. Headcount had grown. Productivity looked solid.

But something felt off.

Morale was slipping. Turnover was rising. The team was quiet, too quiet. The kind of quiet that does not come from focus, but from fatigue.

No one on that dashboard could tell me the last time someone had taken a creative risk. Or had a hard conversation. Or made a decision aligned with our mission, even when it came at a cost.

That is when I realized: we were not measuring the things that actually made us strong.

We were tracking outcomes.

But we were not tracking leadership.

Bold leadership does not show up on a spreadsheet, at least not right away.

It shows up in moments. In choices. In the quiet pivots that happen long before a metric moves.

Traditional indicators, like revenue, market share, or headcount, are lagging signals. They tell you what already happened. But bold decisions happen upstream, in the uncertainty, the tension, the conversations most people avoid.

That is where real growth lives. And that is what Bold Metrics are designed to capture.

Bold Metrics: Measuring What Actually Moves You Forward

Traditional Metrics	Bold Metrics
Revenue	Conversations that challenged the status quo
Headcount	Decisions made in alignment with core values
Market Share	Risks taken before consensus
Productivity	Learning gained from failure or discomfort

These are not feel-good checklists.

They are bold check-ins.

At the end of each chapter, you will find questions designed to help you track your leadership in motion:

- What stretched you?
- What mattered most?
- What did you do when certainty was not available?

Think of these Bold Metrics as your leadership compass.

They help you notice the shift, not just after it has happened, but while it is happening.

Because boldness is not a one-time decision.

It is a discipline.

And what you choose to track becomes what you choose to strengthen.

How This Book Will Lead You

You will not just read about bold leadership here. You will build it. One decision, one conversation, one aligned action at a time.

This book is structured in four parts, each helping you grow as a bold leader from the inside out.

Part I: Bold Awareness

See what is holding you back so you can step into what is next.

I did not realize how much fear was running my decisions until I was praised for playing it safe. That moment hit differently. I had delivered a polished presentation, stayed within budget, avoided risk, and walked away knowing I had played small.

Bold leadership does not begin with action.

It begins with awareness.

Before you can lead differently, you have to see differently.

This section will help you recognize the quiet habits of self-protection that keep you from your boldest moves. You will learn to interpret fear not as a flaw but as a flare. And you will begin to understand the cost of staying in your comfort zone, one unmade decision at a time.

Chapters:

  1. Fear Is Fuel
  2. The Comfort Trap

Part II: Bold Activation

Shift from knowing what is true to acting on it.

The first time I used my voice in a high-stakes meeting, not to agree, but to challenge, I felt like I was shaking from the inside out.

But when the room got quiet and people leaned in, I knew something had shifted. I had not just spoken, I had led.

Awareness opens the door. But action builds the foundation.

This section is about moving from insight to implementation. You will develop the habits, tools, and mindset that help boldness become a repeatable, intentional practice. It is about building momentum, not waiting for the perfect moment.

Chapters:

3. The Bold Advantage

4. Activate Your Bold

5. The D90 Method

Part III: Bold Action

Move with clarity, courage, and trust in your own voice.

Boldness sounds great in theory, until you're standing at the edge of an unpopular decision or facing a room that disagrees.

I have been there, heart pounding, making the call anyway. Not because I had all the answers, but because I knew what mattered most.

This section is where boldness leaves the page and enters the room.

You will learn how to have the conversations most people avoid, how to navigate setbacks without losing your center, and how to trust your instincts when there is no playbook to follow.

Chapters:

  6. Bold Comebacks

  7. Bold Conversations

  8. Bold Data, Instinct, and Courage

Part IV: Bold Alignment

Staying bold as a habit, not a moment.

Boldness does not live in the big keynote or the first launch. It shows up in how you recalibrate after failure, how you stay steady during change, and how you lead when no one is watching.

After I walked away from the C-suite, it was not the bold leap that shaped me, it was the thousand smaller choices that followed. This section is about designing leadership that lasts: clear rhythms, sustainable strategies, and a new way to measure what really counts.

Chapters:

  9. Bold On Repeat

  10. The Bold Leader's Secret

Tools in This Book

This is not a book you read and forget. It is a leadership toolkit designed to create real change in how you lead.

At the end of every chapter, you will find four tools to help you immediately integrate what you have learned:

- **What You Just Learned:** Key bold takeaways to lock in the chapter's core ideas.

- **Bold Truth:** A single distilled insight to carry forward.

- **Your Bold Move:** A real action or reflection to make boldness a daily habit, not a distant goal.

- **Bold Metrics:** Core metrics that enable you to measure what matters most for lasting results.

You will also find Bold Action Moments (BAMs) flagged throughout; these are critical leadership moments when your boldness will be tested and called forward. Think of them as your real-time leadership labs.

This book works only if you work. Every tool, every question, every metric is designed to move you from just reading about bold leadership to living it.

One Last Thing Before We Begin

If you are holding this book, chances are, you are already at the edge of something important. A shift. A knowing. A quiet sense (or maybe a loud one) that the way you have been leading is not fully aligned anymore.

Maybe you are craving more clarity. More boldness. Maybe you are tired of chasing someone else's definition of success. Maybe you have started asking: Is there another way to lead?

There is.

And it starts here, with you.

You do not need to wait for the perfect title, timing, or permission. The bold leader you are searching for is already inside you. The question is not whether you are capable. The question is: *Are you ready to act on it?*

Bold leaders do something different. They choose direction over delay. They embrace risk when it matters. They step forward when others freeze. They trade perfection for progress, and they lead with a kind of clarity that does not demand consensus to be powerful.

And most of all?

They build momentum in moments just like this, when the next step is not fully mapped, but the call to move is undeniable.

Before you begin, pause for just a moment.

Ask yourself: Where am I playing small? Where have I been waiting instead of leading? What bold move has been whispering to me, asking for my attention?

Write it down. Say it out loud. Acknowledge it.

Because this book is not just something to read, it is something to respond to.

A mirror. A map. A moment.

From this point forward, consider this your permission slip, your turning point, and your next bold move. Let's begin, intentionally, and all in.

Part I

Bold Awareness

Learn to See Fear as Information and Break Free From Your Comfort Zone

Ready to challenge what is quietly holding you back? In this foundational section, you will dive deep into understanding how hidden fears and deceptive comfort shape your leadership style. Learn how to transform fear from an obstacle into your most insightful guide. Uncover the subtle traps of comfort zones and break through invisible barriers, reshaping your leadership in truly bold, intentional ways.

Chapter 1

Fear Is Fuel

L et's start here, not with confidence or certainty, but with the moment most leadership books skip over.

The moment you take that deep breath.

Your heart pounds.

Your thoughts race.

And you ask yourself, What if I get this wrong?

> "Every bold decision starts with the courage to listen to fear but not be led by it."

I've been in that moment. More than once.

In boardrooms where the stakes were high, the air thick with expectation.

I was not afraid of presenting, I was afraid of being found out. That somehow, someone would see past the résumé, the extensive experience and into the part of me that still questioned if I belonged there.

It was fear I felt.

And that is exactly where bold leadership begins.

It was supposed to be just another leadership meeting. Slide decks ready, data points lined up—your typical leaning more safe than bold recommendations prepared. But standing there, facing a decision that would redefine the organization's future, I knew this was different. A hinge point. The kind of moment where your next choice echoes far beyond the room.

The traditional playbook was clear: Pause. Gather more data. Build consensus. Wait for greater certainty.

But I also knew what that approach would cost. Momentum. Trust. Impact. The real risk was not in moving boldly, it was in standing still.

The doubt was still there. Fear does not disappear just because you understand the stakes.

It hums under the surface. It tightens your breath. It whispers all the effortless ways to avoid taking your next bold steps. Play it safe. Do not mess this up. Make sure everyone agrees first.

I could have listened. In another life, I might have. But years of leading had taught me something else, fear is not a warning to stop. It is a signal to lean in. In that moment, I did not feel fearless. I felt bold. And that is the difference most people miss. For me, boldness is not about the absence of fear.

"Boldness is about choosing aligned action, even when the fear is still present."

It is not reckless.

It is not impulsive.

It is a decision.

A decision to move, not because everything is guaranteed, but because what matters most is on the line. That day, I made the bold move. Not because it was easy. But because it was necessary. And that choice, like so many others across my career, was grounded in how I was raised. Being bold was part of my DNA. For as long as I can remember, I had witnessed my parents bold choices and how they navigated the most disruptive, unplanned, unwanted, and painful moments in their lives. Our family lost my brother when I was only six.

I say I did not learn boldness through books, schooling, or roles as an adult. I learned it in first grade. That year, my parents experienced a profound loss that changed everything. I was not too young to know, and I understood what was happening. I felt it, the silence, the sadness, the way the world suddenly stopped making sense. And somewhere deep inside me, a truth began to root itself:

life is fragile, and tomorrow is not guaranteed. That early awareness, painful, but powerful, shaped the way I would see risk, boldness, and opportunity for the rest of my life.

Neuroscience tells us that early emotional experiences leave strong imprints on the brain. During childhood, especially between the ages of five and seven, our brains are forming core neural pathways that influence how we respond to fear, uncertainty, and decision-making as adults. The amygdala stores emotional memory. The hippocampus encodes experience. And when those experiences involve loss or trauma, the lessons run deep. For me, that lesson was this: action is always worth more than avoidance. Boldness does not wait. Boldness moves.

So, when people ask me where my boldness comes from, I do not point to a boardroom or a breakthrough. I point to that little girl who learned, far too early, that playing it safe does not protect you from pain but showing up for what matters might. That is the root of my leadership. Not fearlessness, but presence. Not perfection, but truth. And a deep understanding that boldness is something you are taught, it is something you build, decision by decision, starting with the ones no one else can see.

My first job was mowing lawns. Then I unloaded trucks for Federal Express (FedEx) before the sun came up. I managed shipping floors for United Parcel Service (UPS) during college. I have always been curious and open to what I could learn from experiences, connections, and trying something new. I would most definitely be described as spontaneous and open to adventure. Most often the roles I sought were physically and mentally challenging. I did not walk a traditional corporate path. In today's world, I am not sure there is even a traditional path to leadership. What used to be the rule is now the exception. Every move up, every seat at a bigger table, came because I learned to listen to the right kind of fear, the kind that says, *this matters*.

I have always been bold. I just did not have the language for it.

That is part of why I wrote my first book, *Be BOLD Today*, to give you permission to see boldness differently. And now, with this book, *The BOLD Leader*, I am giving you the tools to live and lead from that place with even more clarity, strategy, and heart. Because bold leadership is not just for certain titles, certain roles, or certain moments, or even for when everything feels perfect.

Bold leadership is a practice.

It is built decision by decision, conversation by conversation, move by move.

You do not have to be fearless.

You do not have to be certain.

You must be willing.

To trust yourself.

To move toward what matters.

To be willing to feel the fear and make the bold move anyway.

That is what this book will show you how to do.

Real Talk Moment

When I stood in that boardroom, I was not polished or perfect. I was a leader in real time, heart pounding, fully human. The weight of the decision before me was real. But so was the *clarity*. I knew fear was not trying to sabotage me. It was simply alerting me; this is something very important.

And because I understood that I could stay in the room. I could take a breath, make the call, and move forward.

You can do that, too.

You just must be willing to stay with fear long enough to see what it is pointing to.

Leadership is not about titles or bios or polished press releases. It is about lived experience. The choices you make when the path is unclear. The moments you speak up when silence would be easier. The way you show up, not just when it is going well, but especially when it is not.

And in nearly all of those defining moments, fear is in the room.

So that is where we will begin, right there, in the space where most leadership books skip ahead. With the quiet, gnawing, private kind of fear. The kind that asks, "What if this fails?" or "What if they find out I'm not as put together as they think?"

That fear is real. And it is important.

In this chapter, we will dismantle the myth that bold leaders are fearless. They are not. They have simply learned to lead anyway, to work with fear, not fight it. They know that fear does not mean stop. It means pay attention. And they have built the habits and inner strength to act, even when the outcome is unknown.

This is not about being superhuman. It is about being fully human and choosing boldness anyway.

Definition of a Bold Leader

A bold leader is someone who:

- Moves with clarity even when certainty is not guaranteed.
- Makes decisions aligned with their values, not just comfort.
- Sees fear not as a stop sign, but as a compass pointing to what matters.
- Measures success not by how safe they stayed, but by how true they stayed to their purpose.

Bold leadership is not louder, flashier, or riskier. It is clearer, truer, and deeply committed to moving with integrity toward what matters most.

Bold Action Moment (BAM)
Taking action when you are *not* ready, and letting the action shape the readiness, is a BAM.

Boldness did not arrive all at once. It was built slowly, quietly, through tough decisions, honest conversations, and moments when I was not sure I had any energy left but showed up anyway. I did not learn boldness in a boardroom or from a textbook. I learned it in the in-between: in the hallway after the hard meeting, on the edge of a big choice, at times of the deepest loss, in the silence before I spoke up.

I have doubted it, wrestled with it, rebuilt it. Boldness was not something I found. It was something I practiced.

And now, I am here to walk alongside you, not because I have all the answers, but because I have lived the questions. And I know you can build your boldness, too.

Fear Is Not the Enemy, It Is Your Intelligence System

We have been conditioned to see fear as a weakness, something to suppress, outrun, or hide if we want to be taken seriously as leaders.

But that is not the truth.

Fear is not a flaw in your leadership. It is one of your most powerful signals.

It is saying, *this matters*. This moment holds weight: risk, reward, consequence, or change.

In today's leadership landscape, the fears that rise up are rarely about physical threats. They are about people. Strategy. Culture. Innovation. Integrity.

The presence of fear does not mean you are failing.

It means you are leading where it counts.

The amygdala activates not only in response to physical danger but also when leaders face high-stakes decisions involving uncertainty, risk, and future identity. Neuroscientists now believe fear signals are integral to complex decision-making, alerting leaders to choices that carry meaningful, lasting consequences. Far from being a signal to retreat, fear can be one of the clearest indicators that you are standing at the edge of personal and organizational growth.

> "When fear shows up, your brain is not just reacting to danger, it is tuning in to significance."

While we are often taught that fear is about danger, modern neuroscience shows that fear is also about salience. Salience means importance. When your brain activates fear, it is not just scanning for physical threats, it is tagging moments with high emotional or strategic stakes. In leadership, this matters deeply. Fear is not asking, "Are you safe?" It is asking, "Will this matter to your mission, your people, your future self?" When you learn to listen to fear through this lens, it becomes one of your highest-valued internal advisors.

When fear surfaces in leadership moments, your brain is not telling you, "You're not ready." It is telling you, "Pay attention. This matters." Fear is a high-precision alert system, not a disqualifier. And how you manage that alert changes everything.

Research shows that when you name a fear, whether by speaking it aloud, writing it down, or even labeling it internally, you activate the prefrontal cortex, the rational, executive center of the brain responsible for planning and decision-making. This simple act of emotional labeling reduces amygdala reactivity by as much as 50%, shifting you from reactive mode into strategic clarity. In leadership, that distinction is critical.

This is why bold leadership is not about being fearless. It is about being fear aware. Exceptional leaders are not those who never feel fear, they are those who know how to recognize fear, decode its meaning, and lead anyway. Fear does not stop them. Fear sharpens them. They move through it with awareness, not avoidance.

Fear Is Fuel

You cannot manage or direct what you do not measure. And most leadership development focuses on lagging indicators, results that show up weeks, months, or even years after the bold decisions that created them.

The Bold Leadership Compass is different. It tracks your courage in real time, measuring the moments when you choose growth over comfort, action over analysis, and alignment over approval.

Think of it as your leadership GPS. Instead of waiting to see if you end up where you want to go, it shows you exactly where you are right now and guides your next bold move. Whether you are building your first bold leadership habits or fine-tuning your courage at the next level of your leadership, the compass meets you where you are and shows you where to stretch next.

ACTIVITY: Measuring the Business Impact of Bold Leadership

Bold leadership is not just about being brave, leadership is about driving real, measurable outcomes. But to understand its true value, you have to measure more than just revenue and headcount. Bold leadership leaves its mark in momentum, decision-making, innovation, and the confidence to do what others will not.

Let's track what actually matters.

Start Simple: Track in Three Timeframes

Quick Wins (0–90 Days)

Notice the early shifts bold leadership creates:

- How fast is your team making decisions now?
- Are people more engaged, energized, or taking more ownership?
- What unaligned or ineffective projects did you stop early?

Building Momentum (3–12 Months)

Look for strategic movement and momentum:

- What competitive advantages have emerged?

- How many new innovations, offers, or ideas launched?

- Are you attracting and keeping better talent?

Long-Term Impact (1–3 Years)

Measure what compounds over time:

- What revenue can be traced back to a bold strategic decision?

- How did your team handle crisis moments compared to peers?

- How has your reputation, brand value, or market trust shifted?

The Bold Leadership Value Question

Instead of defaulting to traditional ROI formulas, ask:

"What became possible because I made that bold move, would not have happened if I had played it safe?"

That is the real return.

Bold decisions do not always show up in neat quarterly reports. Sometimes they show up in:

- A culture that innovates faster than your competition.

- A team that trusts itself to speak up and move forward.

- A reputation that opens doors before you even knock.

So yes, track the numbers, but don't miss the stories.

Because the full value of bold leadership lives in what your team can do now that others still hesitate to try.

Bold leadership is not just about courage; it is about results. But measuring bold moves requires tracking different metrics than traditional ROI calculations.

ACTIVITY: Bold Leadership Compass Scale

You have made bold moves. But have you measured what they've made possible?

This tool helps you translate action into insight. Choose one bold decision from the past 90 days and use the prompts below to track the ripple effects, not just the outcome, but the shifts in behavior, energy, and clarity that bold leadership sparks.

Start Here: One Bold Decision

Write it down and reflect:

1. **What was the decision?** What did you choose and when?

2. **What shifted?** What did you notice afterward (team momentum, clarity, confidence, direction)?

3. **What became possible?** What new door opened that wouldn't have without your boldness?

4. **What would you do differently next time?** Boldness is a practice not a performance.

Monthly Reflection Prompt

Review one bold move each month. Over time, you'll see patterns— where you're thriving and where hesitation still holds power.

The Bold Leadership Compass Scale

This is not about scoring yourself to impress anyone. It is about building awareness.

Use this scale to rate your most recent decision or leadership moment. Then, choose 3–5 metrics that best represent your current growth edge.

> "Over time, leaders who track their bold decisions, not just their wins, build the clearest, strongest muscle of all: intentional courage."

Score	Zone	Definition
5	**Bold Zone**	You acted with conviction, stepped into risk, and created real movement.
4	**Builder's Edge**	You took meaningful risks, initiated hard conversations, or disrupted inertia.
3	**Stretch Space**	You made progress, but played it safe in key areas.
2	**Safety Loop**	You saw the bold move—but didn't make it.
1	**Comfort Trap**	You avoided the decision, deferred action, or ignored the discomfort.

Reminder: A low score doesn't mean you failed. It reveals where your next opportunity lives. Bold leaders do not just act. They reflect, adjust, and rise stronger.

Bold Metrics That Actually Matter

Most leadership books measure success in outcomes: revenue, ROI, retention. But bold leadership isn't just about results, it's about the decisions, conversations, and actions that create them. To lead boldly, you need to measure differently. Not just after the fact, but in real time.

I created the Bold Metrics model after watching too many leaders stall out, not because they lacked talent, but because they waited for perfection, played it safe, or mistook silence for alignment. These leaders often came to me after the fact: after their best team member quit, after the product failed, after the board lost confidence. They didn't need better instincts. They needed a new way to track boldness before the damage was done.

This chapter introduces seven categories of bold leadership. Each reflects a core capacity you'll need to strengthen. I've paired each with examples, so you can see what boldness looks like in real-life leadership, not as theory, but as action.

Bold Leadership Compass Categories

1. Decision-Making Boldness

This is the foundation. Leaders who cannot move forward without perfect data become bottlenecks.

> "Bold leadership means building your tolerance for uncertainty."

Experienced leaders who routinely make decisions with partial information demonstrate greater cognitive efficiency and lower stress reactivity.

Why it matters: Bold decisions made with 80% certainty train the brain to tolerate ambiguity and increase confidence over time.

- I made a decision with 80% of the information
  (e.g., Selected a vendor based on fit, not just data).
- I set and honored a decision deadline
  (e.g., "We decide by Friday at 3:00 p.m.").
- I chose the harder right over the easier wrong
  (e.g., Addressed poor performance instead of reassigning work).

2. Communication Courage

Most leadership failures come from the conversations that never happen. Bold leaders don't avoid the hard talks, they lean into them. Avoiding difficult conversations activates the brain's threat response (amygdala), which can lead to chronic stress and decision fatigue. In contrast, clear and timely communication activates the anterior cingulate cortex, which supports emotional regulation and social awareness.

Why it matters: Practicing communication courage builds neural pathways that reduce conflict avoidance and increase leadership effectiveness.

- I had the conversation I was avoiding
  (e.g., Gave feedback to an underperforming teammate).
- I spoke up when others stayed silent
  (e.g., Challenged a flawed strategy in a leadership meeting).
- I addressed problems directly
  (e.g., Told someone their presentation missed the mark).

3. Risk and Innovation

Bold leaders create momentum by experimenting wisely and knowing when to stop. Innovation is not just launching new things, it's learning fast and letting go of what does not work. Dopamine levels rise in the brain when taking calculated risks, creating a reward pathway that fuels motivation and learning. Innovation activates the brain's default mode network, a region associated with creativity and big-picture thinking.

Why it matters: Leaders who take pragmatic risks increase the brain's adaptability, encouraging a culture of innovation.

- I took a calculated risk
  (e.g., Led a cross-functional initiative outside my domain).
- I pushed "safe" ideas further
  (e.g., Asked, "What if we doubled the goal?").
- I stopped a failing initiative
  (e.g., Shut down a lagging project six weeks in).

4. Values Alignment

This is what separates credible leaders from performative ones. Bold leaders act in integrity, even when it costs them. The ventromedial prefrontal cortex helps us evaluate choices based on personal values. When leaders act in alignment with their core principles, this region is activated, reinforcing long-term well-being and decision satisfaction.

Why it matters: Bold leaders who consistently act from their values show higher resilience and lower burnout.

- I chose values over popularity
  (e.g., Defended necessary but unpopular budget cuts).

- I made a hard, right call
  (e.g., Promoted based on merit, not politics).

- I stood for something that mattered
  (e.g., Advocated for employee retention despite pressure).

5. Team Impact

Bold leadership is not a solo act. It multiplies. The mark of a bold leader is a bold team. Psychological safety correlates with lower cortisol levels and higher oxytocin release in team members, fostering trust and collaboration.

Why it matters: When leaders model boldness, they create a neurochemical environment where others are more likely to innovate and take ownership.

- People bring me bolder ideas
  (e.g., A team member proposed a new product line).

- My team takes risks because they see me model it
  (e.g., A direct report launched an ambitious pilot).

- I created psychological safety
  (e.g., Team openly admits mistakes and adjusts fast).

6. Growth Mindset

Bold leaders are learners. They admit what they don't know and extract value from every outcome, especially the imperfect ones. A growth mindset activates the brain's neuroplasticity, particularly in the dorsolateral prefrontal cortex, enhancing learning and adaptive behavior.

Why it matters: Admitting gaps and learning from failure strengthens executive functioning and positions leaders for long-term success.

- I said, "I don't know, but here's how we'll figure it out"
  (e.g., Outlined a plan in front of the board).
- I acknowledged and adjusted quickly
  (e.g., Corrected a hiring mistake within 30 days).
- I captured the learning from failure
  (e.g., Reviewed a product that didn't meet goals).

7. Speed and Action

"Analysis paralysis" is the silent killer of boldness. Bold leaders take action, then adapt. Rapid decision-making under time pressure stimulates the locus coeruleus, which regulates and impacts your heart rate, breathing, and other physiological responses. Leaders who act quickly and adjust build cognitive agility, a key trait in high-performing executives.

Why it matters: Taking timely action reduces overthinking, promotes forward momentum, and rewires the brain for decisive leadership.

- I moved fast on a new idea
  (e.g., Launched a pilot within two weeks of conception).
- I chose momentum over perfection
  (e.g., Released a 90% solution rather than delaying).
- I acted while others waited
  (e.g., Hired top talent while competitors hesitated).

Bold leadership is not a personality type. It's a pattern of behavior.

Track your bold decisions the same way you would track financial results or sales performance.

Make them visible. Make them matter.

And when in doubt, ask yourself: What would I do if I were already the boldest version of myself?

Bold Category	Why It Matters to Leaders
1. Decision-Making Boldness	Trains brain to tolerate ambiguity and builds decision confidence over time.
2. Communication Courage	Builds emotional regulation and reduces conflict avoidance; supports psychological safety.
3. Risk and Innovation	Fuels motivation and creative thinking by activating reward and ideation centers in the brain.
4. Values Alignment	Strengthens resilience and decision satisfaction; enhances credibility and long-term well-being.
5. Team Impact	Promotes trust, ownership, and collaboration through a culture of psychological safety.
6. Growth Mindset	Activates neuroplasticity and builds adaptability, positioning leaders for sustainable growth.
7. Speed and Action	Reduces overthinking, promotes momentum, and increases executive cognitive agility.

The First Leadership Frontier

Bold leaders are not strangers to fear. You have already made high-stakes decisions. You have spoken up when it mattered. You have taken the next bold step, often before you felt fully ready.

But even for the boldest among us, fear still finds a way in.

And often, it does not announce itself.

It shows up dressed as logic.

It sounds like strategy.

It moves through your team as silence, hesitation, or delay.

You know the lines:

- "Let's get a little more input first."

- "We should build a second backup deck—just in case."

- "Maybe now isn't the right time."

These are not just cautious phrases.

They are often fear in disguise.

I have seen brilliant leaders, with track records of bold moves, get quietly stuck here. Not because they lack experience, but because boldness requires constant renewal. Fear evolves with success. The stakes get higher, the visibility sharper, the risks more personal.

And at a neurological level, this makes sense.

Even when your rational mind is ready to lead forward, your nervous system might still be negotiating with the past.

"The amygdala, your brain's built-in alarm system, is not wired for reinvention. It is wired for survival. It scans for risk. It flags uncertainty. And it does not care whether the change ahead is your next brilliant innovation or a complete collapse, it reads both as *danger.*"

But here is where boldness begins again.

Not in pushing past fear, but in recognizing it.

Research shows that simply naming the emotion, *I feel afraid,* can calm the amygdala and reactivate the prefrontal cortex, the seat of reason, focus, and executive decision-making. This is not self-help fluff. This is how the brain is built.

So if you find yourself hesitating, not loudly, but subtly, pause and ask:

Is this strategy? Or is this fear in disguise?

You are not starting from scratch. You are starting from strength.

Bold leadership is not about pretending fear is gone.

The Delay That Was Not About Data

> "Bold leaders are not fearless. They are fluent in fear and still choose to move forward."

A few years ago, I was working with a senior executive at a global healthcare company. She was known for her bold instincts, someone who had led major product launches, restructured teams with clarity and heart, and often made the call before others even realized a decision was needed.

But this time was different.

She was sitting on a major strategic pivot. One that had cross-functional implications, a shift in messaging, and high executive visibility. And week after week, she delayed.

"We just need a bit more data," she told me in our session. "I'm waiting on a few final pieces from the team before I present to the board." But the data kept trickling in, and still, no movement.

Finally, I asked her a simple question: What are you actually waiting for?

She paused.

Then, with a half-laugh and complete honesty, she said,

"I think I'm waiting to not feel afraid of being wrong."

That was the real fear, not the decision itself, but the weight of what it meant if she got it wrong, this far into her career. From that moment on, everything shifted. Not because the fear vanished, but because it was no longer in charge. She named it. She understood it. And she led forward anyway.

Within 10 days, she presented the pivot with confidence. The board approved it. The project launched. And six months later, her division posted record performance. But the win was not just in the outcome.

> "When bold leaders delay, it is rarely about the plan. It is often about the pressure of being the one who decides."

The real win was in the moment she realized fear had been shaping her timeline, and she reclaimed the lead.

The Indecision Loop: Why Waiting Feels Safer but Is Not

Every bold leader knows the feeling: the quiet urge to wait.

To postpone the hard decision until more data arrives.

To gather one more round of feedback.

To seek one more piece of reassurance.

It feels strategic. It sounds wise. But it is often a trap.

I call it the Indecision Loop, a cognitive pattern where leaders get stuck cycling through analysis and hesitation, mistaking delay for diligence. The longer the loop runs, the more paralyzed we become.

And the science explains why.

Our brains are wired to overestimate the pain of making the wrong move and underestimate the cost of not moving at all. Behavioral economists call this loss aversion, the tendency to feel the pain of loss twice as strongly as the pleasure of gain. Add to that status quo bias, and we become neurologically inclined to favor inaction, even when doing nothing guarantees we fall behind.

> "Fear does not mean you are wrong. It means you are awake."

Fear Is Fuel

But the real driver? Anticipated regret.

The fear of being wrong becomes so amplified that no option feels safe enough. And so we delay, not forever, just *a little longer*. Until the window closes.

The longer a leader stays in this loop, the less likely they are to act at all. Prolonged uncertainty depletes willpower and creates what researchers call decision fatigue, a neurobiological drain that pushes leaders toward the path of least resistance: the safest, smallest, or most familiar option. Or worse, no option at all.

And yet here is the paradox: The real leadership risk is not moving too boldly. It is never moving at all.

Hesitation has a cost.

Every month a leadership team delays major decisions correlates with:

6% drop in employee engagement,

7% delay in time-to-market, and

Up to a 5% decrease in customer satisfaction.

Fear-based hesitation is not just emotionally exhausting.

It is operationally expensive.

That is why the first step to leading boldly is not eliminating fear.

It is naming it.

Boldness is not just about grit or resilience.

It is not just about bouncing back, it is about shifting forward.

And that requires a new kind of strength, cognitive agility.

Leaders with high cognitive agility do not just recover faster; they adapt sooner, decide quicker, and innovate under pressure. They are able to pivot perspectives, regulate emotions, and lead through complexity, not because they have full certainty, but because they know how to move without it.

In a leadership landscape where change is constant and clarity is rare, bold leaders do not just survive challenge.

They flex. They shift. They lead.

The most valuable leadership trait today is not stamina, it is the ability to shift gears, mentally and emotionally:

From fear clarity.

From control to curiosity.

From protection to progress.

Let's dig into the Fuel Formula.

The Fuel Formula: Turning Fear Into Forward Motion

Forward Motion-Turning Fear Into Fuel

If fear is a signal, not a stop sign, the real question becomes: What do you do with it?

Because recognizing fear is not enough.

Leading through fear, that is where bold leadership is forged.

That is why I developed a method I call the Fuel Formula.

This is not a corporate exercise.

It is a leadership necessity.

Whether you are facing a board decision, a pivotal hire, a major reinvention, or a deeply personal crossroads, the Fuel Formula is designed to help you translate fear into forward momentum.

Here is what the science tells us:

Anticipatory fear, the fear we feel before we act, is often more intense than the fear we feel in motion.

Our brains are predictive machines.

When facing uncertainty, they fill in the blanks with worst-case scenarios.

Neuroscience shows that during periods of hesitation, the brain's fear circuitry (especially the amygdala) becomes hyperactive, exaggerating risks and catastrophizing outcomes that have not and may never occur.

In other words: The longer you wait, the scarier it feels.

Not because the risk increased, but because your brain did what it is wired to do, protect you from the unknown.

But here is the breakthrough:

Once you take action, fear diminishes.

Movement sends a powerful signal back to the brain: *I am not stuck. I am doing something.*

Even small action quiets the amygdala and re-engages the pre-frontal cortex, restoring clarity, confidence, and a sense of agency.

That is why bold leaders do not wait to feel fully ready.

They move.

They speak.

They decide, *while* the fear is still present, knowing that clarity often follows commitment, not the other way around.

> "Action shrinks fear. Inaction feeds it."

This is not just about mindset. It is about momentum, neurological, emotional, and operational.

When you name the fear, the amygdala calms.

When you reframe the story, your options widen.

When you take action, even a small step, the brain shifts from panic to power.

The Fuel Formula At a Glance

- **Face It:** Name the fear without dressing it up.
- **Focus It:** Ask what it is protecting. Find the value underneath.
- **Fuel It:** Take one step forward aligned with that value.

Boldness does not wait for clarity.
It builds it.

Yet most leaders were never taught how to turn those emotionally overloaded moments into movement.

That is why I created the Fuel Formula, a practical, repeatable tool to help you convert fear into forward motion.

It is bold. It is simple. And it works.

Here is the method I teach leaders across every industry to help them turn fear into fuel so they can lead with momentum, clarity, and courage when it matters most (See Figure 1.1).

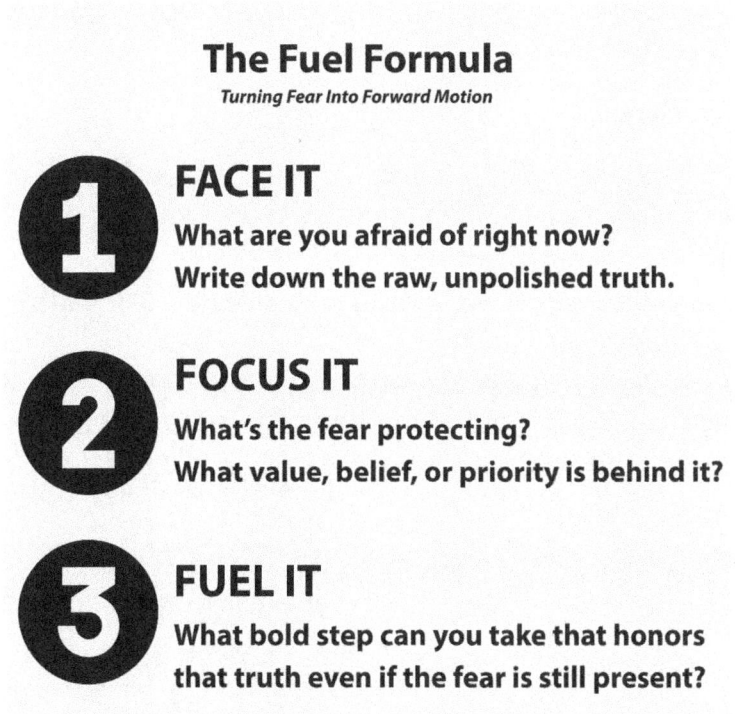

The Fuel Formula

Turning Fear Into Forward Motion

1 FACE IT
What are you afraid of right now?
Write down the raw, unpolished truth.

2 FOCUS IT
What's the fear protecting?
What value, belief, or priority is behind it?

3 FUEL IT
What bold step can you take that honors that truth even if the fear is still present?

Figure 1.1 The Fuel Formula

The Fuel Formula: Three Steps to Turn Fear Into Forward Motion

You are on the edge of something that matters.

The decision is real. The risk is real. And the fear is louder than usual. That is not a flaw in your leadership, it is a signal. A sign that this moment counts.

You do not eliminate fear by thinking harder.

You move through fear by working with it.

That is what the Fuel Formula is designed to do.

When fear shows up, whether in a boardroom, a hiring decision, or a quiet personal reckoning, these three steps help you turn hesitation into clarity, and clarity into bold action.

Step 1: Face It

A senior executive once told me, "I've built my whole career being decisive, but this one move? I'm stuck."

She was not stuck because she lacked information.

She was stuck because she had not named the fear underneath.

Get radically honest:

What are you actually afraid of?

Not the polished version.

Not the one you would share in a team meeting.

The raw one.

"I'm afraid I'll lose credibility."

> "Fear thrives in ambiguity. It shrinks when you name it. Do not overanalyze. Just call it what it is."

"I'm afraid I'll look like I don't know what I am doing."

This is where most leaders get stuck. Not because they are weak, but because they are practiced at hiding fear behind logic.

But bold leadership starts where the mask ends.

Fear cannot lead when you are the one naming it.

Leadership reflection: What fear are you dressing up as strategy?

Bold Action Moment (BAM)

A BAM is a micro-inflection point, where fear and leadership collide.

Naming a fear is a BAM. Moving through it is another.

Stack enough BAMs, and you do not just change your outcomes. **You change who you become.**

Step 2: Focus It

Once you name the fear, ask:

What is this fear trying to protect?

Because fear is not always the enemy.

Sometimes, it is a distorted form of care.

"This fear is guarding the reputation I've built."

"This fear is protecting how much I value trust."

"This fear is reminding me that this next step matters deeply."

Fear almost always points to something important, something that matters to you.

It is rarely random. It is a map.

When you frame fear through the lens of values, you shift from shame to curiosity.

Instead of feeling weak for being afraid, you begin to see what fear reveals:

Integrity. Impact. Belonging. Growth.

Fear shows you what is at stake, because it shows you what you care about.

Use it.

Leadership reflection: What does this fear say about what you value?

Step 3: Fuel It

> "Focused, aligned action is how you reclaim agency from fear."

Now that you know what matters, ask yourself:

What is one bold step I can take that honors this value and moves me forward?

Not a leap.

Not a grand gesture.

Just one real step.

This is not about reacting. It is about responding with clarity.

Maybe it is scheduling the hard conversation.

Maybe it is sharing the bold vision.

> "Courage is not what you feel before you act. Courage is what you build by acting while you still feel fear."

Maybe it is saying yes to something you have secretly wanted but were too afraid to own.

Action breaks fear's momentum. Every time.

Leadership reflection: What is one bold step that would feel meaningful even if it is not perfect?

Why It Works: The Neuroscience of Boldness

Here is what the science says, simply:

- **When you name a fear,** your brain's fear center begins to calm down.

- **When you reframe it with values,** your brain becomes more focused and regulated.

- **When you take action,** even a small one, your brain shifts out of survival mode and back into clarity and momentum.

That is neuroplasticity in action.

Each time you act with courage, you are literally rewiring your brain.

Just like muscles adapt to resistance, your brain adapts to emotional risk.

What once triggered fear becomes familiar ground.

What once felt impossible becomes easier to move through.

Boldness is not a lightning strike.

It is a trained response. A practiced habit. A leadership skill.

And the more you move through discomfort instead of retreating from it, the more instinctive your boldness becomes.

What the Brain Needs to Be Bold

Step 1: Face It

When you name a fear out loud, even just to yourself, your brain begins to settle down.

You move from reaction to reflection.

That is because naming the fear helps quiet the part of your brain that's wired for survival, and reactivates the part that is built for leadership.

Step 2: Focus It

When you reframe fear and connect it to something that matters, like your values or purpose, your brain becomes more focused and calm.

You stop spinning, and start thinking clearly again.

The fear is still there, but it's not running the show anymore.

Step 3: Fuel It

Action changes your brain.

Even one small, values-aligned step sends a signal to your brain: *We're not stuck. We're doing something.*

And the more often you move through discomfort instead of avoiding it, the more natural bold action becomes over time.

The One-Step Email

I once worked with a VP in the tech space, sharp, strategic, and respected. She had a bold new idea for a cross-functional innovation sprint, but she was sitting on it. Not because the idea lacked merit, but because she was afraid.

When we walked through the Fuel Formula together, the fear became clear:

"I'm afraid I'll lose credibility if this fails in front of senior leadership."

She named it. That was Step 1.

Then we reframed it:

"This fear is trying to protect my reputation—but also shows how much I care about bringing real value."

That was Step 2.

Her Step 3? Not launching the sprint.

Just sending an email to the COO to pitch the concept.

A single bold step.

By the end of the week, she had buy-in. Three months later, the sprint had driven the most cross-departmental engagement her team had seen in years.

And she told me afterward: *"The hardest part wasn't the pitch. It was sending the email."*

Because bold leadership is not built in sweeping leaps.

It is built in the decision to move anyway.

Rethinking Risk: Alignment Over Adrenaline

When you hear "risk," what do you picture? Skydiving? Starting a business? Walking into a boardroom and betting on your career? Big, flashy moves? That is not what bold leadership risk really looks like. Real risk is quieter.

It is the risk of telling the uncomfortable truth in a room full of those that say yes, and you say no. It is the risk of betting on a long-term vision when the short-term numbers scream otherwise. It is the risk of aligning your leadership with who you really are, not who the world expects you to be. The best leaders I know, the ones you admire, are not adrenaline junkies. They are alignment junkies.

And they know: *Staying comfortable is far riskier than stretching boldly*.

"Boldness is not how loud you are. It is how aligned you are."

Boldness Built Over Time

I did not wake up one day as a bold leader. No one does.

My first lessons in boldness were not in a boardroom. They were mowing lawns at age 12, learning that showing up consistently mattered more than being the fastest. They came from driving Federal Express trucks in the early morning darkness, being the only woman on the shift and proving myself through performance, not politics. They happened when I stepped into chaotic classrooms to bridge the gap between IT and education, translating complex systems into language teachers could use and apply through new innovative approaches.

Later, I found myself rebuilding research infrastructure at top academic health centers, where million-dollar decisions could not wait for perfect consensus and patient outcomes hung in the balance.

Each moment demanded the same thing: act even when you feel the fear, you may even feel unclear or at times uncertain. Act because the cost of inaction was always higher than the risk of imperfect action. Act because clarity lives on the other side of action, not the other side of analysis.

What I discovered along the way is that boldness is not a personality trait with which you are born. It is not about being fearless or having all the answers. It is about building your tolerance for discomfort, one decision at a time. It is about learning that "I don't know, but I'll figure it out" is often the most honest and most powerful thing a leader can say.

From Repetition to Resilience

Every time you take action when fear is present, you are not just "being brave," you are building your leadership brain. Boldness becomes easier, not because the fear goes away, but because *you've trained yourself to move anyway.* Like strength training for your decision-making muscles, courage compounds.

Every time I chose to speak up instead of staying silent, to try something new instead of sticking with the safe choice, to address a problem instead of hoping it would solve itself, I was building the bold muscle. Some moves worked brilliantly. Others taught me valuable lessons the hard way. All of them made me stronger. All of them created new learnings.

Boldness was not a badge I earned. It is a muscle I built and continue to build every day.

That is the truth about bold leadership, it is not about dramatic moments or big gestures.

"Being a bold leader is about the accumulated weight of small, courageous choices that compound over time into something powerful."

ACTIVITY: Reflection Prompt: Look Back at the Last 12 Months

What is one moment, big or small, where you acted even while uncertain?

What did it teach you about your own boldness?

Now ask: *What decision in front of me today deserves the same courage?*

The Real Costs of Indecision in Leadership

Boldness is not about volume.

It is about alignment.

It is about taking intentional action, even when fear is present.

Especially when fear is present.

That is what separates the bold from the burned-out.

Neuroscience Check-In: Why Boldness Works

Your brain is not wired for boldness by default.

It is wired for protection. But the Fuel Formula helps you rewire your default pattern.

Here is what happens neurologically:

- When you name fear, you calm the amygdala, the brain's threat detector.
- When you explore the fear, you engage the prefrontal cortex, the part of the brain that regulates emotions and drives rational thinking.
- When you take aligned action, you trigger dopamine release, reinforcing courage and building momentum.

The Fuel Formula is not just about mindset.

It is biology. It is strategy. It is leadership.

Real Leader Moment

When I use the Fuel Formula with clients, from executives overseeing million-dollar portfolios to founders navigating unplanned pivots, the same thing always happens:

They do not feel fearless. They feel clear.

And clarity is where real boldness lives.

Reframing Risk: What Bold Leaders Understand

Most people hear the word *risk* and picture danger, exposure, or vulnerability.

That is not wrong, but it is incomplete.

Risk is not the enemy.

Misunderstood risk is.

One of the hardest and most liberating shifts a bold leader can make is this:

Playing it safe is often the riskiest move of all.

Here is why:

- When you overprotect, you lose momentum.

- When you stall, you lose trust.

- When you avoid bold moves, you invite irrelevance.

We often assume that boldness threatens psychological safety, that courage and connection are opposites. But research tells a different story:

Bold leadership and psychological safety are not at odds. They are deeply connected.

When leaders act with transparency, admit uncertainty, take aligned risks, and model honesty around mistakes, psychological safety increases, not decreases.

Teams do not need perfect leaders. They need real ones.

They need leaders who move forward—even when the outcome is not guaranteed.

Safety is not built through certainty. It is built through shared boldness.

In the most innovative organizations, resilience and risk-taking do not happen despite bold leadership.

They happen because of it.

Why Bold (Even Imperfect) Moves Build Momentum

Boldness is not about being reckless.

It is about knowing that clarity is built through action not over-analysis.

In fast-paced, high-stakes environments, decisive leaders outperform hesitant ones.

Not because they are always right, but because they adapt faster.

Real-world feedback beats hypothetical planning. Every time.

In fact, bold leaders who move quickly even when imperfect are seen by their teams as 31% more inspiring and 23% more trustworthy than overly cautious counterparts.

And here's the real secret:

It's cumulative.

Every small risk taken every "micro-bold" move builds the flexibility, trust, and momentum that allow you to make bigger ones later.

Momentum does not come from waiting until you are sure.

It comes from moving while still unsure and learning as you go.

Leadership Myth to Break

Most people assume caution is always the smartest strategy.

But here is the uncomfortable truth:

Caution is only wise when it serves the mission.

Otherwise, it is just fear in disguise.

Bold leaders ask sharper questions:

- Is this decision aligned with our highest priorities?
- Does silence cost more than speaking up?
- Is waiting actually safer or just more comfortable?

Strategic caution moves you forward.

Fear-based caution keeps you still.

"Courage is not a gift with which you are born. It is a neural pattern you build one bold decision at a time."

BOLD Leader Mantra

Risk is not about danger. It is about alignment.

If you are protecting a belief, strategy, or culture that has already expired, you are not managing risk.

You are multiplying it.

The Brain on Boldness

Every time you take action through discomfort instead of away from it, you reinforce the brain's wiring for clarity, resilience, and decision-making.

Boldness is not just a mindset.

It is a muscle.

And it grows through reps.

Action Cue

The next time you feel fear or hesitation, try this simple reframe:

"This is my brain building strength."

Then take one small, real step forward.

Your future bold self is counting on it.

Boldness in Action

A healthcare executive I coached once sat on a transformative innovation strategy for six months paralyzed by a need for certainty that never came.

The turning point?

A single reframing question:

"If you do not act, what future are you choosing?"

That question cut through the noise. It helped them realize that inaction was not safety it was a slow surrender.

> "Bold leadership is not about being reckless. It is about refusing to protect what no longer serves the mission."

They launched the initiative not perfectly, but aligned.

Six months later, the results spoke for themselves:

Streamlined operations.

Improved care delivery.

Recognition across the organization.

Not because they played it safe.

But because they moved when it mattered.

Inaction Is a Decision, Too

Every time you delay, hesitate, or defer bold action,
you are still making a decision:
A decision to stay still.
Ask yourself:

- What am I risking by doing nothing?
- What future am I forfeiting by avoiding this decision?
- What bold move could create momentum right now?

Bold leaders do not just manage risk.
They manage opportunity.

Building Your Bold Muscle

If fear is your fuel, and alignment is your compass then action is your training ground.

Your brain is wired to avoid loss more than it is to pursue gain.

This is known as loss aversion, and it creates a hidden trap for leaders: The pain of making the wrong move feels more urgent than the thrill of creating a breakthrough.

But bold leaders recognize the trap and reframe it.

Instead of asking, *"What could go wrong?"*

They ask, *"What opportunity am I risking if I do nothing?"*

Inaction carries a cost.

And it is often the highest one.

The Reps That Rewire You

When you first lead this way boldly, imperfectly, truthfully it will feel awkward.

You will doubt yourself.

You will wonder if you are pushing too far or moving too soon.

Good. That is your signal.

You are stretching.

You are not supposed to feel 100% ready.

You are supposed to feel 100% aligned.

Start small.

Say the bold idea in the meeting even if your heart pounds.

Speak the hard truth even if your voice shakes.

Pitch the new vision even if no one has done it before.

And then: do it again. And again.

Every time you choose aligned action over protective hesitation, you build your bold muscle.

You are not just shaping your leadership, you are reshaping your brain.

Forward, Not Fearless

You will not get it perfect.

You will second-guess decisions.

You will stumble.

That is not failure.

That is growth.

In fact, research shows it is not the *first* brave move that rewires your brain.

It is the second. The fifth. The fiftieth.

The moment you choose courage again, even while still uncomfortable, you teach your brain something powerful: *I chose courage. And I made it through.*

That imprint strengthens.

It becomes your identity: *I am someone who acts boldly even when it's hard.*

Most leadership books skip this truth: Courage is not what you feel before you act. It is what you build because you acted.

You do not wait for the fear to leave.

You move with it. Through it. Because of it.

And that movement, repeated, becomes momentum.

That momentum becomes mastery.

> "You are not rewiring your fear. You are rewiring your rhythm."

What You Just Learned

- Fear is not a flaw to fix, it is a signal to decode.
- The Fuel Formula (Face It, Frame It, Fuel It) turns hesitation into bold, aligned action.
- Bold leadership reframes risk, from danger to alignment.
- Boldness is not built in one moment. It is strengthened through daily practice.

You have learned that fear is not a personal weakness, it is one of your brain's most intelligent alerts. When fear shows up, it is not always a sign to stop. Often, it is a sign that something important is at stake.

The Fuel Formula helps you move through fear with intention.

It does not require you to be fearless.

It requires you to be honest, aligned, and in motion.

You have also learned that bold leadership is not about reckless decisions.

It is about strategic courage, knowing when the cost of staying still is greater than the cost of moving forward.

Every courageous choice, no matter how small, expands your capacity to lead with boldness, clarity, and purpose.

Bold Truth

Boldness is not about being fearless. It is about moving with your fear, not against it.

Your Bold Move

Look at one decision you have been avoiding. Apply the Fuel Formula today.

Face It: Name the fear.

Fuel It: Find the value it is protecting.

Focus It: Choose one bold, aligned action.

Then take that step, however small. Today. Because bold leadership does not start when everything is clear. It starts when you move anyway.

Bold Metrics

Bold leadership is not about eliminating fear. It is about building the capacity to move with it. In this chapter, you learned to decode fear as a leadership signal, not a flaw. The real test is not whether fear shows up. It is whether you move anyway. Using the compass in this chapter to regularly assess your progress and your momentum needed for your bold leadership.

Track Your Boldness

Did I name the fear clearly instead of avoiding it?
Did I take one step aligned with my core mission, even while fear was present?
Did I reframe fear as information, not inhibition?

Boldness Rating Scale

For each chapter, you will use the Boldness Barometer to track your current bold leadership alignment. Each Bold Metric is rated on a scale from 1 to 5, helping you and, if you choose, your team, self-assess how intentionally and boldly you are leading. This simple check-in reveals where you are stretching, where you are hesitating, and where your next bold move lies.

Bold Metric	Scale Description
1	Not at all I avoided bold action or stayed entirely in comfort/fear.
2	Rarely I noticed the need for boldness but did not act on it.
3	Sometimes I made small bold moves but stayed cautious overall.
4	Often I stretched beyond my comfort zone with intentional bold action.
5	Fully I led boldly, aligned with my values, even when it was hard.

Fear Is Fuel

Bold Barometer

Bold Metric	Rating (1–5)				
	1	2	3	4	5

(1 = Avoided bold action, 5 = Fully acted with aligned boldness)

	1	2	3	4	5
I named my leadership fear clearly.	☐	☐	☐	☐	☐
I moved forward with aligned action.	☐	☐	☐	☐	☐
I used fear as a focusing signal, not a stop sign.	☐	☐	☐	☐	☐

"Comfort lulls leaders into protecting what is, instead of creating what could be."

Setting the Stage for What Comes Next

In Chapter 2, we are going to unpack the second leadership trap that can quietly, and devastatingly, cost you everything, the comfort trap. There were seasons in my leadership where I thought staying steady was the only move I could make, where keeping things running smoothly felt like the goal. But smooth is different from strong. And staying comfortable? It almost cost me the very impact I set out to make.

Comfort, when left unchecked, becomes one of the greatest risks to bold leadership. It does not announce itself with alarms or flashing lights. It slides in quietly, wearing the mask of stability, good enough, or this is how we have always done it. Playing it safe feels responsible, until it starts to disrupt your growth from the inside out.

If Chapter 1 challenged you to rethink your relationship with fear, Chapter 2 will invite you to reconsider your relationship with comfort. Comfort is not simply a reward for success or a cozy destination, it is often a subtle, early warning sign that growth has stalled. If you are feeling a bit too comfortable right now, it is not something to criticize or brush off. It is a powerful realization. Recognizing comfort means you are already alert, prepared, and perfectly positioned to break free from patterns holding you back. It signals that you are ready to lean into discomfort, step forward boldly, and answer the call to your next level of leadership.

Chapter 2

The Comfort Trap

You have learned that fear is not a flaw, it is a signal. Now we turn to fear's quieter, more dangerous cousin: comfort. If fear triggers hesitation through doubt, comfort triggers hesitation through ease. It lulls leaders into standing still. It convinces you that stability equals success. It feels responsible, prudent, and wise, until the true cost of standing still becomes too big to ignore.

I learned this the hard way.

I remember sitting in a leadership retreat a few years ago, reviewing quarterly metrics. Everything looked good. Growth was steady. Employee engagement scores were high. The kind of meeting where everyone leaves feeling satisfied.

But underneath the metrics, I felt something else. The team's innovation energy had dulled. Big ideas were being deferred. Caution had replaced curiosity. And when I looked closer, I saw it in myself, too.

I had stopped asking bigger questions. I had stopped stretching for bolder possibilities. I had started managing the organization instead of leading it. Success had become my comfort zone, and comfort had become my trap. I had entered the comfort zone and taken on the native characteristics of the organization that valued harmony over everything else.

That moment broke something open for me. I realized boldness was not just for seasons of crisis or disruption. Boldness was a daily discipline. And I was failing at it, I had "gone native."

Here is what neuroscience tells us—our brains are wired to seek predictability and minimize cognitive load. Familiar patterns deliver small dopamine hits, making us feel good when we repeat the same actions, even when they are no longer serving us.

The result? Momentum fades. Innovation slows. Relevance erodes.

Comfort does not announce itself like a crisis. It seeps in quietly, disguised as wisdom and success. And that is exactly what makes it so dangerous.

Now, we turn to the second frontier of bold leadership, recognizing and rejecting the Comfort Trap. If fear tempts you to freeze, comfort tempts you to settle. And make no mistake, comfort is stealthier. It is quieter. It does not announce itself with flashing lights and alarm bells.

It wraps itself in the illusion of stability. It sounds like, "Things are working fine. Why rock the boat?" It feels like security. But it often marks the beginning of leadership decline.

Emerging leadership research suggests that complacency, not risk-taking, is now the biggest career limiter among mid- and senior-level executives. Leaders who plateau in comfort zones stagnate not because of failure, but because of their unwillingness to disrupt themselves when they are still winning.

Bold leadership is not just about moving through fear. It is about refusing to be seduced by comfort. Because comfort is not the reward for boldness. It is the resistance to your next evolution.

In this chapter, you will learn how comfort quietly creeps into leadership, how it reshapes your risk tolerance without you even noticing, and how to systematically spot and shatter the patterns that keep you stagnant.

It is time to stop mistaking stability for success.

It is time to get uncomfortable on purpose.

It is time to lead boldly forward.

The Slow Fade Into Comfort and Why I Refused to Settle

The Comfort Trap occurs when the desire for stability overtakes the drive for growth. It tricks leaders into prioritizing ease, familiarity, and reputation over innovation, adaptability, and bold action.

On the surface, everything looks fine. But underneath, leadership capacity is quietly eroding.

Here is how it works: When you maintain familiar routines, your brain delivers small hits of dopamine, this is the satisfaction of predictability. Over time, this builds what behavioral scientists call habit loops: stability becomes the reward, and boldness starts to feel emotionally risky, even when you intellectually know it is necessary.

The signs are subtle:

- You find yourself solving the same problems with the same old solutions.

- Innovation feels like a nice-to-have rather than urgent necessity.

- You hesitate to question current strategy because "it's still working."

- Praise comes more for keeping things steady than creating change.

- You defend what exists instead of exploring what is possible.

If any of these resonate, you are not failing. You are being called forward and need to take action.

Comfort does not announce itself like a crisis. It does not crash through the door.

It seeps in quietly, disguised as "stability," "wisdom," "success." And

"Because the uncomfortable truth about leadership is if you are not actively stretching, you are slowly becoming irrelevant."

for many leaders, it is tempting. After all, the climb to leadership is hard-won. Once you have built something that works, that runs smoothly, that looks good on paper, it is easy to believe the work is done.

But not for me. Not then. Not ever. I have never been wired to settle for comfort.

Every major move I have made, whether it was launching a new division, stepping away from a stable C-suite role, or building Bold Industries Group from the ground up, came from one fundamental truth, progress demands boldness, even when comfort is available.

I understood something that many leaders miss until it is too late, comfort is not neutral. Comfort is a slow erosion of progress and so much more damaging. The world does not stand still. Markets shift. People grow. New ideas emerge. If you stop evolving, you do not stay where you are, you fall behind.

Neuroscience backs up what my instincts already knew. When the brain operates in low-stakes, repetitive environments, the default mode network (DMN) becomes dominant. While the DMN is essential for creativity and internal reflection, when over-activated, it pulls leaders into self-reinforcing loops of complacency and disengagement. Without challenge, your brain defaults to comfort, and comfort leads directly to drift. And organizational research confirms this as well. Companies that over-prioritize operational efficiency at the expense of bold growth initiatives experience a higher decline in employee engagement and innovation output within just two years.

What is more dangerous, leaders in comfort often miss weak signals, the early warnings of needed change. If you are not intentionally stretching, you are silently shrinking. That is why I have always chosen the harder road. Even when stability was an option. Even when staying put would have been easier. Even when others advised "don't rock the boat," and, "keep your head down."

Bold leadership is not just about stepping up in crisis. It is about moving forward before crisis forces your hand. It is about refusing to let comfort calcify your clarity, your ambition, or your impact. That is why you are here. Because deep down, you know this too. You were not built to settle. You were built to move.

If fear tries to freeze your movement, comfort tries to convince you that movement is not necessary. Next, we will break down exactly how the Comfort Trap operates and why bold leaders must learn to spot it early before it costs them more than they realize.

Comparing Fear and Comfort

While fear and comfort are often misunderstood as emotional states to avoid, they are two of the most powerful internal signals a leader can receive. Each carries distinct neurological, strategic, and leadership implications. Fear, when decoded properly, acts as a high-value salience signal, alerting leaders to moments of meaningful risk, growth, or mission-critical decisions. It engages the amygdala initially but can activate the prefrontal cortex when leaders intentionally name and process it.

In contrast, comfort feels stable but neurologically shifts leaders toward the brain's default mode network, favoring routine and minimizing adaptability. When comfort goes unexamined, it erodes innovation, underestimates change and increases the risk of becoming irrelevant.

Understanding these two forces side by side reveals a deeper truth: bold leadership is not about eliminating fear or clinging to comfort. It is about learning to recognize what each signal is telling you and leading with intentional alignment. Table 2.1 summarizes the key differences, offering a field guide to interpreting and acting on these powerful internal cues.

Table 2.1 Fear vs. Comfort

Category	Fear	Comfort
Primary Signal	Threat to mission or identity	Perceived success or stability
Neuroscience Response	Amygdala activation + prefrontal cortex engagement when processed correctly	Default mode network activation, prioritizing efficiency over innovation
Risk if Unmanaged	Overreaction, paralysis, poor decision-making	Stagnation, loss of relevance, underestimation of change
Potential for Growth	High: Activates learning, resilience, strategic innovation	Low: Reinforces past patterns, inhibits adaptation
Leadership Action	Decode fear and move with alignment (Fuel Formula application)	Recognize comfort as a potential signal to stretch beyond current success

ACTIVITY: Bold Leadership Team Check-In: Fear vs. Comfort

Step 1: Diagnose Where You Are *As a team, honestly assess your current state:*

If the team feels...	You are likely...	Common Warning Signs
Safe but stagnant	**Stalled by Comfort**	Fewer new ideas, over-reliance on past success
Overthinking and avoiding decisions	**Paralyzed by Fear**	Endless meetings, delayed launches, missed pivots
Busy but uninspired	**Drifting in Complacency**	High activity, low strategic momentum
Frustrated but unfocused	**Misaligned with Purpose**	Conflicting priorities, unclear sense of mission

Step 2: Choose Your Bold Move
After diagnosing, agree on one next action to break the pattern:

"Comfort protects what was. Boldness builds what is next."

Bold Move Options	When to Use
Launch a high-visibility project aligned with core mission	If stuck in Comfort or Complacency
Make a bold, time-bound decision without perfect consensus	If stuck in Fear or Overthinking
Sunset an initiative that no longer fits the future vision	If drifting or feeling friction around priorities
Initiate an open "truth-telling" session about risks and opportunities	If feeling restless or disconnected as a team

The Science of Comfort

Why does comfort feel so good and yet lead us so far off track? Neuroscience offers some answers. The human brain is wired to seek predictability and minimize cognitive load. Known as the predictive brain model, this tendency rewards familiar patterns and routines with small dopamine hits, making us feel good when we repeat the same actions, even if they are no longer serving us.

In leadership, this creates a dangerous dynamic where familiar decisions feel safer than bold ones, even when conditions have changed. Past success gets mistaken for future-proof strategy. And the illusion of stability masks emerging risks.

This is called the competency trap in organizational psychology, where prior success becomes the barrier to future adaptation. In simple terms, comfort rewards your brain today and risks your mission and vision tomorrow.

Quick Brain Check

- Predictability triggers dopamine.

- Novelty requires more cognitive effort.

- Boldness demands a willingness to disrupt easy reward loops.

That is why bold leaders consciously disrupt their own comfort cycles. They know that comfort is not a reward for past boldness. It is a signal that new boldness is needed.

Fear vs. Comfort Pocket Matrix: Where Are You Right Now?

In leadership, fear and comfort are not just emotional states; they are strategic signals that shape decision-making and momentum.

The Fear vs. Discomfort Matrix (Figure 2.1) offers a simple but powerful way to self-diagnose whether you are pausing at the edge of growth or settling into patterns that can quietly erode innovation and impact. Fear, often mislabeled as weakness, is actually a salience signal, your brain's way of flagging what matters most. It invites leaders to pay attention, reflect, and choose action aligned with their mission. Comfort, by contrast, can masquerade as success but frequently signals complacency. Studies show that leaders and organizations who prioritize stability over adaptation are at greater risk of decline. The Fear vs. Comfort Matrix helps you quickly locate where you or your team are operating: Are you overanalyzing, drifting, playing it safe, or strategically stretching? Each quadrant offers a diagnostic checkpoint and most importantly, a call to a bold next move. Bold leadership is not about eliminating fear or rejecting comfort entirely; it is about interpreting these signals wisely and moving forward with intention.

Figure 2.1 Fear vs. Discomfort Decision Matrix

The Comfort Trap

- **Stalled Potential: High Fear, High Comfort** You know you are meant for more. You feel it in your gut. But comfort has its grip on you, convincing you it is safer to stay where you are. Every bold instinct gets rationalized away.

- **Your Next Bold Move:** Choose one stretch goal that both excites and scares you. Something just outside your current rhythm. Boldness is not built by staying steady. It is built by stretching deliberately.

- **Leadership Crossroads: High Fear, Low Comfort** You are restless. The anxiety is real. You know you cannot stay where you are, but the way forward feels overwhelming or unclear. This is a crossroads moment and hesitation will only magnify the discomfort.

- **Your Next Bold Move:** Name the fear. Apply the Fuel Formula (Face it. Fuel it. Focus it.). Take one small but aligned step forward today. Bold clarity is earned through action, not analysis.

- **Complacency Drift: Low Fear, High Comfort** Everything looks good on the outside. Meetings are calm. Metrics are stable. But underneath? You feel it: a slow drift away from growth. Comfort is quietly turning into stagnation.

- **Your Next Bold Move:** Do not wait for disruption to force your hand. Proactively seek a challenge. Launch a bold new idea, take a stretch assignment, shake your thinking loose. Growth must be chosen on purpose.

- **Misalignment Burnout: Low Fear, Low Comfort** You are not scared; you are disconnected. The work no longer resonates. The fire that once fueled you feels faint. You are not just tired. You are misaligned.

- **Your Next Bold Move:** Reconnect with your mission. Ask: "What do I want to be bold for?" Redesign your leadership around meaning, not just momentum. Real energy returns when alignment does.

Why Understanding the Comfort Trap Matters

Comfort can masquerade as success. It tells you that because things are not broken, they do not need to evolve. It whispers that the safest move is to stay exactly where you are. But in leadership, safe is often the most dangerous move you can make. If fear was the first force you learned to work with, comfort is the second force you must learn to challenge, every single day. Because here is the uncomfortable truth about leadership, if you are not actively stretching, you are slowly becoming irrelevant.

What the Comfort Trap Really Is and Why It Is So Dangerous

At its core, the Comfort Trap is not just a feeling. It is a cognitive, emotional, and cultural pattern that subtly rewires how leaders think and act. From a neuroscience perspective, comfort is not just a preference. It is a reward system. When leaders maintain familiar routines, the brain delivers small, reinforcing hits of dopamine, the neurochemical associated with satisfaction and reward. Even when the external world demands innovation, the brain's internal wiring encourages staying with the known.

Researchers have found that under uncertainty or stress, the brain naturally defaults to habitual behavior rather than adaptive learning. In leadership, this means that when pressure rises, a leader's instinct may not be to boldly innovate, but to double down on what has already been done.

Over time, this builds what behavioral scientists call habit loops with three elements that include cue, routine, reward. Stability becomes the reward, and boldness starts to

> "The brain is wired for survival, not significance. Bold leadership rewires it."

feel emotionally risky, even when intellectually leaders know it is necessary. Bold leaders break the loop on purpose. They recognize the lure of familiarity and choose conscious, values-driven disruption over comfortable repetition.

Definition

The Comfort Trap occurs when the desire for stability overtakes the drive for growth. It tricks leaders into prioritizing ease, familiarity, and reputation over innovation, adaptability, and bold action.

On the surface, everything looks fine.

But underneath, leadership capacity is quietly eroding.

The Science Behind Comfort

Neuroscience shows that the human brain is wired to seek comfort because familiar patterns require less energy. This preference is known as the effort minimization principle, where the brain instinctively favors routines and predictability to conserve cognitive resources.

But in dynamic environments, the kind leaders face daily, this preference becomes a liability. Organizations that prioritize operational stability over adaptation are 2.5 times more likely to underperform their peers during periods of disruption. Comfort feels efficient in the moment, but it quietly sabotages resilience, relevance, and results.

Spotting the Comfort Trap Early

How can you tell when you are slipping into the comfort trap? Spotting the comfort trap early can save you from stagnation and lost momentum. Pay attention to subtle clues. You find yourself tackling the same problems with the same old solutions. Innovation starts to feel like a nice-to-have rather than an urgent necessity. You hesitate to question the current strategy because, after all, it is still working. Praise comes more often for keeping things steady than for creating meaningful change. And perhaps most telling of all, you begin to defend what currently exists instead of exploring what could be possible. Recognizing these signs early is key to breaking free and reclaiming bold momentum.

If any of these resonate, you are not failing. You are simply being called forward. This transitions the leader from exploitation, maximizing current advantages, to exploration, seeking new opportunities. Bold leaders must balance both.

How to Recognize When You Are Stuck in the Comfort Trap

The comfort trap does not show up as obvious complacency. It shows up as subtle shifts in thinking, decision-making, and behavior. There are early warning signs every bold leader must learn to recognize before comfort becomes a trap. It often starts with defaulting to what has worked before, without pausing to question whether those approaches still serve the mission. Leaders may quietly avoid stretch goals, rationalizing that what we have is good enough, even when deeper instincts say otherwise. Innovation initiatives stall, not because they are strategically unsound, but because the emotional discomfort of change outweighs the perceived payoff. Success begins to be measured by stability and harmony rather than growth or evolution, even when the market, the team, or the mission itself is signaling a need to move. Approval-seeking becomes more comfortable than alignment-seeking, because rocking the boat feels riskier than standing still. Left unchecked, these patterns silently erode impact, credibility, and relevance, long before the consequences become visible.

People naturally tend to protect what they have rather than pursue what they could gain, a bias known as loss aversion. For leaders, this instinct often results in clinging to the status quo, even when bold action could lead to greater success. In bold leadership, unchecked loss aversion does not just maintain the present; it quietly erodes your potential for meaningful impact.

Why Comfort Erodes Trust Faster Than You Realize

It is easy to believe that playing it safe will protect your credibility. But in reality, prolonged comfort slowly erodes trust. Psychological safety on teams actually declines when leaders fail to stretch, challenge, and evolve with the needs of their teams. Employees sense when leadership prioritizes their own comfort over the organization's mission. They disengage not because leaders push too hard, but because leaders stop pulling forward.

People trust leaders who are willing to *move* even when it is hard, not those who stay silent, still, or stuck. Comfort does not just quietly erode innovation at the top. It ripples downward, eroding energy, trust, and engagement across teams. When leaders unconsciously prioritize stability over stretch, teams sense it. Initiative declines. Creative risks stop. A culture of silent frustration sets in.

Emotional disengagement starts long before formal turnover does and has shown that people will withdraw emotional, cognitive, and physical presence when they do not see a meaningful future ahead. When leadership avoids bold moves, teams unconsciously interpret it as a lack of vision and they respond not with rebellion, but with quiet retreat. Bold leadership does not just protect innovation. It protects belief. It tells teams, We are moving. We are stretching. We are moving forward.

"When leaders stop reaching, teams stop believing."

Escaping the Comfort Trap

To break free from the Comfort Trap, bold leaders must shift the fundamental leadership questions they ask, instead of, is this safe enough? A Bold Leader asks, is this aligned enough? instead of will this feel comfortable? A Bold Leader asks, will this move us toward what matters? This cognitive reframe draws from research in psychological flexibility, the capacity to adapt behavior based on goals and values rather than momentary comfort. Psychological flexibility, not rigid adherence to comfort, is now seen as one of the strongest predictors of leadership resilience, innovation, and long-term success. Comfort is not a reward for good leadership. It is often the first red flag that leadership is at risk.

ACTIVITY: The Bold Questions Audit

Step 1: Catch Your Current Questions
For the next three days, notice what questions you ask yourself when making decisions. Write them down exactly as they occur to you.

Step 2: Identify Your Comfort Questions
Review your list and mark any questions that prioritize safety, consensus, or avoiding discomfort over mission alignment and growth.

Step 3: Reframe to Bold Questions
For each comfort question you identified, create a bold alternative using this framework:

Comfort Question	Bold Question
"Is this safe enough?"	"Is this aligned with our mission?"
"Will everyone approve?"	"Will this move us forward?"
"What if it fails?"	"What happens if we do not try?"
"Can we wait longer?"	"What is the cost of delay?"
"Will this disrupt things?"	"Will this create the change we need?"

Step 4: Practice Bold Questions

For the next week, deliberately ask your reframed questions before making any significant decision. Notice how different questions lead to different choices and different results.

Your Bold Questions Template: Write your three most common comfort questions and their bold alternatives here:

Comfort: _____

Bold Reframe: _____

Comfort: _____

Bold Reframe: _____

Comfort: _____

Bold Reframe: _____

Building a Bold Practice of Discomfort

Building a bold leadership practice means getting comfortable with being uncomfortable on purpose, and every single day. True boldness is not a lightning strike. It is a rhythm you create by stretching yourself in ways that sharpen your edge: speaking first when you would rather wait, pitching the raw idea before you polish it, challenging assumptions even when it rattles the room. Bold leaders track these moments, not just in their minds, but in real time. They may even keep a bold moves journal, documenting each stretch, each win, and each moment they moved instead of stalled because momentum does not just happen, it is built. They celebrate action over perfection, knowing that boldness is not about getting it right the first time; it is about having the courage to move before certainty arrives. Most importantly, they learn to call out the Comfort Trap fast.

The second the voice of hesitation says, "Maybe next quarter..." or "Let's wait a little longer...," they do not negotiate. They move. Because bold leadership is not built in the moments you feel ready, it is built in the moments you choose to move anyway.

Brain science tells us that when you deliberately challenge yourself, even in small ways, you actually change your brain. Each time you stretch beyond comfort, whether you speak up in a meeting, make a decision without perfect information, or try something new, you build stronger neural pathways.

Your brain grows through challenge, not just success. Small, repeated acts of deliberate discomfort signal your brain to adapt and strengthen. The more you practice being uncomfortable on purpose, the more your brain becomes wired for boldness. Bold leaders are not born with a different brain. They build one, through daily stretch.

You are rewiring your brain for agility, innovation, and boldness.

How the Comfort Trap Erodes Boldness

When leaders prioritize comfort over evolution, three critical damages occur. Examples can include:

- **Stagnation:** Without bold new bets, your strategy becomes stale. Companies that focus solely on short-term stability without innovation see a significant decrease in market relevance.

- **Credibility Loss:** Teams lose trust in leaders who appear more interested in protecting their position than pursuing the organization's future. Bold leadership, courageous, aligned, and transparent, builds psychological safety and commitment.

> "Safe leadership feels responsible in the moment, but looks irrelevant in the rearview mirror."

- **Legacy Erosion:** Your leadership is not judged by how perfectly you preserved the status quo. It is judged by how bravely you shaped what came next.

The Neuroscience of Bold Disruption

Want more proof that disrupting comfort is essential?

Studies show that exposure to positive stress, situations where leaders stretch beyond their comfort zone without being overwhelmed, actually strengthens neuroplasticity and adaptive leadership behaviors. In other words, bold action keeps your leadership brain healthy.

Leaders who avoid disruption at all costs gradually lose not only external relevance, but internal resilience, too. The ability to tolerate discomfort, to step into new arenas without guarantees, to innovate under uncertainty. These are mental muscles that atrophy without use.

> "Bold leadership is a living system that is nurtured and practiced. Use it or lose it."

Facing My Own Comfort Trap

I remember sitting in a leadership retreat a few years ago. We reviewed quarterly metrics. Everything looked good. Growth was steady. Employee engagement scores were high.

But underneath the metrics, I felt it, the team's innovation energy had dulled. Big ideas were being deferred. Caution had replaced curiosity. And when I looked closer, I saw it in myself too. Sometimes we feel we have to assimilate to fit in and be accepted, even as a leader. I had stopped asking bigger questions. I had stopped stretching for bolder possibilities. I had started managing the organization, instead of directing and leading it. I realized boldness was not just for seasons of crisis or disruption. Boldness was a daily discipline and that I was misaligned with my values as a leader and as an individual. That realization changed the trajectory of my leadership and it can change yours, too.

What You Have Learned

You have learned that while comfort in leadership can feel safe, it often signals subtle erosion rather than true strength. Neuroscience confirms that our brains naturally gravitate toward energy-saving habits, which means bold leaders must intentionally interrupt this autopilot tendency. It is loss aversion, not laziness, that explains why many leaders become stagnant, clinging to what is familiar instead of venturing into growth. You also discovered that psychological safety does not shrink in the face of bold action; it actually expands. Ultimately, bold leadership is not about occasional dramatic leaps but about intentionally choosing small, daily moments of discomfort that steadily stretch you and your team toward greater possibilities.

Bold Truth

If you are not intentionally stretching, you are unintentionally slipping.

Your Bold Move

Identify one place in your leadership where you have been playing it safe out of habit, not strategy.

Ask: "What future am I sacrificing by staying comfortable here?"

Choose one aligned, uncomfortable move and take it within 48 hours.

Bold Metrics

Disrupting Comfort with Purposeful Stretch

Comfort feels safe, but in leadership, it quietly erodes innovation, momentum, and trust. In this chapter, you learned to spot the signs of comfort drift, and why bold leaders must stretch even when success feels steady.

Track Your Boldness

Did I intentionally step outside of my leadership comfort zone this week?

Did I notice where comfort was masking stagnation?

Did I design a purposeful stretch aligned with future growth?

Bold Metric	Rating (1–5)				
	1	2	3	4	5
(1 = Avoided bold action, 5 = Fully acted with aligned boldness)					
I identified an area where comfort was holding me back.	☐	☐	☐	☐	☐
I proactively pursued a growth opportunity.	☐	☐	☐	☐	☐
I moved toward discomfort in service of my mission.	☐	☐	☐	☐	☐

Setting the Stage for What Comes Next

In Chapter 1, we redefined fear. You learned that fear is not a flaw to eliminate but a signal to decode. Fear points to what matters most. When you understand this, fear becomes fuel for aligned action rather than a barrier to progress.

In Chapter 2, we exposed the hidden costs of comfort. You discovered that while fear announces itself loudly, comfort seeps in quietly, disguising stagnation as stability. You learned to spot the comfort trap early and understand that if you are not intentionally stretching, you are unintentionally slipping.

Now you have the awareness. You can recognize when fear is offering valuable information and when comfort is quietly eroding your impact. But awareness alone does not create results. Knowledge without application is just interesting information.

In Chapter 3, we take everything you have learned and transform it into your Bold Advantage. Because boldness is not just about surviving risk or managing discomfort. Boldness is about using aligned risk as a strategic force multiplier, for your leadership effectiveness, your team performance, and your organizational results.

You will discover how bold leaders create competitive advantage not by avoiding uncertainty, but by moving through it faster and more strategically than their competitors. You will learn why innovation and boldness are inseparable, and how to build systems that turn calculated risks into breakthrough outcomes.

The foundation is set. The awareness is built. The skills are ready to be activated.

It is time to claim your Bold Advantage.

Part II

Bold Activation

Turn Insight into Impact with Actionable Frameworks and Tools

Insights alone will not change your world, actions will. Here, you will master the BOLD Framework, Believe, Own, Learn, Design, to move from clarity to action. You will also implement the game-changing D90 Method, a precise 90-day action plan designed to translate bold intentions into tangible, measurable leadership wins. No more waiting, it is your time to lead boldly and decisively.

Chapter 3

The Bold Advantage

You have crossed two of leadership's most invisible thresholds. You learned that fear is not your enemy, but one of your most sophisticated intelligence systems. You uncovered how comfort, when left unchecked, becomes a slow, silent killer of innovation and momentum.

> "Momentum is not magic, it is deliberate leadership math."

Now we shift forward.

Bold leadership is not just about surviving fear or resisting comfort. It is about using aligned risk as a force multiplier. It is about understanding that innovation, growth, and impact are not accidents, they are outcomes of boldness practiced on purpose.

Welcome to the Bold Advantage.

The Myth of Momentum

Momentum is not magic. It is leadership math.

For years, I believed what many do, that momentum was something you could catch, like a lucky tailwind. That if you worked hard enough, built the right teams, made the right calls, momentum would take shape and appear. That is not how it works. Not in real leadership.

Momentum is not given. It is generated. And bold leadership is the engine.

Here is what I learned the hard way—waiting does not create momentum. Action does. Movement creates motivation. Bold leaders move first, not because it feels easy, but because it is the only way momentum is built.

Real momentum, the kind that fuels innovation, deepens trust, and accelerates impact, comes from leaders who are willing to move before conditions are perfect. Leaders who stretch into discomfort not because it feels safe, but because it feels aligned. And neuroscience agrees. Studies show that action taken in uncertainty increases dopamine activation, reinforcing learning loops that sustain adaptive behavior and innovation. Action taken under uncertainty activates the brain's dopaminergic reward system, the circuits that reinforce adaptive behavior and emotional resilience. When you move forward, your brain rewards you. When you hesitate, it defaults into threat mode, feeding doubt and disengagement. In simple terms, bold movement creates its own momentum. Waiting halts your momentum and any movement forward.

Boldness vs. Busyness

Busyness can feel satisfying. You are checking boxes, attending meetings, filling your calendar. But boldness is different. It asks, "Is this movement aligned with what matters?"

✔ **Bold leaders create velocity toward purpose.**

✘ **Busy leaders create velocity toward exhaustion.**

Research in organizational behavior shows that leaders who prioritize "movement aligned with mission" achieve 2.4× higher goal attainment compared to those who simply maximize hours worked. It is not how much you do. It is how *meaningfully* you move.

Why Innovation Demands Boldness

Innovation is not the result of brainstorming sessions, sticky-note marathons, or quarterly hackathons. It is not about how many creative ideas you can generate. It is about what you are willing to activate before the outcome is certain, before the risk is fully measured, before the world agrees it is safe.

Innovation belongs to the bold.

Organizations that consistently acted on imperfect but mission-aligned decisions outperformed their perfection-driven competitors. The companies that moved earlier, even without full consensus or flawless information, captured more opportunity, built adaptive cultures, and scaled faster. The real differentiator was not creativity. It was action.

In fact, additional research by McKinsey found that the top 10% of innovative organizations had leadership teams that made major strategic decisions 45% faster than their industry peers, even when they had access to the same limited information. The speed of bold action created competitive separation long before product advantages emerged.

From a neuroscience perspective, this phenomenon is deeply wired into how the brain handles decision-making under uncertainty. Decision Urgency Theory shows that when the brain encounters ambiguous or incomplete information, it is biologically more advantageous to act on a meaningful signal rather than delay action indefinitely in search of certainty. The brain's prefrontal cortex, responsible for rational thought, integrates signals until a good enough threshold is reached, then pushes for action.

Leaders who ignore this wiring by delaying action excessively fall prey to paralysis by analysis, leading to cognitive fatigue, slower learning loops, and missed opportunities. And the stakes are even higher today.

"Waiting does not protect innovation. Waiting makes innovation impossible."

Organizations operating in high-uncertainty environments, such as post-pandemic markets, that waited for high levels of certainty before launching new initiatives missed market shifts by an average of 8–12 months, costing them both customer loyalty and revenue acceleration.

My Experience

In my own leadership experience, whether launching new business lines, advising healthcare and business leadership teams, or coaching C-suite executives, every major breakthrough I witnessed started not in certainty, but with the choice of strategic boldness.

The leaders who moved first did not have it all figured out. They did not have unanimous support. They did not have any guarantees. But they had alignment. Alignment with their mission, values, and vision. And alignment always beats assurance.

Because bold leadership does not guarantee the first move is perfect. It guarantees you are in motion when it matters most, and motion, intelligently directed, will always outpace analysis paralysis. Bold leadership creates bold results.

The Neuroscience of Bold Activation

> "Boldness is not just psychological, it's neurobiological."

When leaders act aligned with a meaningful mission, even in uncertainty, two critical brain systems activate. The dopaminergic reward system, which reinforces adaptive behavior through positive feedback loops. And the salience network, which heightens attention to what matters most while reducing noise from irrelevant threats.

In simple terms, bold action rewires your brain for focus, resilience, and momentum.

Waiting, by contrast, reinforces the brain's threat response. Extended hesitation activates the amygdala and anterior cingulate cortex, regions associated with fear, hypervigilance, and emotional exhaustion. This is why long periods of indecision or playing it safe do not just slow progress externally. They erode internal resilience over time.

Boldness is not being reckless. It is a biologically strategic move that keeps leaders adaptive, energized, and cognitively flexible in fast-changing environments.

> "Boldness is not innate. It is built."

The most resilient leaders are not those who feel no fear. They are the ones who act meaningfully before fear has a chance to create paralysis. Neuroplasticity research shows that when leaders repeatedly act with courage in small moments, they physically strengthen the brain circuits responsible for decision-making, confidence, and emotional resilience. Every bold act, even microsized moves, makes the next bold move easier. Each bold step leads to more experience and confidence which then leads to more agency in your leadership role and in your life.

Boldness in Action

Early in my career, I was sitting in a quarterly planning meeting when I noticed something others had missed. We were approaching a critical infrastructure project the same way we had for years, but the landscape had changed. New technology, different user needs, shifting regulations, everything was pointing toward a completely different approach.

I had two choices: stay quiet and let the meeting proceed as planned, or speak up with an untested idea that would challenge the entire room.

The room was full of seasoned leaders, people with decades more experience than me. The budget was already approved. The timeline was set. The safe move was to keep my mouth shut.

But I could not shake the feeling that we were about to spend six months and significant resources building something that would be obsolete before we finished.

So I spoke up.

"What if we are solving the wrong problem?" I said. The room went quiet. I could feel the skepticism, but I pushed forward. I outlined a completely different approach, one that would require us to possibly scrap our current plan and start over, but would position us ahead of our competitors.

The questions came fast. The pushback was real. Some people thought I was being naive. Others wondered if I understood the complexity involved.

But here is what happened next, the conversation shifted. Instead of rubber-stamping the old approach, we started exploring possibilities. Three other leaders in the room admitted they had similar concerns and now voiced them. The financial leader started running numbers on my proposal.

Two weeks later, we pivoted to the new approach. The project launched four months early, came in under budget, and became a model that other divisions adopted.

That decision, to act boldly in a moment that could have easily led to hesitation, changed more than just the project trajectory. It changed my trajectory. It built trust with leadership who saw I was willing to take risks for the mission. It sparked momentum across the team who realized bold ideas were welcome. It modeled for others that leadership is not about waiting until you are 100% ready, or defined by your tenure in an organization, it is about moving when the mission calls, even if the path is not fully paved.

The lesson? Boldness is not about having all the answers. It is about being aligned with what matters most and moving with that alignment, even when the outcome is still unfolding.

The Problem with Playing Catch-Up

Too many leaders believe innovation is the job of someone else, but real innovation starts with you. It is in how you think. What you challenge. What you refuse to tolerate. What you are willing to risk. Organizations that innovate consistently do so because their leaders act boldly, not recklessly, but with clarity and conviction.

Bold leaders will ask:

What is possible here that has not been tried?

What assumptions are we treating as facts?

Where are we underestimating our own potential?

They do not wait for perfect conditions. They move with imperfect information.

And they create a culture where experimentation is safe, stretch is expected, and feedback is fuel.

It is not just about moving. It is about moving aligned and early.

The Bold Leadership Triangle

Boldness. Innovation. Growth.

At first glance, these concepts might seem like independent elements of leadership, each valuable but separate. But in reality, they are deeply interconnected, forming a powerful, self-reinforcing triangle essential for transformative leadership.

Boldness sparks the cycle. It is the courageous first step that breaks through inertia, the decision to move forward when the path is not fully clear. Boldness is not about fearless leaps into the unknown; it is about intentional action fueled by deep alignment with your vision, purpose, and core values.

From boldness comes Innovation. True innovation is not simply iteration or incremental improvement, it is what happens when boldness meets possibility. When you are bold enough to question the status quo, you open the door for new ideas, creative solutions, and opportunities you might have otherwise missed. Innovation thrives where boldness disrupts familiar patterns and invites fresh perspectives.

"Growth is both the result and the reward of choosing boldness and embracing innovation consistently."

The natural outcome of innovation, sustained through consistent bold action, is growth. Genuine, sustainable growth is not accidental or sporadic. It arises from purposeful experimentation, continuous learning, and intentional alignment over time.

A key point to remember as a leader, you cannot shortcut this triangle.

- Growth without innovation is fragile and accidental, easily lost as conditions change.

- Innovation without boldness merely results in small refinements, never truly transforming or achieving meaningful breakthroughs.

- Boldness without alignment becomes noise, chaotic action without lasting purpose or impact.

Bold leadership recognizes and harnesses this powerful cycle intentionally. It moves beyond understanding boldness, innovation, and growth as separate elements and integrates them into a unified strategy. By consistently aligning boldness with your vision, translating courage into innovation, and channeling innovation into purposeful growth, you create an unstoppable engine of progress that continually elevates your leadership and amplifies your impact.

ACTIVITY: Map Your Bold Leadership Triangle

Take a few minutes to reflect on a recent major initiative, project, or pivot you were part of as a leader in your organization.

Ask yourself:

What was the bold move? What decision or action disrupted the status quo?

What innovation did it unleash? Did it open new opportunities, insights, or solutions?

What growth resulted or did not? Was there measurable progress, and what lessons emerged?

Now look ahead at your current priorities: Where is boldness missing right now? Where could a single bold move unleash new innovation and future growth?

Boldness is not reserved for special moments.

It is built, activated, and multiplied, one move at a time.

The Team That Stopped Apologizing

A mid-sized healthcare technology company came to us stuck in hesitation. They had a promising new platform, but they had delayed launch twice, second-guessed strategy, and buried themselves in internal reports. Every meeting opened with, "We know we're behind, but…" They were not just stuck operationally. They were stuck emotionally. So we asked them one question: If you believed you were ahead of the curve, how would you lead? Everything shifted. They stopped apologizing for where they were not and started leading toward where they could be.

Within 45 days, they made three bold product decisions. Launched a user pilot and secured two new ideas for partnerships. What changed was not the platform. It was their leadership posture, from defensive to bold.

The Difference Between Motion and Momentum

There is a difference between being busy and building momentum. Motion looks like endless meetings, reports, and second-guessing. You know, those meetings to have a meeting to set another meeting. Admit, you have either been in them or maybe you have been the person who has created this crazy cycle of meetings. It is painful when the indecision loops set in and micromanagement is leading the team tiny step by tiny step.

Momentum feels like meaningful stretch toward a clear destination, not an incremental crawl toward a goal. If your team is moving but not progressing, if your strategy looks good on paper but feels lifeless in action, what is missing is not a better plan. It is your bold factor.

Your brain loves patterns, it gives you a little dopamine reward every time you choose the familiar. That's why old strategies feel safer, even when they are quietly costing you momentum. Bold leadership literally wires the brain for innovation.

> "Boldness doesn't just accelerate your pace, it expands your potential."

Why Boldness Accelerates Innovation

Let us get a little technical for a moment.

You have probably noticed that your best innovations do not come from comfort zones or crisis zones. They come from somewhere in between when there is enough pressure to think differently but not so much that people shut down.

There is actually science behind this. Researchers call it "the edge of chaos," that sweet spot where there is just enough disruption to force adaptation without falling into disorder.

Think of it like this:

- **Too much stability** = innovation dies. Your team gets comfortable, stops questioning, stops stretching. Everything feels safe, but nothing new emerges.

- **Too much chaos** = the system breaks down. People become overwhelmed, trust erodes, and energy gets wasted on damage control instead of progress.

- **The edge of chaos** = innovation thrives. There is enough tension to spark creativity, enough safety to take risks, and enough direction to channel energy productively.

Bold leadership allows you to dance at that edge. You push when the team needs a stretch. You stabilize when trust needs rebuilding. You create enough productive tension to spark new growth without breaking what already works.

"Innovation is not an accident. It is a strategic side effect of intentional boldness. This is not bravado. This is strategy."

This is why bold leaders do not just generate ideas, they generate the conditions where breakthrough thinking becomes inevitable.

ACTIVITY: Bold Innovation Sprint

Pick one major challenge your team keeps circling but not solving. Now answer the following questions.

- What is the boldest solution you have been afraid to name?
- What is the smallest test of that solution you could launch within 30 days?
- Who needs to be involved in that first small move?

Innovation is not a brainstorming exercise. It is an act of bold alignment.

The Internal Advantage

Bold leaders do not just scale companies. They scale themselves. They build internal clarity that cannot be shaken by external noise. They model courageous decision-making so consistently that it becomes contagious across teams. They do not just build strategies. They build cultural momentum.

Boldness becomes embedded, not episodic. And over time, that leadership posture, clear, courageous, and consistent, becomes the advantage that no competitor can copy.

Bold leadership does not just drive innovation, it also acts as a magnet for top talent and attention. Leaders who demonstrate courage and creativity can transform ordinary individuals into visionary leaders by inspiring decisive and innovative action. This approach fosters a culture where employees feel involved and valued, creating ideal conditions for innovation to flourish.

Real Talk Moment

Boldness is not a burst. It is a rhythm. You build it one aligned decision at a time.

One brave conversation at a time. One leap forward, even when no one else is ready, at a time.

Bold leadership often entails venturing into uncharted territory, which can be a solitary journey. Research indicates that senior leaders are twice as likely to report feelings of isolation compared to their junior counterparts. This loneliness stems from the heavy burden of leadership and decision-making, not necessarily from a lack of social connections. Acknowledging and addressing this emotional challenge is crucial, as it can impact both personal well-being and organizational effectiveness.

> "Boldness is not about moving fast for the sake of speed. It is about moving true for the sake of what matters most."

The Advantage Within

Boldness is not something you have to find. It is something you have to remember.

Think back to a moment when you acted with complete conviction, maybe as a child standing up for a friend, or early in your career when you spoke a truth others would not say. That boldness was not borrowed. It was yours.

What happened along the way? You learned that leadership was supposed to look cautious, calculated, and maybe even were taught it was about conforming. You absorbed the message that good leaders wait for permission, build consensus, always have harmony, and avoid making waves. You started second-guessing the instincts that once served you well.

The bold leader you are becoming is not a future version of yourself waiting somewhere out there. It is the fullest version of you that already exists, buried under layers of conditioning and doubt.

You do not need to add something artificial to be bold. You need to remove the barriers that have made you hesitate, hide, and second-guess your instincts.

You need to free the part of you that already knows:

- How to move toward growth even when it feels uncomfortable.
- How to lead with conviction even when the outcome is unclear.
- How to build momentum not from perfection, but from purpose.

That leader is not missing. That leader is waiting.

The question is not whether you have what it takes to be bold. The question is whether you are ready to stop hiding what you have always had.

What You Have Learned

This chapter was not about teaching you to become someone new. It was about reminding you who you already are, and showing you the strategic, psychological, and organizational power that comes when you choose boldness on purpose.

The Bold Advantage you now hold is more than a mindset. It is a movement inside you. It is the decision to lead differently, to create, disrupt, and stretch not just because you have to, but because you can. It is the realization that innovation is not for the lucky few. Growth is not for the reckless few. Impact is not for the loudest few. It is for the bold ones, the ones willing to move when most people wait, to speak when most people stay silent, to choose clarity over comfort, and to bet on something bigger than their fear.

You have that capacity now. You have always had it. And now, you are learning how to use it with precision, with alignment, and with a resilience that does not burn out when the road gets tough.

Bold Truth

Boldness multiplies impact. One aligned, courageous action creates far greater results than endless safe choices combined.

Your Bold Move

Grab a pen and reflect on the following questions:

Where are you stretching boldly?

Where are you waiting for permission, you do not actually need?

Did I stretch beyond what was comfortable?

Did I make one decision that scared me a little?

Where did I default to busyness instead of boldness?

What bold action am I delaying and what is the real cost of that delay?

Weekly reflection accelerates bold leadership habits far more powerfully than quarterly reviews or annual self-assessments. Because boldness, like any leadership muscle, is strengthened in repetitions, not resolutions.

Bold Metrics

Use the scale below to assess where your bold leadership stands today:

	1	2	3	4	5
I initiate bold ideas before perfect conditions.	☐	☐	☐	☐	☐
I encourage stretch experiments within my team.	☐	☐	☐	☐	☐
I move toward innovation even when outcomes are uncertain.	☐	☐	☐	☐	☐
I model decisiveness aligned with a bold vision.	☐	☐	☐	☐	☐

Setting the Stage for What Comes Next

In the next chapter, we are moving beyond simply recognizing boldness as an advantage, we are going to dive into how you can actively build it into your leadership as a reliable, daily practice. Think of this as constructing a powerful, repeatable system you can count on, especially when the world feels chaotic or uncertain. This is where you will start mastering the heart of bold leadership and the framework I created when I was figuring out my next bold move, The BOLD Framework: Believe, Own, Learn, Design. You will explore how to ground your leadership deeply in belief, truly own your voice, choices, and direction, learn purposefully through both intentional action and honest reflection, and thoughtfully design your next moves, guided not by fear or doubt, but by your core values and vision. You have the awareness. You understand that boldness is not just an advantage, it is *the* advantage. The gap most leaders face is knowing boldness matters and actually building it into your daily leadership are completely different challenges.

I faced this exact moment five years ago. I was standing at my own leadership crossroads, knowing I needed to make a bold move but having no reliable system to guide me through it. The traditional leadership frameworks felt too safe, too slow, too disconnected from the reality of leading in uncertainty.

That is when I created the BOLD Framework. Not in a conference room or strategy session, but in the messy middle of my own leadership transition. When I needed something practical, something I could count on when the stakes were high and the path was unclear.

In Chapter 4, you will learn this framework, the same system that guided me from executive burnout to building Bold Industries Group. The framework that our clients use to make decisions that matter, have conversations that count, and create momentum when everyone else is stuck in analysis paralysis.

This is not academic theory. This is leadership math that works when everything else feels uncertain.

Your Bold Advantage is waiting. Let me show you how to activate it.

Activate Your Bold

By now, you have faced fear and realized it is not your enemy, it is your intelligence system. You have named comfort for what it is, a trap in disguise. You have seen how boldness fuels innovation, ignites growth, and creates real results in messy, unpredictable, high-stakes moments.

> "Most leaders think boldness is about big moves. It is actually about building the inner structure that makes every move aligned."

Now we pivot, from concept to commitment. This chapter is not about understanding boldness. It is about activating it. Every day. In how you decide. How you show up. How you shape the space around you. Because leadership without self-leadership is just performance. And bold leadership? It begins from within.

This chapter is where your boldness becomes real. It is not about what you know; it is about how you lead. It is time to move from concept to practice. From knowing the principles to living them. This is where you take action through each bold step that you make as a leader.

Your Personal Leadership Operating System

The BOLD Framework is not just a model I created. It is the structure I lived through. It is how I led myself out of burnout. It is how I built and bootstrapped Bold Industries Group from scratch. It is how

I coach other leaders to move, not with action for action's sake, but intentional impact coupled with alignment.

BOLD stands for Believe, Own, Learn, Design and can be applied this way in leadership:

- **Believe:** What you believe shapes what you build. Your mindset becomes your blueprint. If you believe you have to prove your worth, you will lead from fear. If you believe you are already enough, you will lead from a space of personal power and stand in your value.

- **Own:** Radical ownership of your presence, your patterns, and your potential. Bold leaders take full responsibility, not just for outcomes, but for energy, voice, and integrity.

- **Learn:** Every outcome is data. Bold leaders do not fear failure, they metabolize it. Reflection replaces reactivity. Learning becomes momentum.

- **Design:** Bold leadership does not default. It designs. It does not just respond to what is; it builds what is next, on purpose.

> "Boldness becomes real when you choose it daily, not just when the pressure is high, but when the stakes feel invisible."

This framework and its parts are not a to-do list. They are a loop. A rhythm. A living operating system you return to again and again.

What You Believe Shapes What You Build

When I left my corporate role, it was not a lack of strategy that scared me. It was the quiet voice that asked, do I really know how to be a successful entrepreneur? That is the power of belief. Before any bold move, there is a belief, either inherited or chosen, that whispers what you think is possible. Bold leadership begins long

before strategy meetings, pitch decks, or metrics dashboards. It begins inside you, with what you believe about yourself, your role, your team, and what is possible.

Beliefs are not just thoughts. Neuroscience shows that beliefs operate as internal predictive models, shaping how you filter information, interpret risks, and decide which opportunities you pursue. Your brain, wired for efficiency, tends to seek evidence that confirms your core beliefs and dismiss evidence that challenges them. This phenomenon, known as confirmation bias, can either trap leaders in old patterns or empower them to stretch into bold new realities.

If you believe that boldness is reckless, you will filter every new opportunity through caution. If you believe that boldness is alignment in action, you will move forward with clarity even when conditions are imperfect.

> "Your beliefs are the blueprint your leadership builds upon. Upgrade them, and you upgrade your outcomes."

Belief Drift Warning Signs (Subtle signs you are leading from a limiting belief):

- You hesitate to share ideas in high-stakes rooms.
- You say "yes" to things that drain you because you do not want to seem difficult.
- You over-prepare before speaking up.
- You tell yourself, "Once I get X, *then* I'll feel ready."

The Bold Leader's first job is not to predict the future. It is to clarify the internal beliefs shaping how they meet it.

Example:

> **Old belief:** "I can't speak up until I have all the data."
>
> **Bold belief:** "My insight has value even when the picture isn't complete."

Belief is not just personal. It is cultural. Bold leaders rewire belief systems inside teams, too. They ask, "What do we believe is possible and is it holding us back or pulling us forward?"

The Science of Belief Formation

Beliefs are not static, they are living neural networks, flexible and rewritable under conditions of emotional salience and intentional action. When you consistently act in alignment with a new, empowering belief, your brain begins to physically rewire, reinforcing the new pattern while weakening the old. This is called self-directed neuroplasticity, and it is why small bold acts, repeated over time, do far more than just change outcomes, they change leaders at the identity level.

> "Your calendar and how you choose to spend your most important resource, time, always reflects your core beliefs. The question is, whose beliefs are they?"

Your Leadership Belief Audit

- What beliefs about your leadership do you hold right now, about your capacity, your worth, your voice?

- Who or what planted those beliefs?

- Which beliefs expand you? Which limit you?

- What bold belief would you choose to lead from today, if you could rewrite the script?

Why Belief Matters More Than Strategy

You can have the best playbook in the world, but if you believe you are not capable, worthy, or ready, you will hesitate. You will discount your instincts. You will lead small when the moment demands bold. Leaders with strong self-efficacy beliefs, belief in their ability to influence outcomes, were more likely to lead strategic pivots successfully compared to leaders with low self-efficacy, even when experience levels were equivalent. Translation? Belief is not nice to have. It is the foundation of strategic execution under uncertainty.

Real Talk Moment: The Bold Leaders Collective

When I first launched The Bold Leaders Collective Membership in late summer of 2023, I had the idea fully mapped out. I had the vision. The structure. The heart. But I also had a belief playing quietly in the background that nearly kept me from hitting "publish."

The belief? No one will join unless I prove this is worth it.

It was a belief rooted in years of corporate conditioning, the need to validate, to have the data, to stack every credential before I could invite someone into something new. Even though I had coached hundreds of leaders and built bold results before, my belief still whispered that this time was different.

So I hesitated.

I tweaked the landing page 12 times.

I delayed the launch date.

I wondered if I needed more testimonials, more structure, more polish.

But then I stopped. And I did the work I now teach others. I ran that belief through my Bold Belief Upgrade Process:

- **Spot It:** No one will join unless I prove this is worth it.

- **Source It:** That belief did not come from me, it came from old systems that taught me worth was something to earn, not something I already held.

- **Stretch It:** What if I believed the opposite? The right women will join because it is bold, aligned, and real.

- **Seed It:** I launched with what I had. I spoke directly from my why. I shared the heart behind the work, and within two weeks, the first cohort was full.

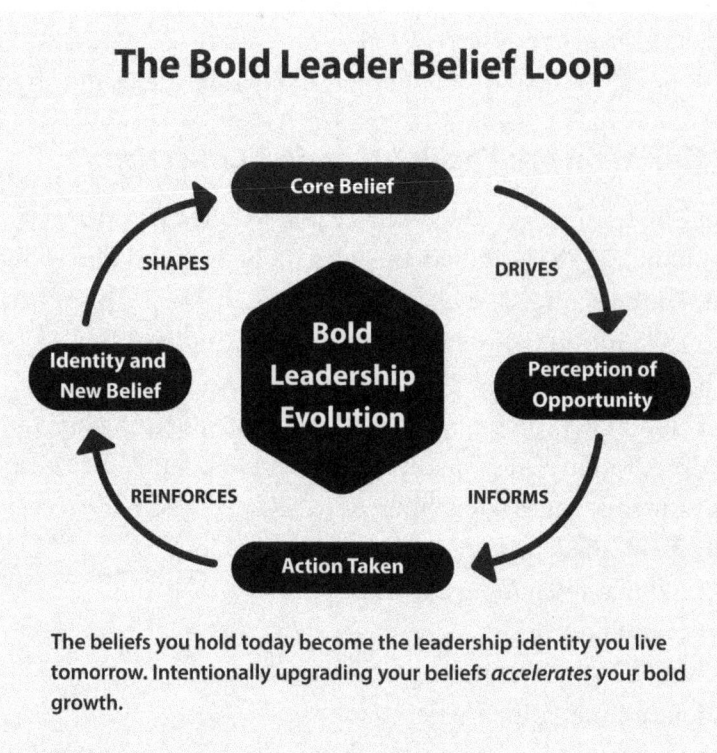

Figure 4.1 The Bold Leadership Belief Loop

That moment rewired something permanent in me. I did not need to prove my worth. I needed to believe in the worth of the bold space I was building (see Figure 4.1). And when

"Every bold step you take becomes evidence that the new belief is true."

I did, others did too. That is how belief works. It does not wait to be proven. It asks you to lead as if it is already true. Now you can try your own leadership Belief Upgrade.

ACTIVITY: Belief Upgrade Exercise

Instead of just listing your current beliefs, take it further:

1. **Spot It:** Write down one leadership belief that feels constraining.

2. **Source It:** Where did it come from? Whose voice is it really?

3. **Stretch It:** Imagine you believed the opposite. What new moves would that unlock?

4. **Seed It:** Choose one micro-action this week that reinforces the new bold belief.

Example:

- **Old Belief:** "I'm not experienced enough to drive change."
- **Source:** A former mentor who favored seniority over creativity.
- **Stretch Belief:** "Innovation favors clarity, not tenure."
- **Action:** Speak up in the next strategy meeting with your vision, even if no one else has yet.

Spot the Belief in Action

Your leadership behavior is often a mirror of your core beliefs. But most of those beliefs do not shout, they whisper. They run in the background, shaping how you show up in ways that feel automatic. Here is how to spot the belief behind the behavior and how to reframe it boldly:

Situation	Default Belief	Bold Reframe
You hesitate to share an idea in a meeting.	I need more data to be credible.	My lived experience is valuable even when the picture is not perfect.
You price your offer lower than you intended.	I do not want to scare them off.	Right-fit clients are drawn to clarity and confidence, not discounts.
You avoid giving feedback to a peer.	It will create conflict.	Truth builds trust, silence builds resentment.
You delay launching something until it is perfect.	If I get this wrong, I will lose credibility.	Progress creates credibility, perfection is not required.
You let your calendar fill with misaligned meetings.	Saying no will make me seem ungrateful.	Every yes I give should be in service of what matters most.

Use this chart to spot your own patterns. Next time you feel resistance, ask yourself: What belief is underneath this? Is it serving my bold leadership or is it shrinking it?

The Cost of Default Beliefs

Default beliefs are not just mindset fluff, they influence the actual way you lead, price, decide, and grow. Default beliefs in action can look like this:

- **In Conflict:** If you believe tension equals danger, you will avoid hard conversations. But if you believe tension is where trust gets built, you will lean in with courage.

- **In Pricing:** If you believe your value is tied to approval, you will underprice and overprove. If you believe your value is rooted in alignment and results, you will price with clarity.

- **In Risk-Taking:** If you believe mistakes equal failure, you will hesitate to act. If you believe mistakes are data, you will move with curiosity and make bolder calls.

> "Your leadership isn't defined by what you believe in theory, it's shaped by what you believe in the moment."

- **In Visibility:** If you believe recognition makes you a target, you will stay small. If you believe visibility gives your mission reach, you will step into the light.

Radical Ownership for Your Leadership

If belief is where bold leadership begins, ownership is where it comes to life. Owning your boldness is not about being the loudest person in the room. It is about being the clearest. Clear about who you are.

> "You do not have to control everything to own your leadership. You just have to stop giving your power away."

Clear about what you are here to do. Clear about the impact you are willing to create, even when it is uncomfortable. It is about claiming the full spectrum of your leadership, both your strengths and your areas for growth.

The True Meaning of Ownership

Most leaders excel at ownership when it is tied to visible success, for example, goals hit, awards earned, wins celebrated. But bold leadership requires something more. It demands radical responsibility, not just for your strengths, but for your energy, your presence, your blind spots, your choices, and the impact you create, whether intentional or not. It means leading even when the outcomes are murky, the feedback is tough, or the path is not clear. It means choosing agency over avoidance. Intention over inertia.

When you own your leadership, you stop outsourcing your power. You stop waiting for the perfect condition, the ideal environment, or someone else's permission to lead. You choose to show up, not in response to circumstances, but in alignment with who you are and what you stand for.

This is where leadership often falters. When pressure mounts or plans derail, the default response is deflection. We blame the system. The timing. The team. The market. The CEO. But bold leadership asks a different question: What part of this do I own?

> "Ownership is not about blame it is about agency. And agency is where boldness begins."

This question does not diminish your power, it amplifies it. It grants you agency. And agency fuels boldness.

What Ownership Is (and Is Not)

Ownership is not about taking everything on yourself because there is no one else to do it. Trust me, that will lead you straight to burnout, like it did for me. It is not about being the hero. It is not about shouldering everyone's burdens or having all the answers. Instead, true ownership is about agency, the understanding that you are responsible for how you show up, how you influence, and how you evolve.

Examples of owning your BOLD could include:

- Owning your voice in the meeting no one else wants to lead.
- Owning your vision, even when no one else sees it yet.
- Owning your boundaries, calendar, and focus.
- Owning your part in missteps and mistakes with humility and clarity.
- Owning your capacity to grow without waiting for someone else to tell you it is time.

The Neuroscience of Ownership and Agency

When we take psychological ownership of a challenge (see Figure 4.2), viewing it within our sphere of influence, the brain's reward circuitry activates more strongly. When we own something, we become more motivated to improve it, protect it, and invest in it. Conversely, when we distance ourselves from problems, our brain's emotional regulation systems begin to shut down. We become passive observers rather than active participants. This is crucial in leadership because bold decisions often involve ambiguity, conflict, or high stakes. If you unconsciously shift into "not my problem" mode, you sacrifice your effectiveness before the decision process even begins.

When it comes to agency (see Figure 4.3), ownership taps into the internal locus of control, a belief that your actions influence outcomes. And here is where it gets interesting: agency is trainable. Each time you make a bold choice and stand in it, even when the result is uncertain,

What is radical ownership?

Not This...	But This...
"I didn't get clear feedback."	"I'll clarify expectations and ask direct questions."
"The team didn't follow through."	"Where did I under-communicate or miss accountability?"
"This wasn't my idea, so it's not on me."	"I'm here to lead, regardless of where the idea started."

Figure 4.2 What Radical Ownership Looks Like

Figure 4.3 Agency, Compliance, and Avoidance

you reinforce neural pathways for self-leadership. You build self-efficacy, a belief in your own ability to influence events and outcomes (see Figure 4.4). The more you own, the more capable you feel. And the more capable you feel, the more boldly you lead. This is exactly why I say every bold step leads to more confidence which then leads to greater agency in your life and in your ability to lead boldly.

Beyond Mindset

This is not just mindset. It is wiring. When you own your voice, your brain strengthens the neural pathways that reinforce agency, confidence, and decisiveness. Over time, bold decisions become less emotionally taxing and more instinctive. Taking ownership does not mean micromanaging everything or bearing every burden alone. Bold ownership means taking 100% responsibility for your response, not for every external outcome. Ownership builds trust. It models courage. It invites accountability without shame. It tells your team, we move forward, even when it is messy.

Neural Region	Role in Ownership
Prefrontal Cortex	Planning, reflection, impulse control
Anterior Cingulate Cortex	Decision-making under conflict
Dorsolateral Prefrontal Cortex	Mental resilience and goal tracking
Amygdala	Regulates emotional response

Figure 4.4 The Neuroscience of Ownership

97

Quick Reframe

Not Owning: I have no control over this.

Bold Leader Ownership: What part of this do I own and how will I lead from that place?

It means:

- Owning your energy in the room.

- Owning your presence in the silence.

- Owning your tone in difficult conversations.

- Owning your decisions when you lack complete clarity.

"You do not need a perfect plan to lead boldly. You need the courage to take full responsibility for the space you already occupy."

ACTIVITY: Own the Room

Select one leadership interaction from the past week, a meeting, a 1:1 conversation, an email, or even a moment of silence.

Ask yourself:

1. What energy did I bring into that space?
2. What part of the outcome do I fully own?
3. What would bold ownership have looked like in that moment?
4. What will I adjust next time?

Now, make a commitment: Choose one upcoming opportunity where you will bring full ownership. Document it. Set your intention.

What Activating Boldness Looks Like in Real Leadership

When I left my corporate role and launched Bold Industries Group, there were moments that I felt an overwhelming weight of responsibility and it made me think about waiting. Waiting for better timing, waiting for more savings, waiting for certainty, or waiting to see if I could handle it and the timing would be better. But the bold move for me was not waiting. The bold move was owning what I knew, what I believed, and what I had to offer. I had to own the decision to lead a new kind of work fed by my years of experience, one centered on bold clarity, not just strategy.

That ownership did not come without fear. But it did come with *freedom*.

"Bold leaders do not wait to feel ready. They own what's true, and lead from there."

When you take radical responsibility for your leadership, you free yourself from perfectionism. You stop confusing caution with wisdom. And you begin to lead in a way that energizes others, because nothing is more contagious than someone leading with conviction.

ACTIVITY: Own Your Leadership Audit

Grab a notebook and answer these prompts as honestly as you can:

1. What parts of your leadership are you fully owning right now?
2. Where are you still waiting on permission, validation, or conditions to change?
3. Where are you outsourcing responsibility or playing small?
4. What would it look like to lead from full ownership this week?

Leadership Fatigue vs. Ownership Fatigue

I have observed that many leaders confuse exhaustion with effort. If you feel chronically drained, it is not always because you are doing too much, it is often because you are not owning the right things. You are reacting instead of initiating. You are managing instead of leading. You are stretching in the wrong direction. Leaders who aligned their actions with clear ownership, as opposed to passive response or avoidance, reported higher energy retention and greater clarity in daily decision-making. Ownership does not drain you. It grounds you.

> "When you own your leadership, you own your energy."

The Bold Ripple Effect

When you embrace radical ownership, your team sees it. They do not just see your actions, they witness what is possible. Your example gives them permission to do the same. Leadership teams that demonstrated visible ownership, especially during uncertain conditions, experience higher trust and faster decision-making cycles across departments.

Bold ownership accelerates culture. It creates clarity. It shrinks the distance between vision and action. And it begins with one decision, to stop waiting and start leading from within.

Signs You Are Not Fully Owning It

Ownership does not always look like bold proclamations, big stages, or confident speeches. Sometimes, it is quieter. And so are the ways we avoid it. You might be in a leadership moment right now and not realize where you are handing away your power. Look out for these subtle red flags:

- You are waiting for permission to make the next move.
- You are blaming lack of clarity for inaction.
- You are deferring your opinion until someone else speaks up.
- You are saying "yes" to things that are not aligned with your values.
- You are downplaying your influence, even in rooms where you have power.

These are not failures. They are invitations to step back in.

What Radical Ownership Sounds Like

- "I don't have the answer yet, but I'm willing to find one."

- "This did not go as planned. Here is what I have learned."

- "That is on me. Let us talk about how to move forward."

- "This matters to me. Here is why."

This language builds trust. It models clarity. And it reminds others that leadership is not about control it is about courage.

Owning the Room When It Is Hard

During a leadership retreat, I worked with a woman who had just been promoted but was struggling to feel seen in the new leadership circle. She kept shrinking back because she did not want to be seen as arrogant or too aggressive in her approach. Does this sound familiar?

We practiced her re-entry into a space she already belonged in. She began by owning one meeting a week with full clarity, speaking first, setting the agenda, and claiming her seat. Two months later, she was not just more vocal, she had redefined how decisions were made in her department. Not by waiting. But by owning.

How to Model Ownership for Your Team

"Ownership is not about having control. It is about leading with clarity and letting others do the same."

Bold leaders do not just own their leadership, they show others how to do it too.

When you model radical ownership, you create a culture where accountability is shared, initiative is expected, and growth is not outsourced. But modeling ownership is not about always having the answers. It is about being the kind of leader who goes first, with clarity, courage, and transparency.

Here is how to model it in real time:

1. **Narrate your decision-making.**

   Say things like, "Here's what I know, here's what I don't, and here's why I'm deciding this way." This teaches your team how to think not just what to think.

2. **Take responsibility without deflection.**

   When something does not go well, say, "That one is on me. Here is how I am adjusting." Owning mistakes publicly builds massive trust and gives your team permission to do the same.

3. **Celebrate ownership in others.**

   When someone owns a stretch goal, a hard truth, or a new idea, name it and honor it. This reinforces ownership as a cultural norm, not a leadership exception.

4. **Ask bold reflection questions.**

   Instead of saying, "Why didn't this work?" ask, "What did we own fully and what did we hesitate to claim?" This shifts your team from blame to clarity.

5. **Model boundaries.**

   Owning your energy, calendar, and focus is just as bold as owning your outcomes. When leaders protect their time and values, they show teams how to do the same without guilt.

Turn Every Outcome into Insight

If belief is the foundation and ownership is the engine, then learning is the accelerator. Bold leaders do not just act, they reflect. They

> "Every bold move is a teacher. You are either learning or applying what you learned."

pause not to retreat, but to decode. They ask sharper questions. They metabolize every outcome, especially the uncomfortable ones, and turn them into fuel for what is next.

Why Bold Decision-Making Rewires Your Leadership Brain

I bet you did not know that every bold decision you make is not just a professional choice, it is a neurological event, literally reshaping your brain. The intersection of neuroscience and leadership reveals a critical truth, the brain does not just learn from experience, it learns through the process of making decisions, particularly bold decisions under uncertainty.

Understanding this can shift your relationship with risk, transform your approach to mistakes, and amplify your leadership impact.

> "Your brain is not shaped by perfection, it is shaped by participation. Bold decisions, successful or not, accelerate growth at a neurological level."

Bold decisions trigger neuroplasticity, the brain's extraordinary ability to reorganize itself by forming new neural connections throughout life. When you step into uncertainty, whether launching a new product, leading a challenging conversation, or changing career directions, your brain perceives this as a significant, emotionally charged event. Emotional salience, the brain's signal for importance, activates heightened attention and accelerates the encoding of new neural pathways. This is not theoretical, it is neurological. Your brain is literally rewiring itself with each bold action.

Moreover, bold leadership decisions engage the brain's reward and prediction system, specifically, the dopaminergic pathways. Dopamine, often called the reward chemical, does more than just create pleasure and it reinforces learning loops. When you make a courageous decision and experience positive outcomes, even something as simple as personal growth, new insights, or meaningful recognition, your brain releases dopamine, strengthening the neural circuits associated with confidence and adaptive decision-making.

But it is not just successful decisions that reinforce bold learning. Neuroscience shows that your brain learns as profoundly from decisions that do not go as planned, provided you approach them with curiosity rather than criticism. In fact, regions of the brain involved in reflective processing and strategic adjustment, such as the prefrontal cortex and anterior cingulate cortex, become highly active following experiences that challenge expectations or lead to perceived setbacks. These areas of your brain are responsible for insight, perspective-taking, and emotional regulation, essential qualities in resilient, bold leaders.

This has powerful implications for leaders at all experience levels. If you are leading from a place of caution, defaulting to what is known or waiting for absolute certainty, you are neurologically limiting your potential. Conversely, every bold step you take in the face of uncertainty accelerates your brain's ability to adapt, learn, and lead effectively under future uncertainty.

Your reflective practice after bold actions matters deeply. Reflection activates your prefrontal cortex, linking strategic insight and emotional regulation pathways. Consistently reflecting on bold decisions, particularly challenging ones, accelerates adaptive learning loops in your brain.

Practical Neuroscience in Real Leadership Moments

"Boldness isn't just brave behavior, it neurological conditioning for resilience, clarity, capacity and impact."

Think of it this way. When you walk into a high-stakes negotiation or deliver critical feedback, your brain is immediately scanning for risk and reward cues. If you hesitate or second-guess yourself, the brain's threat networks activate more strongly, leading to heightened anxiety and diminished cognitive performance. But if you have trained your neural pathways through repeated bold actions, your brain shifts into reward mode. You are calmer, clearer, and more cognitively flexible. This is not accidental. It is neurological preparation.

This underscores why boldness is not optional if you are committed to growth-oriented leadership. Every bold decision wires your brain for greater capacity. Every hesitant retreat rewires your brain toward caution. The choice and neurological consequence is always yours.

ACTIVITY: Neuroplasticity in Action

Reflect on a recent bold decision (successful or not).

Write briefly about:

- What was the decision?
- How did it initially feel?
- What did you learn (neurologically reinforced)?
- What new neural pathway (habit, belief, insight) did this create?

Your brain is always learning. The question is, are you teaching it to default or to decide boldly?

The Bold Leader's Mindset: Everything Is Data

Bold leadership is not about perfection. It is about iteration. It is not about never failing, it is about never wasting what failure can teach you. This is not just mindset talk. Neuroscience shows that learning from experience activates the brain's default mode network, particularly in moments of introspection. Leaders who regularly engage in self-reflection show higher activation in the medial prefrontal cortex, the area linked to self-awareness and adaptive decision-making.

Before bold action can happen, bold belief must take root. But belief is not something you simply decide once, it is something you strengthen through intentional practice. That is where the Bold Belief Upgrade Map comes in. Figure 4.5 is a tool that walks you through the four-step process of identifying a limiting belief, uncovering its origins, upgrading it, and reinforcing the new belief through aligned action. It is not about positive thinking. It is about belief in motion. Every time you step into a room, make a decision, or lead a conversation, your beliefs are driving the outcome. This framework helps you take back the wheel.

"Bold learning does not wait for hindsight. It happens in real time."

107

Activate Your Bold

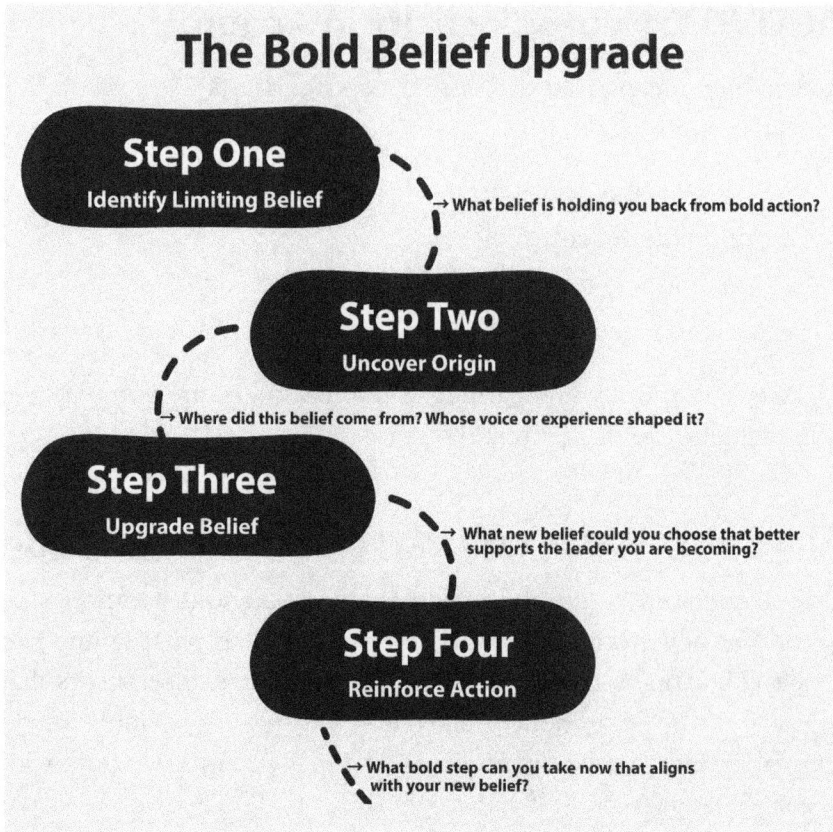

Figure 4.5 The Bold Belief Upgrade

When you reflect, your brain does not just store memory, it strengthens pattern recognition. This is how learning becomes wisdom. And wisdom fuels boldness. But most leaders are moving too fast to reflect. They default to action as a way to avoid the discomfort of introspection. That is why bold learning is not reactive. It is ritualized.

Bold Learning in Practice

Want to become a leader who learns fast, adapts faster, and leads with clarity?

Start here:

- **Post-Moment Pause:** After every key meeting or decision, ask: What did I notice? What surprised me? What stretched me?

- **Weekly Debrief:** Carve 15 minutes every Friday to review: What did I learn? What did not go as planned? Where did I lead in alignment?

- **Team Learning Loop:** Normalize reflection across your team. Do not just ask for wins, ask what each person learned and how it shifted their approach.

Why Most Leaders Stop Learning

The higher you rise in leadership, the easier it becomes to confuse experience with insight. But experience does not guarantee learning. Only reflection does. In fact, leaders with high positional power often

> "Bold leaders do not just fix what went wrong. They listen to what it is trying to teach."

engage in less feedback-seeking behavior and underestimate the gap between intent and impact. Why? Because power can create the illusion of certainty. That is why bold leaders disrupt their own assumptions on purpose. They ask: What am I pretending not to see? Where is my ego louder than my listening? What outcome am I calling failure that might actually be a data point?

ACTIVITY: Bold Leadership Learning Loop

Choose one experience this week that did not go the way you planned and then ask yourself:

1. What happened?

2. What belief or behavior shaped the result?

3. What did I learn?

4. What would I do differently next time?

Now, take one bold action that incorporates what you learned. Learning is not just insight, it is integration.

What Learning Looks Like in Bold Work Cultures

- Mistakes are shared, not hidden.

- Lessons are celebrated, not punished.

- Debriefs are expected, not optional.

- Reflection is seen as strategy, not sentiment.

- Feedback is not personal, it is fuel.

Designing Your Leadership

"Bold leadership does not require certainty. It requires clarity."

When I hit burnout in my corporate career, one of the paths I seriously considered was interior design. I was intrigued by the seven core principles designers use (Balance, Rhythm, Emphasis, Proportion, Contrast, Unity, and Negative Space) and realized these principles could directly shape how we lead ourselves and others. Just like a thoughtfully designed room can transform how you feel and function, intentionally designing your leadership creates environments where people and purpose thrive. Design from within, a key part of the BOLD Framework, helps you approach leadership as a creative process, ensuring every decision, action, and interaction aligns meaningfully with your values and vision. It is not about adding more complexity, it is about crafting your leadership deliberately, removing distractions, embracing clarity, and empowering yourself and your team to grow.

What You Have Learned

In this chapter, you have shifted from understanding boldness as a concept to fully owning it as a daily practice. You have discovered that bold leadership begins within, guided by the BOLD Framework (Believe, Own, Learn, Design). You have seen how your beliefs shape your outcomes, influencing decisions far more than strategy alone, and you have learned how upgrading those beliefs rewires your brain for confident, intentional action. You now understand radical ownership, not just of successes, but of your presence, energy, and the full spectrum of your leadership, amplifying your agency rather than waiting for conditions to change. You have explored how every bold decision physically strengthens your brain's capacity for resilience and adaptability through self-directed neuroplasticity, making courage easier with each action. Finally, you have embraced reflection as a crucial learning accelerator, turning outcomes, especially challenging ones, into strategic insight. Bold leadership is not about being perfect, it is about becoming intentional, clear, and aligned, building your leadership deliberately rather than by default.

Bold Truth

Bold leadership is not a title, a trait, or a destination. It is a choice, one you must make daily. It is deciding to believe in your capability even when doubt whispers, taking radical ownership even when it is uncomfortable, and choosing to learn deliberately from every outcome rather than hiding from the lessons it offers.

Your Bold Move

This week, intentionally apply the BOLD Framework to one key decision or situation:

Believe Name one empowering belief you will choose to lead from.

Own Clearly define your role and responsibility in that situation.

Learn Afterward, pause to capture insights without judgment.

Design Adjust your next action based on what you have learned, not what you feared.

Document your reflections. Notice the difference bold clarity makes.

Bold Metric

Rate your leadership practices this week on the following dimensions. For each statement, check the box that best represents your experience on a scale of 1 (lowest) to 5 (highest).

Believe

I consciously chose an empowering belief to guide my leadership this week.

	1	2	3	4	5
Rarely or never chose empowering beliefs.	☐	☐	☐	☐	☐
Occasionally recognized limiting beliefs but did not shift them.	☐	☐	☐	☐	☐

	1	2	3	4	5
Sometimes intentionally selected empowering beliefs.	☐	☐	☐	☐	☐
Frequently guided decisions with empowering beliefs.	☐	☐	☐	☐	☐
Consistently led from consciously chosen empowering beliefs.	☐	☐	☐	☐	☐

Own

I fully owned my voice, decisions, and influence in challenging moments.

	1	2	3	4	5
Avoided responsibility or deferred to others.	☐	☐	☐	☐	☐
Took partial ownership in comfortable situations only.	☐	☐	☐	☐	☐
Claimed ownership in most situations.	☐	☐	☐	☐	☐
Consistently owned my leadership presence.	☐	☐	☐	☐	☐
Demonstrated complete ownership even in highly challenging contexts.	☐	☐	☐	☐	☐

Learn

I actively sought insights from outcomes rather than dismissing or deflecting them.

	1	2	3	4	5
Defended or explained away unexpected outcomes.	☐	☐	☐	☐	☐
Acknowledged outcomes but without deeper reflection.	☐	☐	☐	☐	☐
Reflected on some outcomes to identify learning.	☐	☐	☐	☐	☐
Regularly extracted meaningful insights from most experiences.	☐	☐	☐	☐	☐
Transformed all outcomes into valuable learning opportunities.	☐	☐	☐	☐	☐

Design

My next decisions clearly reflect learning from previous experiences.

	1	2	3	4	5
Repeated past patterns despite previous results.	☐	☐	☐	☐	☐
Made minor adjustments to approach.	☐	☐	☐	☐	☐
Applied some lessons to future decisions.	☐	☐	☐	☐	☐
Consistently integrated past learning into new approaches.	☐	☐	☐	☐	☐
Deliberately designed next steps based on comprehensive learning integration.	☐	☐	☐	☐	☐

16–20: Bold Leadership—You're consistently applying the BOLD framework

11–15: Developing Boldness—You're building strong foundations

6–10: Emerging Boldness—You have clear opportunities for growth

1–5: Boldness Block—Significant barriers may be limiting your leadership impact

Setting the Stage for What Comes Next

Now it is time to take boldness off the page and onto your calendar because awareness may inspire you, but activation is what truly transforms you. The difference between leaders who create lasting impact and those who merely hold good intentions always comes down to execution. In Chapter 5, you will discover the D-90 Method, a structured, proven approach I have designed, tested, and refined both personally and alongside countless other bold leaders. This method turns clarity into measurable outcomes within just 90 days. You will learn how to plan strategically, act intentionally, and consistently measure your bold results.

You already have the tools, you know how to strengthen your beliefs, fully own your influence, and turn every experience into deeper insight. But lasting leadership is not built on occasional actions, it is built on intentional habits. It is about embedding boldness into your daily rhythm and routine, not just when the spotlight's on or when conditions are perfect.

It is time to bridge bold intention and real-world impact. No more waiting for permission, no more hesitation. You are moving from a bold mindset into powerful momentum, from intentions to tangible results. This is where clarity meets breakthrough. This is where your bold leadership comes to life.

Chapter 5

The D90 Method

You've decoded fear, navigated comfort, embraced your bold advantage, and fully activated the BOLD Framework (Believe, Own, Learn, and Design) in real-time leadership moments. You understand that bold leadership isn't about reckless leaps, but strategic alignment.

Now it's time to put a timeline to your boldness.

This chapter introduces the D90 Method, my signature process for translating your bold intentions into measurable, meaningful impact within just 90 days. It's designed to compress a year's worth of clarity, momentum, and growth into three focused months. Boldness without deadlines remains a dream, and deadlines without boldness remain tasks. Combine them, and you create impact.

> "Bold moves aren't made in years. They're made in days, moments, and choices repeated intentionally."

You have the awareness. You have the framework. Now it is time to put a timeline to your boldness.

This chapter introduces the D90 Method, my signature process for translating bold intentions into measurable impact within 90 days. It

> "Boldness without deadlines remains a dream, and deadlines without boldness remain tasks. Combine them, and you create impact."

compresses a year's worth of clarity, momentum, and growth into three focused months.

Because boldness without deadlines remains a dream. Deadlines without boldness remain tasks. Combine them, and you create impact.

Why 90 Days Works

The 90-day window is not arbitrary. It is strategically designed to work with your brain's natural systems for motivation and habit formation (see Figure 5.1).

30 days = Too short for substantial transformation.

365 days = Too long to maintain focus and urgency.

90 days = The sweet spot for sustained change with maintained urgency.

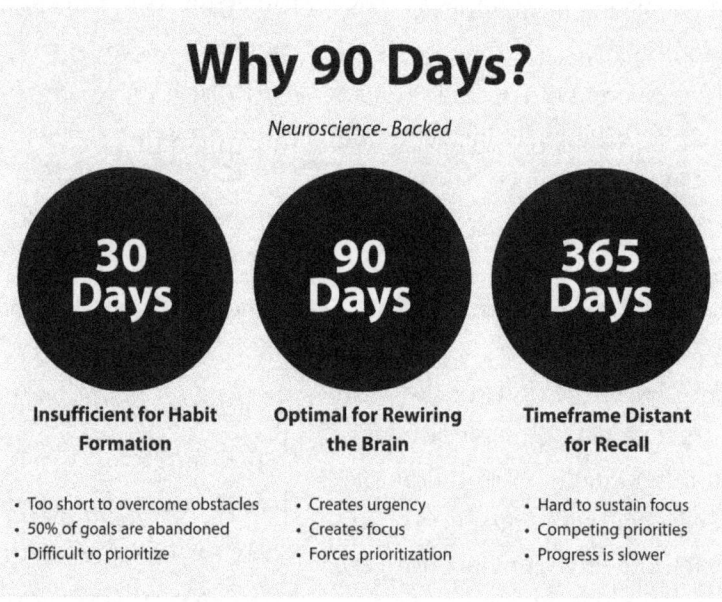

Figure 5.1 The Science of 90 Days

When goals extend beyond 90 days, your brain treats them as abstract and distant, defaulting to old habits. Within 90 days, goals feel achievable yet urgent, activating your brain's reward systems to drive motivation and decisive action.

This is not just psychology, it is neuroscience. The 90-day framework leverages three critical brain systems:

The Brain Benefits of 90 Days

Prefrontal Cortex: Thrives with clearly defined goals and timelines.
Dopamine System: Releases motivation through achievable milestones.
Basal Ganglia: Forms new habits through 60–90 days of consistent action.

The D90 Method turns these brain systems into your competitive advantage. It's strategically designed to work with your brain's natural motivation and habit-forming systems. When we examine successful transformation, whether personal, professional, or organizational, a pattern emerges. Sustained change requires enough time to embed new patterns, but short enough to maintain urgency and focus. Neuroscience research shows that the brain thrives on short-term, tangible milestones.

The corporate world has long recognized this through quarterly planning cycles. But the D90 Method takes this further by creating a deliberate framework for bold transformation, not just incremental progress.

The Neuroscience of Achievement

Understanding the neuroscience behind the D90 Method underscores why this structured, time-bound approach effectively transforms intentions into bold results. Your brain is wired to respond

The D90 Method

positively to structured deadlines and incremental progress, and the D90 Method capitalizes precisely on this neurological advantage.

First, let's consider the role of the prefrontal cortex (PFC), the executive center of the brain responsible for planning, decision-making, and regulating behaviors. Neuroscience research indicates that the PFC thrives in environments of clearly defined goals and timelines. When goals are ambiguous or timelines overly extended, the PFC struggles to maintain consistent focus and efficient decision-making. However, a clearly defined 90-day window aligns perfectly with the PFC's capabilities, enhancing its ability to prioritize, maintain clarity, and execute strategic decisions effectively.

Second, the D90 Method leverages the brain's dopamine reward system, a critical component of motivation and goal-directed behavior. Dopamine is released when your brain anticipates achieving a meaningful goal, creating feelings of pleasure and satisfaction that reinforce ongoing action. Long-term goals often lack this consistent dopamine reinforcement because the reward feels distant and abstract. Conversely, the 90-day window activates a series of short-term, achievable milestones, continually stimulating dopamine release, thereby maintaining motivation and momentum throughout the process.

The reticular activating system (RAS) also plays a vital role within the D90 framework. This neural network acts as your brain's gatekeeper, determining what information is filtered into your conscious awareness. When you set a clear 90-day goal, your RAS starts filtering your environment to highlight relevant opportunities and resources previously unnoticed. This heightened awareness significantly accelerates progress toward your bold objectives.

Finally, consider the basal ganglia, your brain's habit-formation center. Research indicates that repeated actions performed consistently over approximately 60 to 90 days transition from conscious effort to automated habit. By structuring bold moves within this scientifically validated timeframe, the D90 Method ensures that strategic bold actions become deeply embedded habits, reducing the cognitive load on your PFC and freeing mental resources for new initiatives and creative problem-solving.

In essence, the D90 Method isn't merely a strategic choice, it's a neurological advantage. By aligning your bold initiatives with your brain's natural mechanisms for motivation, attention, decision-making, and habit formation, you significantly enhance the likelihood of achieving sustained, impactful leadership transformation.

A Systematic Approach to Bold Results

D90 (see Figure 5.2) stands for Designed in 90 Days. It's your path to clarity, alignment, and action. Unlike traditional goal-setting frameworks, D90 integrates both strategic clarity and tactical execution within a unified system that is supported by regular looping assessments of progress and course corrections.

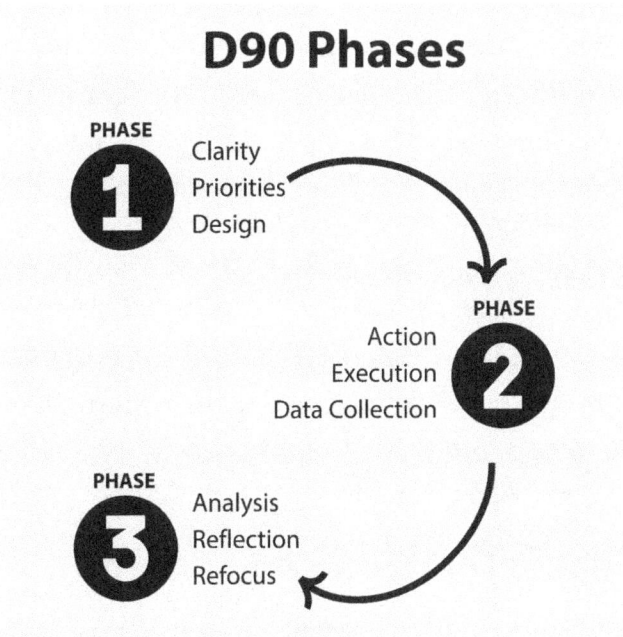

Figure 5.2 Overview of the D90 Phases

The D90 Method

The D90 Method: Three Phases

Days 1–30: CLARITY

- Define your single bold outcome
- Identify 3–5 high-leverage actions
- Create commitment structures that ensure follow-through

Days 31–60: ACCELERATION

- Take consistent daily action toward your outcome
- Gather feedback and adjust tactics weekly
- Maintain momentum through the "messy middle"

Days 61–90: INTEGRATION

- Cement bold actions into sustainable habits
- Document what worked and what did not
- Design your next 90-day cycle

This methodology isn't about cramming more into your calendar. It's about creating focused intensity around what matters most. The structure creates a container for transformation, clear boundaries that foster creativity, commitment, and courage.

Each phase builds on the previous, creating compound momentum that transforms bold intentions into measurable results.

"Your boldest vision deserves clarity. Your clarity deserves urgency. Your urgency deserves action."

What Makes D90 Different

Let's be real, most traditional planning methods have some major blind spots. They often overlook how crucial it is to sequence your actions strategically, treating every task as equal instead of recognizing that certain steps lay the groundwork while others rapidly accelerate your progress. They also tend to ignore the psychological barriers, the doubts, beliefs, and fears, that quietly hold you back from bold moves. And perhaps most frustratingly, these methods frequently separate planning from execution, creating an artificial divide where momentum fizzles and good intentions stall.

That's exactly why I developed the D90 Method, to close these gaps. D90 deliberately sequences your initiatives based on their psychological and strategic significance, helping you build confidence while laying a strong foundation. It tackles mindset and action simultaneously, so you're not just taking bold steps, you're shifting the beliefs that support them. Most importantly, D90 ensures a seamless flow from vision to action, keeping momentum strong from start to finish. This isn't just another plan on paper, it's your roadmap from intention to real, measurable impact.

Clarity and Commitment Days 1–30

Boldness begins with ruthless clarity. Many leaders confuse busyness with effectiveness, activity with achievement. The result is scattered effort and diluted impact. Bold leaders know clarity always precedes speed.

The first 30 days of the D90 Method focus on three critical steps:

1. **Define Your Bold Outcome:** What's the single boldest result you want in 90 days?

2. **Identify Your High-Leverage Actions:** Which few bold moves will create disproportionate impact?

3. **Secure Commitment:** How will you commit yourself and your team to relentless focus?

Let's explore each step in detail.

Defining Your Bold Outcome

Your bold outcome isn't just a goal, it's a declaration of what matters most. It's specific, meaningful, and slightly uncomfortable. It stretches you beyond incremental improvement into transformation.

A well-crafted bold outcome has these characteristics:

Singular Focus: One clear priority, not a list of competing objectives.

Measurable Clarity: Defined in specific, observable terms.

Meaningful Impact: Connected to larger purpose and vision.

Stretching Yet Achievable: Requiring bold action without being impossible.

The power of a well-defined bold outcome is that it creates immediate clarity about what deserves your attention and what doesn't. It becomes a filter for decision-making, resource allocation, and daily prioritization.

Identifying High-Leverage Actions

Not all actions create equal results. The second step in the clarity phase is identifying the vital few moves that will create disproportionate impact. These high-leverage actions should:

- Directly advance your bold outcome.
- Address root causes rather than symptoms.
- Create compounding benefits over time.
- Usually feel uncomfortable or challenging.

I recommend identifying no more than 3–5 high-leverage actions. This constraint forces strategic thinking and prevents the dilution of effort that comes with longer lists.

Securing Commitment

Clarity (see Figure 5.3) without commitment is merely information. The final step in the first 30 days is creating structures that ensure follow-through when resistance inevitably arises.

Effective commitment mechanisms include making a clear public declaration by sharing your bold goals with key stakeholders, establishing accountability through regular check-ins with trusted mentors or peers, and intentionally designing your environment, both physical and digital, to reinforce your top priorities. Aligning your calendar by proactively blocking time for high-impact actions, along with developing simple decision filters, guiding questions you can use daily to maintain focus, will ensure your bold intentions translate consistently into meaningful outcomes. My commitment wasn't just internal, I shared it publicly with my network, enhancing accountability. I restructured my calendar to prioritize aligned conversations

Creating Bold Clarity

Ask yourself the following questions:

☑ **Is this aligned with what matters most right now?**

☑ **Does this outcome move the needle meaningfully?**

☑ **Am I pursuing this for impact, not perfection?**

☑ **Is the action connected to my values or priorities?**

☑ **Can I clearly communicate this outcome to others?**

☑ **Does this stretch me beyond my current comfort zone?**

☑ **Am I willing to take responsibility for the next step?**

Figure 5.3 Creating Bold Clarity

The D90 Method

The Bold Clarity Exercise

Take 30 minutes to complete this foundational exercise:

1. **Draft Your Bold Outcome:** Write a single sentence describing the most meaningful result you want to achieve in the next 90 days.

2. **Test It:** Does this outcome stretch you? Is it specific and measurable? Does it excite and slightly frighten you? Refine until your answer is yes.

3. **List Potential Actions:** Brainstorm 6–10 actions that could contribute to this outcome.

4. **Identify Leverage:** Circle the 3–5 actions that would create the greatest impact. Be ruthless in your assessment.

5. **Design Commitment:** Write down three specific ways you'll ensure follow-through when motivation wanes.

above all else. And I created a simple decision filter: Will this action directly contribute to enrolling aligned members, yes or no?

Overcoming Clarity Obstacles

In the first 30 days, leaders typically encounter several obstacles: I have summarized what to look for and be aware of so you can identify when you may be hitting the obstacles.

The Clarity Paradox: Sometimes, gaining clarity requires taking action, yet action without clarity feels risky. Break this cycle by treating your initial bold outcome as a working hypothesis, clear enough to guide action, flexible enough to evolve with new insights.

Perfectionism: Many leaders delay commitment until their plan feels "perfect." Remember that boldness isn't about perfect planning but decisive action. A clear direction now creates more impact than a perfect plan later.

Competing Priorities: When everything seems important, nothing receives the focus it deserves. The D90 Method requires temporary de-prioritization of competing initiatives. This isn't abandonment. It's strategic sequencing. By the end of the first 30 days, you should have unwavering clarity about your bold outcome, your high-leverage actions, and your commitment structures. This foundation makes the acceleration phase not just possible but powerful.

Acceleration and Alignment Days 31–60

With clarity established, the next 30 days are about taking accelerated action and refining as you go. Bold leaders know that clarity without action is wasted potential. Here, your goal isn't perfection, it's momentum. The neuroscience of this is that your brain's basal ganglia, the habit center, thrives on repetitive actions. During this phase, your consistent bold moves start becoming instinctive, shifting from effortful to effortless.

Creating Bold Momentum

The secret to momentum isn't occasional large levels of effort but consistent, aligned action. During days 31 to 60, prioritize small yet meaningful daily bold moves by selecting one specific action each day that directly advances your bold outcome (see Figure 5.4). These daily steps create compound impact over time. In addition to daily actions, dedicate each week to accelerating efforts in one targeted area, progressively intensifying your focus to prevent stagnation and build deeper confidence. Bold leaders actively seek rapid feedback, applying insights immediately rather than waiting for formal quarterly reviews. Finally, proactively identify and address potential obstacles early, whether through initiating tough conversations, strategically reallocating resources, or adjusting processes, ensuring sustained momentum and consistent progress toward your bold goals.

Bold Course Correction

Bold action doesn't mean rigid plans. Weekly reflection allows bold leaders to pivot quickly, realigning their efforts with evolving realities without losing momentum. Consider these questions when assessing whether a course correction is needed:

1. Is the bold outcome still relevant and compelling?

2. Are our current actions creating the progress we anticipated?

3. What unexpected insights have emerged that might alter our approach?

4. If we continue this exact path, will we achieve our bold outcome by day 90?

Changing tactics or steps isn't abandoning boldness, it's expressing boldness through adaptability.

The Midpoint Assessment

Day 45 marks the halfway point of your D90 journey, a critical moment for deeper assessment. While weekly reflections keep you aligned, the midpoint assessment takes a more comprehensive view.

Gather key stakeholders for a candid discussion about the following measures:

Progress Indicators: What measurable progress have we made toward our bold outcome?

Method Effectiveness: Which approaches are working, and which aren't?

Resource Allocation: Are our time, attention, and resources optimally deployed?

Roadblock Analysis: What persistent obstacles require creative solutions?

Acceleration Opportunities: Where could we intensify efforts for exponential results?

This assessment isn't just evaluation, it's preparation for the final 30-day sprint. The insights gained should inform specific adjustments to maximize your impact in the integration phase.

When I reached the midpoint of my Bold Mastermind enrollment period, I noticed that while my one-on-one conversations were highly effective, they weren't scalable enough to meet my target. This insight led me to add small group sessions to my approach, maintaining the quality of connection while increasing reach.

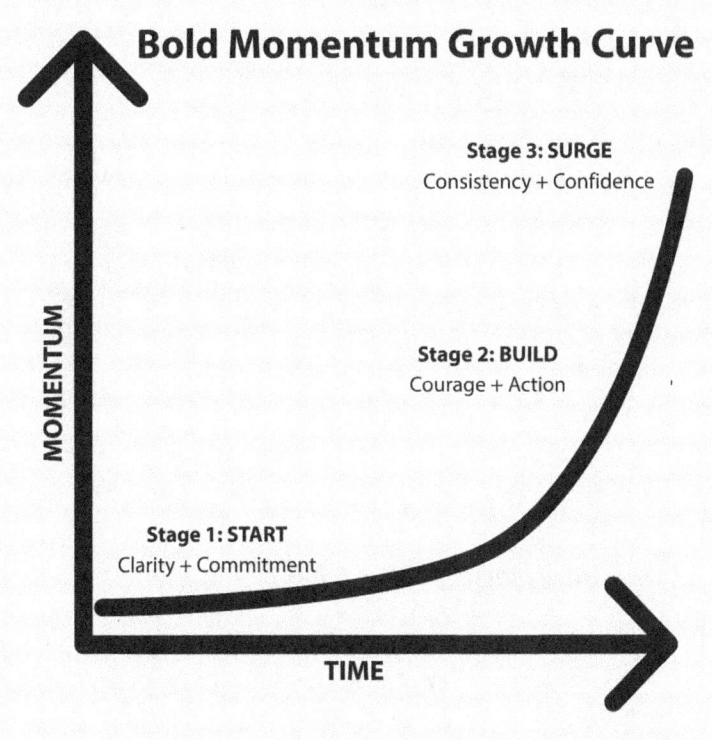

Figure 5.4 Bold Momentum Growth Curve

The D90 Method

The Psychology of Momentum

Understanding the psychological dynamics of the acceleration phase helps you navigate its unique challenges connected to lack of clarity, consistency, and shifts in focus.

- **The Messy Middle:** In any 90-day initiative, days 40–60 often feel chaotic and uncertain. Initial excitement has faded, yet substantial results have not fully materialized. This messy middle is where many bold initiatives falter. Recognize this as normal, not a sign of failure.

- **The Consistency Threshold:** Research in habit formation reveals that consistency matters more than intensity. Showing up imperfectly every day creates more momentum than perfect execution occasionally. During this phase, prioritize regularity over perfection.

- **Identity Reinforcement:** As you consistently take bold action, your identity shifts. You begin seeing yourself as someone who follows through, who embraces discomfort, who leads boldly. This identity shift makes subsequent bold actions easier and more natural.

By day 60, bold actions that once required tremendous effort should feel increasingly routine. Your clarity has transformed into consistent execution, setting the stage for integration and lasting impact.

Impact and Integration Days 61–90

The final 30 days are about solidifying the bold impact you've initiated. Now, boldness is not a series of actions, it is a sustainable operating rhythm embedded in your daily leadership.

Here is what happens neurologically, repeated bold action strengthens neural pathways in your prefrontal cortex and striatum, reinforcing decision-making clarity and rewarding bold choices.

Cementing Your Bold Impact

The integration phase is about cementing your bold impact through four focused activities. First, systematize your success by turning effective methods into repeatable systems. Document your processes, develop clear templates, and establish straightforward protocols to ensure bold actions become the natural choice. Second, deepen mastery by intentionally refining and practicing the skills most essential to your bold outcome. Third, expand engagement by involving additional stakeholders in your initiative, creating opportunities for others to contribute, broadening your impact, and sharing ownership. Finally, measure your results comprehensively, collecting both quantitative data and qualitative insights. Clearly document not only what you have achieved but precisely how you achieved it.

Your Integration Rhythm

To get the most from this phase, set up a clear, repeatable rhythm that fits seamlessly into your daily routine. Each day, choose one simple action that makes boldness feel second nature and sustainable. Maybe that's refining your workspace, simplifying a key process, or building a specific skill. At the start of each week, take a step back to ask yourself how your bold approach could stretch beyond your initial focus. Could other teams, projects, or goals benefit from this momentum? Finally, every two weeks, pause to clearly document the real impact you are creating, both measurable results and meaningful shifts. This regular reflection keeps you accountable and helps you see the powerful difference you are making through intentional, bold leadership.

The D90 Completion Assessment

At the end of 90 days, conduct a comprehensive assessment of your bold journey:

What measurable results did we achieve?

Which actions created the greatest impact?

What unexpected outcomes (positive or negative) emerged?

Which approaches should become standard practice?

What did we learn about ourselves and our organization?

How do we integrate these bold moves into sustained practices?

This assessment serves two critical purposes. It celebrates and solidifies your achievement while laying the groundwork for your next bold initiative. The end of one D90 cycle should seamlessly flow into the beginning of the next, creating continuous bold momentum.

Beyond 90 Days Creating Bold Cycles

The true power of the D90 Method emerges when you stack multiple 90-day cycles. Each cycle builds on the previous, creating compound impact over time.

Successful leaders typically sequence their D90 cycles in one of two ways:

Depth Sequencing: Using consecutive 90-day cycles to go deeper into a single area, creating mastery and comprehensive transformation.

Breadth Sequencing: Addressing different areas in sequential 90-day cycles, creating balanced growth across multiple dimensions.

Neither approach is inherently superior, the right sequencing depends on your specific context, priorities, and organizational needs.

What matters most is maintaining the momentum. The space between D90 cycles often becomes a vulnerable time where gains can be lost. Plan your transitions carefully, ensuring one cycle completes as the next begins.

Your D90 Blueprint From Concept to Action

You understand the method. You know the science. Now it is time to make this real (see Figure 5.5).

The D90 Blueprint is not just another planning exercise, it is your bridge from bold intention to measurable impact. This is where abstract concepts become concrete commitments, where good ideas transform into scheduled actions, and where your next 90 days become the most focused and productive period of your leadership.

Take the next 30 minutes to complete your blueprint. Do not overthink it. Bold action begins with bold planning.

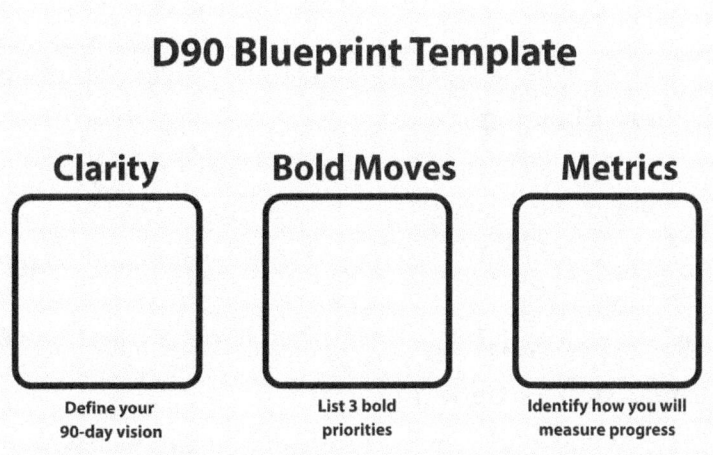

Figure 5.5 D90 Blueprint Template

The D90 Method

ACTIVITY: Your D90 Blueprint

Grab your notebook and outline your D90 plan right now:

1. Bold Outcome Definition

What specific, measurable result will you achieve in 90 days?

Why does this matter deeply to you and your organization?

How will you know when you have succeeded?

2. High-Leverage Actions Identification

What 3–5 actions will create disproportionate impact?

Which action, if taken consistently, would make other actions easier or unnecessary?

What bold move have you been avoiding that needs to be on this list?

3. Commitment Design

How will you hold yourself accountable daily, weekly, and monthly?

Who needs to know about your bold initiative to support your commitment?

What structures will you put in place to ensure follow-through?

4. Phase Planning

Days 1–30: What specific activities will establish clarity and commitment?

Days 31–60: How will you accelerate action and incorporate feedback?

Days 61–90: What integration activities will solidify your impact?

5. Bold Metrics Definition

How will you measure progress throughout the 90 days?

What leading indicators will show you are on track?

How will you capture both quantitative and qualitative impact?

Completing this blueprint creates not just a plan but a commitment. It transforms your bold intention from possibility to inevitability by creating a clear path forward.

Navigating the Predictable Obstacles

While every D90 journey is unique, certain challenges consistently emerge. Anticipating these challenges allows you to address them proactively rather than being derailed when they arise.

Challenge 1 The Enthusiasm-Execution Gap: Many leaders begin with tremendous enthusiasm but struggle to maintain momentum when initial excitement fades. The solution lies in creating structures that do not rely on motivation, clear daily actions, accountability partnerships, and visual progress tracking.

Challenge 2 The Priorities Collision: Your D90 initiative will inevitably collide with other priorities. Rather than abandoning your bold outcome, look for integration opportunities. How might addressing your bold outcome simultaneously advance other priorities? Where can you create synergy rather than competition?

Challenge 3 The Feedback Resistance: When feedback suggests your approach is not working, it is tempting to either ignore the data or abandon the outcome. Bold leaders take a third path: they honor the feedback by adjusting their approach while maintaining commitment to the outcome.

Challenge 4 The Complexity Creep: As your initiative progresses, it is natural to add complexity, more actions, more metrics, more considerations. This complexity dilutes focus and drains energy. Combat this by regularly returning to the essential question: "What's the simplest way to achieve our bold outcome?"

Challenge 5 The Success Plateau: Early wins often lead to a plateauing of effort. You have made progress, so the urgency diminishes. Counter this by establishing progressive targets throughout the 90 days. Each achievement should trigger a new level of challenge, maintaining the productive tension that drives bold action.

Boldness becomes real in deadlines and action. The D90 Method is not just productivity, it is identity formation. It turns your bold vision from possibility to reality by putting you in motion every single day.

Power of Commitment

The difference between those who achieve bold outcomes and those who merely dream about them is not capability, talent, or perfect timing. It is commitment. I have worked with hundreds of leaders who possessed brilliant strategies, deep expertise, and clear vision. Some transformed their organizations and careers within months. Others remained stuck in analysis, planning, and "getting ready" for years.

What separated them? The bold ones committed before they felt ready. They chose a start date and honored it. They declared their intentions and stood by them. They moved from "I should" to "I will" to "I am."

Right now, you stand at that same decision point. You have everything you need, the awareness from previous chapters, the BOLD Framework, and now the D90 Method. The question is not whether you are capable; you are. The question is whether you will commit.

Commitment is not a feeling. It is a decision followed by consistent action. It is choosing your bold outcome over your comfort zone every single day. It is honoring your plan when motivation fades, when obstacles arise, when others question your approach.

Real commitment is demonstrated in bold leadership through several routes, including:

Calendar Commitment: Block time now for your D90 activities. Treat these appointments with yourself as seriously as you would treat meetings with your CEO.

Social Commitment: Tell someone about your bold outcome. Choose someone who will ask you about progress, not someone who will let you off the hook when things get difficult.

Financial Commitment: Invest something meaningful in your success. Whether it is hiring a coach, buying tools, or setting aside resources for your initiative, genuine commitment and investment changes everything.

Identity Commitment: Start calling yourself someone who follows through. Stop saying "I will try" and start saying "I will do." Your language shapes your reality.

System Commitment: Create structures that make success inevitable. Remove obstacles, eliminate distractions, and design your environment to support your bold moves.

Your D90 cycle begins the moment you commit, not the moment you feel ready. Choose your start date. Choose your bold outcome. Choose commitment over comfort.

The world needs what you are here to build. But it will exist only if you decide to build it.

Commit publicly or privately to your first bold D90 cycle right now. Declare your bold outcome. Outline your actions. Choose bold over comfortable every day, starting today.

Because every bold leader I know has one thing in common: they started before they felt ready, and they committed before they knew how. Your turn.

> "The leaders who achieve breakthrough results do not wait for perfect conditions. They create commitment structures that carry them through imperfect ones."

The difference between those who achieve bold outcomes and those who merely dream about them is not capability, it is commitment. Right now, you stand at a decision point: Will you commit to your first D90 cycle, or will you remain in the realm of interesting ideas?

What You Just Learned

You have learned why the 90-day window is the sweet spot for transformation, long enough to create meaningful results but short enough to sustain urgency and clarity. You have explored the three-phase framework, progressing strategically from clarity in days 1 to 30, acceleration during days 31 to 60, and integration from days 61 to 90, building consistent momentum along the way. You have discovered the importance of singular focus, understanding that concentrating your energy on one bold outcome supported by a few high-impact actions achieves far greater results than scattering attention across multiple priorities. You now recognize the necessity of deliberate integration, embedding bold initiatives deeply into your systems, processes, and organizational culture to ensure lasting change. Finally, you have embraced that bold leadership is not a one-time effort but a continuous, rhythmic practice, sustained and strengthened through successive 90-day cycles.

Bold Truth

Most leaders never achieve their boldest aspirations because they lack structure. They try to be bold episodically rather than systematically. They pursue bold outcomes without bold methods.

The D90 Method changes this equation by providing both the psychological framework and practical structure for consistent bold action, turning your bold vision from possibility to reality by putting you in motion every single day.

Your Bold Move

The difference between those who achieve bold outcomes and those who merely dream about them is not capability, it is commitment. Right now, you stand at a decision point, will you commit to your first D90 cycle, or will you remain in the realm of interesting ideas?

Your bold move is to make this commitment concrete by:

1. **Setting the Timeline:** Mark your calendar with the start and end dates of your first D90 cycle. This simple act creates immediate accountability.

2. **Declaring Your Outcome:** Write down your bold outcome and share it with at least one person who will hold you accountable. The act of declaration transforms vague intention into specific commitment.

3. **Scheduling the Phases:** Block time on your calendar now for:

   Your initial clarity work (Days 1–5).

   Weekly reflection sessions (every Friday).

   Your midpoint assessment (Day 45).

   Your final integration review (Days 85–90).

4. **Creating Visible Tracking:** Establish a visual system for tracking your progress, whether a simple chart on your wall, a digital dashboard, or regular team updates. Visual accountability dramatically increases follow-through.

Commit publicly or privately to your first bold D90 cycle right now. Declare your bold outcome. Outline your actions. Choose bold over comfortable starting today.

Remember that imperfect action today creates more progress than perfect planning tomorrow. Your D90 approach will refine over time, but only if you begin.

Bold Metrics

To ensure you stay on track throughout your D90 journey, establish a consistent measurement practice. Bold metrics create clarity about your progress and provide early warning signals when adjustments are needed.

Rate your progress in each area by checking the appropriate box (1 = lowest, 5 = highest):

Bold Clarity

	1	2	3	4	5
I have unwavering clarity about my bold outcome	☐	☐	☐	☐	☐
I can articulate why this outcome matters deeply	☐	☐	☐	☐	☐
I consistently communicate this clarity to others	☐	☐	☐	☐	☐
My daily decisions align with this priority	☐	☐	☐	☐	☐

Bold Action

	1	2	3	4	5
I take high-leverage actions daily toward my outcome	☐	☐	☐	☐	☐
I move forward despite uncertainty or discomfort	☐	☐	☐	☐	☐
I focus on impact rather than activity	☐	☐	☐	☐	☐
I consistently prioritize bold moves over urgent distractions	☐	☐	☐	☐	☐

Bold Adaptation

	1	2	3	4	5
I actively seek feedback about my approach	☐	☐	☐	☐	☐
I adjust my methods based on real-time learning	☐	☐	☐	☐	☐
I pivot strategies without abandoning outcomes	☐	☐	☐	☐	☐
I respond to obstacles with creativity rather than retreat	☐	☐	☐	☐	☐

Bold Integration

	1	2	3	4	5
My bold actions are becoming habitual	☐	☐	☐	☐	☐
I'm creating systems to sustain my progress	☐	☐	☐	☐	☐
I'm involving others in my bold initiative	☐	☐	☐	☐	☐
I'm documenting learning for future application	☐	☐	☐	☐	☐

Track these metrics weekly, noting patterns and addressing areas where your scores consistently fall below 4. This simple practice creates accountability without complexity, keeping you focused on what matters most.

Total Score: _____ / 80

Setting the Stage for What Comes Next

In the next chapter, we transition from Part Two Bold Activation, of the book and begin Part Three, Bold Action. As we begin Chapter 6, we'll build upon the foundation of the D90 Method to explore bold leadership in challenging contexts. While this chapter focused on creating bold momentum in a structured timeframe, the next chapter examines how to maintain that boldness when facing resistance, setbacks, and organizational complexity.

You'll discover how to navigate bold conversations that most leaders avoid, how to lead boldly even when formal authority is limited, and how to sustain your bold approach when facing inevitable obstacles. The D90 Method provides the structure, now you'll develop the situational agility to apply it under diverse and challenging circumstances.

The coming chapters will also explore how to scale your personal boldness into organizational boldness, creating cultures, teams, and systems that operate with the same clarity, courage, and commitment you've developed through your D90 practice.

Because now that you know boldness isn't about waiting for the right time, it's about creating it, you'll never lead the same way again. You have the framework to transform not just your next 90 days, but your entire leadership trajectory.

Part III

Bold Action

Face Challenges Head-On, Communicate Boldly, and Trust Your Instincts

True boldness is revealed in action. In this section, you'll strengthen your resilience, learning to bounce back stronger from setbacks. You'll master courageous conversations that build trust and credibility. With confidence, you'll balance analytical data with powerful intuition, ensuring your bold vision consistently translates into meaningful, impactful results.

Chapter 6

Bold Comebacks

You have mastered the psychology of boldness, embraced the BOLD Framework, and structured your initiatives using the D90 Method. You have clarity, commitment, and a plan.

But what happens when, not if, you stumble?

Every bold leader falls. Every bold initiative faces unexpected resistance. The question is not whether you will experience setbacks, but how you will respond when they arrive.

This chapter is about the art and science of the bold comeback (see Figure 6.1). Not just recovery, anyone can eventually recover. This is about how bold leaders bounce back, intentionally, not just eventually. It will be built on how you transform your toughest moments into your strongest advantages.

"The ultimate measure of a leader isn't how they perform when things go well, but how they transform when things fall apart."

"Bold comebacks transform setbacks from career threats into leadership accelerants."

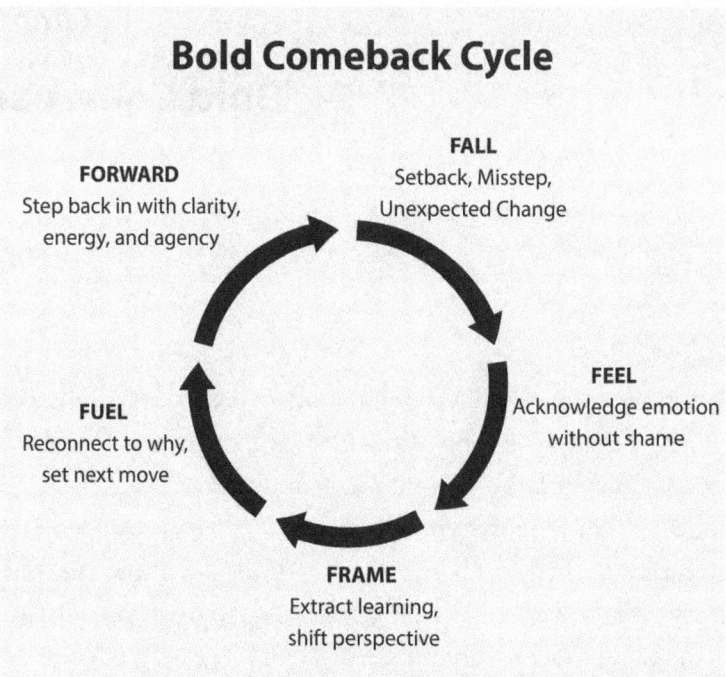

Figure 6.1 The Bold Comeback Cycle

The Anatomy of Setbacks

Before we explore how to rise after a fall, we need to understand the different types of setbacks that bold leaders encounter. Not all setbacks are created equal, and your response should be calibrated to the specific challenge you're facing.

Understanding the Types of Leadership Setbacks

Setbacks aren't simply obstacles; they're defining moments in every bold leader's journey. Understanding exactly what kind of setback you're facing is essential to respond effectively, regain momentum, and learn for the future. Here are five common types of setbacks leaders encounter:

Strategic Failures: When Your Plan Misses the Mark

You crafted the vision and executed faithfully, but the results didn't come. Strategic setbacks happen when your core assumptions don't align with reality, or market conditions change unexpectedly. Perhaps a competitor disrupted the space, customer needs evolved, or critical information was incomplete. Strategic failures aren't about execution. They indicate it's time to pause, reassess your environment, and recalibrate your direction.

Leadership Story: The Pilot That Pushed Too Fast

A few years ago, I worked with a rising healthcare executive, who had just launched a high-profile innovation pilot meant to streamline patient intake across three hospital systems. It was bold, visionary, and well-funded. But there was one issue: the speed of implementation outpaced the readiness of her frontline staff. What was meant to be a breakthrough became a bottleneck.

She was devastated. She had advocated for this pilot for months and felt like the failure reflected poorly on her leadership. But instead of retreating, she called a postmortem meeting, not just with her direct reports, but with the people who had struggled most: the unit nurses, intake clerks, and tech support.

What she learned in that one hour reshaped her entire leadership approach. She did not need to abandon the innovation, she needed to slow down and co-build it. Together, they redesigned the process with frontline input, rolled it out in two phases instead of one, and six months later, the same pilot became a model for the system.

The comeback did not happen because she forced it.

It happened because she paused, listened, and redesigned boldly.

That is what bold comebacks require realignment, not just rebound.

Execution Failures: Sound Strategy, Flawed Delivery

Even the best strategies falter when implementation goes awry. These setbacks might involve missed deadlines, inconsistent quality, insufficient resources, or misaligned efforts across teams. The vision was right, but the path to achieving it stumbled. Execution failures teach leaders the value of disciplined follow-through, detailed planning, rigorous accountability, and clear communication.

Relationship Ruptures: Broken Trust and Misalignment

Leadership fundamentally involves people, and setbacks rooted in damaged relationships often have the most lasting consequences. These happen when trust erodes, communication fails, or priorities clash between you and your team, peers, or stakeholders. Relationship ruptures require more than tactical adjustments; they demand humility, openness, and a genuine commitment to rebuilding trust through dialogue and integrity.

Personal Limitations: Your Skills or Knowledge Need an Upgrade

Sometimes, the setback is deeply personal, highlighting a gap in your own leadership skills or abilities. Perhaps you reached the limits of your current knowledge, struggled with a necessary competency, or found yourself unable to meet the expectations of a new role. These setbacks, while uncomfortable, illuminate exactly where you must grow. Bold leaders embrace these moments as opportunities for focused personal development and transformation.

External Disruptions: Forces Outside Your Control

Even perfectly executed strategies can be derailed by external factors, such as economic shifts, regulatory changes, unexpected market moves, or global events. These setbacks remind leaders that boldness also requires flexibility, resilience, and adaptability. You can't control these disruptions, but you can control your response, finding innovative ways to adapt, pivot, or reposition your vision to weather external storms.

Choosing Your Response and Why Knowing the Setback Type Matters

Every setback type demands a unique, thoughtful response. Strategic setbacks call for recalibration and fresh insights. Execution failures require refined processes, clearer communication, and stronger accountability. Relationship ruptures need honest dialogue, empathy, and trust-building. Personal limitations signal it's time for focused self-development. External disruptions ask leaders to remain agile and creatively responsive.

Bold leadership isn't about avoiding setbacks, it's about understanding them, categorizing them clearly, and responding purposefully. By identifying the nature of the setbacks you encounter, you equip yourself to rebound more quickly, wisely, and powerfully each time, transforming setbacks from obstacles into opportunities for growth.

The Psychology of Setbacks

Every leader experiences setbacks, but how you handle these challenges mentally and emotionally significantly influences your capacity to bounce back. The psychology behind setbacks involves predictable patterns, and understanding these can dramatically improve your ability to recover and grow from each challenge.

Research in cognitive psychology shows that our brains process failures more intensely than successes, a phenomenon called negativity bias. While this once served as a survival mechanism, it poses significant hurdles for modern leaders. Failures become deeply embedded memories that your mind revisits repeatedly, potentially limiting your ability to move forward constructively.

When facing a setback, your brain typically shifts into one of three distinct responses.

Threat Response Protecting Yourself

When setbacks feel threatening, your amygdala, the brain's emotional alarm system, springs into action (see Figure 6.2). It prompts instinctive reactions like fight, flight, or freeze. Your vision narrows, creativity stalls, and you become defensive, withdrawn, or quick to blame. While this reaction is normal, staying in threat mode can severely limit your leadership effectiveness and hinder your recovery.

Comeback Readiness Reflection

What did I learn from this fall that I could not have learned any other way?

Where am I still holding shame or self-blame?

What truth do I need to own in order to move forward?

What support, resource, or mindset shift will fuel my return?

Figure 6.2 Access Your Readiness Reflection

Rumination Cycle Getting Stuck

In the rumination cycle, the default mode network is the mental autopilot that replays mistakes over and over. Initially, this reflection can be beneficial, helping you learn from mistakes. But if unchecked, it quickly becomes unproductive, trapping you in repetitive, negative thought patterns that prevent progress.

Growth Response Moving Forward Strategically

Your brain's decision-making center kicks in, helping you see clearly and learn quickly. This response enables strategic thinking, meaning-making, and adaptive learning. Instead of remaining stuck or defensive, you analyze the setback, gain new insights, and proactively integrate lessons into your future decisions.

Most leaders will cycle through each of these responses when confronting setbacks. The key difference between those who successfully rebound and those who falter isn't whether they experience threats or rumination; it's how swiftly they transition into the growth response. Leaders who quickly shift their mindset from protecting their ego to prioritizing their growth ultimately achieve the boldest comebacks.

> "The speed of your comeback depends on how quickly you shift from protecting your ego to prioritizing your growth."

Why Bold Leaders Face Bigger Falls

Choosing bold leadership is choosing a path marked not only by opportunity and impact but also by heightened vulnerability. When you lead boldly, your decisions and actions naturally become more visible, drawing attention from your peers, stakeholders, and even the broader public. While this visibility can amplify your successes, making your achievements stand out, it can also turn setbacks into highly public and scrutinized events. Facing criticism or judgment publicly can feel intensely personal, adding pressure to the recovery process.

Furthermore, bold leadership frequently involves shaking up the status quo and addressing complex challenges that others might shy away from. These ambitious efforts often require navigating intricate organizational dynamics, resistance from stakeholders, and unforeseen obstacles. Consequently, setbacks can occur more frequently or intensely than in less ambitious pursuits, making resilience a crucial trait for any bold leader.

The depth of personal investment is another key reason why bold leaders face bigger setbacks. When you commit fully to a vision or project, your sense of identity, reputation, and purpose become closely intertwined with its outcomes. A setback, therefore, can feel like a personal failure, creating emotional burdens that go beyond professional disappointment. Learning to manage and separate your self-worth from professional results becomes essential.

Finally, bold leaders tend to maintain exceptionally high standards, setting ambitious goals that may far exceed conventional benchmarks. What others perceive as acceptable or even successful might fall short of your personal expectations, amplifying the sense of failure or inadequacy during setbacks. It's vital for bold leaders to cultivate a healthy perspective, balancing aspiration with self-compassion.

Recognizing these dynamics isn't about discouraging bold action but preparing you to handle setbacks constructively. Bold leadership isn't about avoiding setbacks entirely, it's about embracing the possibility of failure as a necessary step toward meaningful growth and lasting impact.

Your Strategic Setback Assessment

Facing a significant setback? Before you react, pause and use this structured assessment to strategically understand and navigate the situation:

1. Classify the Setback

Identify clearly. Is this primarily a strategic, execution-related, relationship-driven, personal, or externally triggered setback?

2. Evaluate the Impact

Who is affected by this setback, and how deeply? Clearly differentiate between the real impact and perceived or emotional reactions.

3. Clarify Your Contribution

Honestly pinpoint what actions or decisions within your control contributed to the setback. Being specific and objective helps you learn and adjust effectively.

4. Recognize Pattern

Reflect on whether you've experienced similar setbacks before. Notice any repeating patterns or recurring issues to help prevent future occurrences.

5. Extract Key Insights

Consider what this setback uniquely reveals insights, weaknesses, or opportunities, that were previously hidden. These valuable lessons can drive significant growth.

Using this structured assessment positions you to respond thoughtfully and effectively, turning a challenging setback into a powerful opportunity for bold leadership growth and recovery.

The Bold Comeback: How to Turn Setbacks into Powerful Opportunities

Let's be honest, as leaders setbacks are not fun. They can be uncomfortable, frustrating, and sometimes downright discouraging. But here's the exciting truth, they also offer incredible opportunities to grow stronger, wiser, and even more effective as a leader. Let's explore a straightforward, practical way to turn your setbacks into your greatest leadership moments (see Figure 6.3).

Right after experiencing a setback, your instinct might be to jump immediately into action or to pull back entirely. Neither reaction helps you in the long run. Instead, pause intentionally. Take a moment to

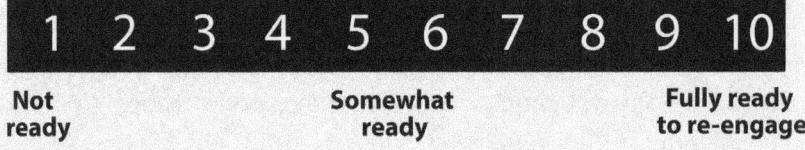

Are you ready for a comeback?

Pause and assess your readiness to move forward after a setback.

On a scale from 1 to 10, rate how confident you feel in taking your next bold step.

| 1 | 2 | 3 | 4 | 5 | 6 | 7 | 8 | 9 | 10 |

Not ready **Somewhat ready** **Fully ready to re-engage**

Then ask yourself: What would help me move just one point higher?

This isn't about achieving perfect confidence, it's about building momentum by acknowledging where you are and identifying what you need. Whether it's clarity, support, rest, or a mindset shift, this scale encourages gentle self-awareness and intentional progress.

I'll know I'm ready when...

Figure 6.3   Assess Your Confidence for Your Comeback

breathe, feel your emotions without guilt, and take care of yourself physically and mentally. Good decisions come from clear thinking, and clear thinking starts with giving yourself the space to process what happened.

After your pause, it's time to find the lessons hidden in your setback. This goes beyond superficial insights. Dive deeply to understand why things happened the way they did. Be honest about your role, recognizing what you could control and what you couldn't. Notice if there's a pattern, something you've seen before. Identifying these deeper insights helps you make real, lasting changes.

Once you've uncovered the wisdom from your setback, carefully shape how you talk about it. Instead of letting others define the story, or worse, letting your inner critic take over, own the narrative yourself. Be truthful but kind in your assessment. Frame the setback as a learning experience, highlighting the insights gained and the possibilities now available to you. When you communicate your narrative clearly and confidently to your team and stakeholders, everyone can move forward together.

When you're ready, re-engage strategically and deliberately. Don't rush back to exactly where things left off. Use what you've learned to refine your goals and actions, rebuild important relationships, and allocate resources more effectively. Timing matters, so re-enter thoughtfully, ensuring you're truly ready and that your environment is receptive.

> "Your boldest achievements often come right after your biggest challenges. Embrace your setbacks as opportunities to leap forward into greater success."

Finally, aim not just to recover, but to build something even better. Use your setbacks as catalysts to redesign your processes, deepen your awareness, and strengthen your leadership capacity. Develop a support network to reinforce areas of vulnerability revealed through your experience. Your bold comeback isn't about returning to the same place, it's about leveraging what you've learned to reach a higher level than ever before.

Psychological Tools to Support Your Bold Comeback

Facing setbacks isn't just about strategic recovery, it's also about managing the internal, emotional challenges you inevitably experience. Here are powerful psychological tools you can use to navigate these internal hurdles effectively and ensure your comeback is meaningful and lasting.

Dealing with Shame and Vulnerability

Leadership setbacks often trigger a deep, uncomfortable feeling of shame. Unlike guilt, which relates specifically to actions like, "I made a mistake," shame attacks your core sense of self, suggesting "I'm not enough." Renowned sociologist Brené Brown emphasizes that shame thrives in secrecy and isolation. To combat it effectively, speak openly about your experiences with carefully chosen, trusted confidants who offer supportive feedback without judgment. It's also crucial to differentiate clearly between making a mistake and being fundamentally flawed. Cultivating compassionate self-talk, and acknowledging mistakes without internal criticism, helps you quickly transition from self-criticism to productive self-improvement.

Rebuilding Your Confidence After Public Failure

Confidence isn't constant, it naturally fluctuates, especially after visible setbacks. Yet confidence can and should be rebuilt intentionally. To counter the negative impact of a setback, deliberately gather evidence of your past successes and current strengths. This practice balances your perspective, reminding you that setbacks don't define your entire leadership story. Additionally, embrace graduated challenges by setting progressively more ambitious but achievable tasks, allowing you to experience incremental wins that rebuild your belief in your abilities. Develop simple routines like power poses, affirmations, or brief mindfulness exercises, to access feelings of confidence when needed most. Finally, spend intentional time with colleagues, mentors, and friends who recognize and reaffirm your leadership strengths, especially during the sensitive initial stages of your comeback.

Separating Helpful Feedback from Unhelpful Noise

During your comeback, expect to receive extensive feedback, some helpful, some less so. Being able to discern meaningful feedback from noise is crucial. Pay close attention to who's providing the feedback. Consider their expertise, intentions, and perspective, and give priority to feedback from credible, trusted sources. Look for repeated themes across multiple sources; these often signal important areas for growth and learning. Evaluate feedback through the lens of your core leadership values and long-term goals, embracing insights that align closely with the kind of leader you aim to become. Prioritize feedback that's specific, actionable, and constructive, rather than vague criticism or generalized praise.

Remember, your bold comeback isn't about absorbing every piece of input. Instead, it's about strategically choosing which insights will truly help you grow and lead even more effectively in the future.

The Resilience Inventory

Rate your current resilience resources in each area from 1 (limited) to 5 (abundant):

		1	2	3	4	5
Physical Resilience	Energy management, sleep quality, physical activity, nutrition.	☐	☐	☐	☐	☐
Emotional Resilience	Emotional awareness, regulation, expression, processing.	☐	☐	☐	☐	☐
Cognitive Resilience	Perspective-taking, meaning-making, creative problem-solving.	☐	☐	☐	☐	☐
Social Resilience	Support network, reciprocal relationships, community connection.	☐	☐	☐	☐	☐
Spiritual Resilience	Purpose, values alignment, meaning, transcendent perspective.	☐	☐	☐	☐	☐

Focus your comeback strategy on strengthening your lowest-rated areas first, as these represent your current vulnerability points.

Bold Comeback Patterns: Discovering Your Path Through Proven Stories

Every leader's comeback is unique, but certain powerful patterns emerge again and again. Recognizing these patterns can give you clarity, inspiration, and comfort as you navigate your own journey back to boldness.

One common pattern in successful comebacks is Integration, which is viewing your setback not as an isolated event but as an essential chapter in your broader leadership story. Leaders who integrate their setbacks effectively embrace these challenges as opportunities to expand their identity and build new capabilities.

Another powerful pattern is Accelerated Learning, where a setback dramatically speeds up personal growth. Leaders experiencing this accelerated learning find their previous assumptions challenged, opening them to new perspectives. They're more willing to experiment, rapidly testing and adapting their approaches. The intense feedback during recovery periods, if embraced constructively, creates an unmatched opportunity for growth in a short timeframe.

The most transformative comebacks often follow the Authentic Transformation pattern. Here, setbacks spark deep reflection, prompting leaders to become more aligned with their authentic values and strengths. This transformation often leads to less energy spent trying to appear perfect and more openness about challenges and vulnerabilities. Leaders shifting into this authentic space frequently find their impact significantly expanded, driven by genuine purpose rather than superficial markers of success.

> "The greatest comebacks don't just restore what you lost, they reveal opportunities and strengths you never knew existed."

Finally, it's important to recognize the unexpected advantages that setbacks can offer. Research shows that difficult experiences often lead to valuable growth not achievable through ordinary, gradual development. Bold leaders who effectively leverage setbacks often gain clearer perspectives, stronger authenticity, deeper resilience, enriched relationships, and a sharper sense of purpose. While setbacks are rarely pleasant, they can become remarkably valuable if you intentionally seek out and embrace these hidden benefits.

Leading Others Through Setbacks

Bold leadership isn't just about navigating your own comebacks, it's about developing this capacity in your teams and organizations.

Bold Comebacks

As you strengthen your comeback capability, consider how to build this same resilience in those you lead (see Figure 6.4).

Building a Culture That Thrives on Comebacks

Imagine if your organization didn't fear setbacks but saw them as steppingstones to greater success. This mindset doesn't happen by accident, it requires deliberately cultivating a culture equipped to turn challenges into strategic advantages.

Start by establishing clear and supportive protocols for responding to setbacks. These processes guide your teams thoughtfully and

Setback to Strategic Steps

Setback	What it Triggered	What I Learned	Strategic Step
Project delay	Frustration and doubt	Resilience in uncertainty	Clarify timelines upfront
Negative Feedback	Self-doubt, Anxiety	Power of active listening	Progress feedback loop

Every setback carries the potential to become a strategic advantage, if we're willing to do the work of reflection. This tool walks you through identifying the setback, naming the emotional or mental trigger it activated, extracting the core lesson, and then defining a clear strategic next move. By mapping your response in this way, you transform a reactive moment into an intentional one. It helps you zoom out, take ownership, and lead forward with greater wisdom and impact.

Figure 6.4 Setback to Strategy Process

systematically through the recovery process, minimizing panic and confusion. To prevent repeating mistakes, a simple, shared library of lessons so the whole organization grows stronger after every setback, ensuring your organization continuously learns and improves.

Flexibility is critical during recovery periods. Equip your organization to quickly redirect resources, time, budget, and personnel, based on new learning and strategic shifts. Alongside practical flexibility, offer robust support networks to help your team members recover effectively. Provide formal resources like coaching and training, as well as informal emotional support, recognizing that setbacks affect both performance and morale.

Companies with these cultural elements don't just bounce back faster, they transform setbacks into powerful competitive advantages, continually enhancing their strategic learning capabilities.

"Organizations that thrive aren't the ones that avoid failure, they're the ones that turn each setback into meaningful growth."

Your Bold Comeback Playbook

Ready to prepare yourself personally for inevitable setbacks? Let's create your own customized Comeback Playbook, your go-to system when challenges arise.

ACTIVITY: Crafting Your Comeback Playbook

Spend time addressing each of these key areas to build your personalized recovery playbook:

1. Early Warning Signs

Reflect on the physical, emotional, and cognitive signs that indicate you're beginning to react defensively. Identify trusted individuals who can help flag these signals when you might overlook them.

2. Strategic Pause

Outline specific actions you'll take to intentionally pause and process without disconnecting from your leadership responsibilities. Clearly communicate your pause plan to those who need to support or respect this critical reflection period.

3. Extracting Insights

Determine the core questions you'll consistently ask yourself to uncover root causes and recurring patterns. Choose a reliable method to document these insights clearly, even during emotionally charged moments.

4. Crafting Your Narrative

Identify key points your setback narrative must include. Select trusted colleagues or mentors who can help ensure your narrative is authentic, constructive, and empowering.

5. Thoughtful Re-engagement

Define clear criteria indicating when you're ready to re-engage strategically. Identify relationships and interactions requiring special attention and proactive repair during your comeback.

6. Building Your Support Team

Identify people who belong in your Comeback Cabinet, individuals who genuinely support and guide you during recovery periods. Clearly specify the type of support you'll seek from each person.

> "You are not behind. You are just being prepared for the boldest chapter yet."

Regularly revisit and update this playbook, integrating fresh insights from your experiences. With this personalized plan, you'll approach setbacks confidently, knowing you're prepared not just to recover, but to return stronger and wiser every time.

Your Comeback Cabinet: Key Allies for Every Bold Leader

You don't have to face setbacks alone, in fact, you shouldn't. Bold leadership means having the right people in your corner when things get tough. Consider building your Comeback Cabinet by including these essential supporters:

The Truth-Teller

This person isn't afraid to give you direct, honest feedback, even if it's uncomfortable. They tell you what you need to hear, not just what you want to hear.

The Perspective-Giver

When you're feeling stuck or overwhelmed, this ally helps you step back, gain perspective, and reconnect with your broader goals and values.

The Confidence-Builder

This supporter genuinely believes in your abilities. They remind you of your strengths, past wins, and capabilities, especially when your confidence takes a hit.

The Practical Strategist

They're skilled at transforming insights into clear, actionable next steps. This person helps you move forward with concrete plans rather than getting stuck in endless reflection.

The Recovery Partner

Someone who cares deeply about your well-being, physically and emotionally, ensuring you prioritize self-care and resilience during tough periods.

Remember, one person might fulfill multiple roles. The key is ensuring your cabinet collectively covers these crucial areas, giving you comprehensive support when you need it most.

Bold Comeback Practices: Building Resilience Every Day, Week, and Month

Resilience isn't just about responding effectively after setbacks, it's about building your comeback muscles proactively. Here's a creative way to embed resilience practices seamlessly into your daily, weekly, and monthly routines, ensuring you're prepared for whatever comes your way.

Daily Resilience Rituals

Reflect and Learn: Take just 5–10 minutes each day to quickly review challenges you faced, focusing on what you learned rather than what went wrong. Treat this practice as strengthening your resilience muscle: small, consistent actions make significant impacts over time.

Mindset Reset Moments: Identify everyday actions like walking through doorways or waiting for your coffee as opportunities to mentally reset. Use these brief pauses to clear your mind, check in emotionally, and shift positively into your next interaction or task.

Cultivate Gratitude: Regularly acknowledging positive moments and successes can powerfully shield your well-being from setbacks. Science confirms that gratitude consistently enhances resilience, helping you bounce back faster and stronger.

Weekly Resilience Check-Ins

Insight Integration: Set aside 20–30 minutes weekly to dig deeper into setbacks, clearly identifying valuable lessons. Integrate these insights deliberately into your leadership approach to continuously enhance your comeback effectiveness.

Strengthen Connections: Intentionally engage with at least one trusted member of your Comeback Cabinet weekly, ensuring strong relationships and support systems are firmly in place before they're critically needed.

Energy Audit: Regularly assess your stress levels, energy reserves, and overall resilience indicators each week. Proactively adjust your workload, rest periods, and priorities to maintain optimal resilience and prevent burnout.

Monthly Resilience Enhancements

Story Calibration: Each month, consciously evaluate how you're framing recent setbacks and challenges. Make sure your internal narrative remains truthful yet empowering, fostering constructive growth rather than lingering self-criticism.

Targeted Development: Choose one resilience-related skill each month to deliberately strengthen, based directly on recent experiences or upcoming challenges.

Celebrate Growth: Monthly, acknowledge and celebrate tangible evidence of your increasing resilience and comeback capability. Reinforcing positive progress enhances motivation and solidifies resilience as part of your leadership identity.

These ongoing practices don't eliminate setbacks but significantly enhance your ability to transform challenges into strategic growth opportunities, positioning setbacks as powerful catalysts rather than obstacles.

"Your boldest bounce-back is not about returning to where you were, it is about rising into who you were becoming all along."

The Bold Truth About Comebacks

> "Ultimately, your greatest leadership legacy isn't built on flawless victories but on the strength, insight, and growth created through your toughest moments."

Let's finish by anchoring your journey with some essential truths about bold comebacks. Every bold leader encounters setbacks along their journey. In fact, the most inspiring leadership stories often highlight periods of struggle and eventual recovery. Exceptional leaders stand out not because they avoid failure, but because they possess the ability to transform setbacks into meaningful opportunities for growth. While initial success might be driven by talent or favorable circumstances, truly lasting impact comes from the resilience gained through navigating repeated challenges. Your reactions to adversity ultimately reveal your core leadership values more authentically than any statement or public declaration ever could. And while some people naturally rebound quickly, the good news is that resilience and effective comeback strategies can be intentionally developed by every committed leader.

What You Just Learned

Navigating setbacks is not about simply overcoming obstacles; it's about transforming challenges into pivotal moments of growth.

You've explored how setbacks differ in nature, like strategic missteps, execution errors, relational breakdowns, personal limitations, and external disruptions, and learned that each type requires its own unique, thoughtful response.

You've gained insights into the psychological dynamics at play, recognizing the critical importance of shifting rapidly from a threat or rumination response to a constructive growth mindset. Understanding these principles empowers you to handle setbacks not just effectively, but strategically.

Bold Truth

Your leadership legacy will ultimately be defined less by your moments of seamless success and more profoundly by your responses to difficulty. Bold leaders don't simply survive setbacks; they use them as powerful springboards to higher levels of clarity, resilience, and influence. Your setbacks, if leveraged wisely, can catalyze unparalleled growth and deepen your authentic leadership impact.

Your Bold Move

Proactively embrace and prepare for future setbacks. Clearly define your personal Comeback Playbook, a robust system ready to activate when needed. Identify your core support team, your Comeback Cabinet, making intentional investments in these critical relationships before crises hit. Implement daily, weekly, and monthly resilience practices that continuously build your comeback muscles. Commit today to reframing setbacks not as threats, but as essential growth catalysts within your leadership journey.

Bold Metrics

Assess your comeback readiness and resilience progress regularly by reflecting on these key indicators:

Response Speed: How quickly do you move from emotional reactions to strategic, solution-oriented responses?

Insight Depth: Are your reflections leading to profound and actionable insights rather than surface-level lessons?

Narrative Clarity: Have you crafted an empowering, truthful comeback narrative that you confidently share with your stakeholders?

Relationship Strength: Is your support network robust, active, and providing balanced feedback and encouragement?

Resilience Habits: Are resilience-building activities firmly embedded in your daily, weekly, and monthly routines?

Regular evaluation and adjustment in these areas will significantly enhance your resilience and comeback capacity over time.

Setting the Stage for What Comes Next

You now know how to transform setbacks into strategic advantages. You understand that bold leaders are not defined by their failures but by their comebacks. You have the tools to rise stronger from whatever challenges you face.

But Here Is the Reality: Many of your biggest setbacks could have been prevented. And your most powerful comebacks will require something most leaders avoid, difficult conversations.

Most leadership setbacks trace back to one thing, conversations that never happened. The expectation that was not clarified. The conflict that was allowed to fester. The difficult decision that was delayed.

In Chapter 7, we move from recovering boldly to communicating boldly. Because bold leaders do not just bounce back, they speak up before bouncing back becomes necessary. You will learn how to have the conversations that most leaders avoid but that every organization needs. The ones that build trust instead of breaking it. The ones that create clarity instead of confusion. The ones that turn potential setbacks into breakthrough moments.

Your next bold move is not just about what you do. It is about what you say, and how you say it.

Chapter 7

Bold Conversations

She knew the team was off-track. Everyone did. But no one said it aloud. Until the missed deadline turned into a lost client. Until morale sank. Until she realized that the conversation she avoided was the one that would have changed everything.

> "The conversation you are afraid to have is the conversation you need to have."

We do not avoid hard conversations because we lack skill.

We avoid them because we overestimate the discomfort and underestimate the cost of silence.

You've embraced the psychology of boldness, implemented the BOLD Framework, structured your initiatives with the D90 Method, and developed the capacity to transform setbacks into comebacks. Your bold foundation is strong. Now it's time to direct this capacity toward one of leadership's most challenging territories: difficult conversations.

Bold conversations are the interactions most leaders avoid but that create disproportionate impact when navigated skillfully. They're the feedback sessions, conflict resolutions, accountability discussions, and courageous challenges that distinguish merely competent leaders from truly transformative ones.

> "The quality of your leadership is determined by the quality of the conversations you're willing to have."

This chapter explores how to initiate and navigate conversations that matter, the ones that clear barriers, deepen trust, challenge limitations, and catalyze breakthrough results. Because bold leadership isn't just about what you do, it's about what you're willing to say when it matters most.

The Bold Conversation Advantage

"When you develop the ability to speak courageously and clearly about challenging topics, you gain access to capabilities that separate exceptional leaders from merely competent ones."

Most leaders know they should have difficult conversations. They understand these discussions are important. But they do not realize that mastering bold conversations creates a compound advantage that transforms every aspect of their leadership effectiveness.

These advantages build on each other, creating momentum that accelerates your impact in ways that extend far beyond any single conversation.

Leaders who master bold conversations surface issues before they become crises. Instead of waiting until problems are undeniable and costly to fix, they address challenges while they are still manageable. This early intervention saves time, resources, and relationships that would otherwise be damaged by prolonged avoidance.

Bold leadership conversations build extraordinary trust through their willingness to speak truth respectfully, even when it feels uncomfortable. This trust is not built through agreement or harmony, but through consistency and courage. When people know you will address issues directly and fairly, they stop wondering what you really think. This clarity creates the psychological safety that drives innovation, engagement, and high performance.

These leaders also access collective intelligence by creating environments where diverse perspectives are genuinely heard and valued. Research shows that teams with the highest performance exhibit specific conversation patterns characterized by energy, engagement, and exploration, all of which require the psychological safety that bold conversations create. When people feel safe to disagree, challenge, and contribute authentically, the quality of thinking and decision-making dramatically improves.

Finally, bold conversations accelerate results by removing the interpersonal barriers that can silently sabotage progress. Unclear expectations, unaddressed tensions, and unspoken concerns create drag in every initiative. When leaders address these issues directly, teams can focus their energy on execution rather than navigation of interpersonal complexity.

The ability to initiate and navigate difficult conversations becomes a leadership multiplier, enhancing the effectiveness of every other leadership capability you possess. It is not just another skill, it is the skill that makes all your other skills more powerful.

The Anatomy of Bold Conversations

Bold conversations differ from routine communication in several fundamental ways (see Figure 7.1). Bold conversations address issues with significant consequences, for individuals, relationships, teams, or organizations. They're the conversations where real impact, positive or negative, is on the line.

Leader's stakes perception directly influences conversation outcomes. When participants perceived high stakes, their physiological responses changed dramatically, with increases in heart rate variability and cortisol levels that impacted cognitive function.

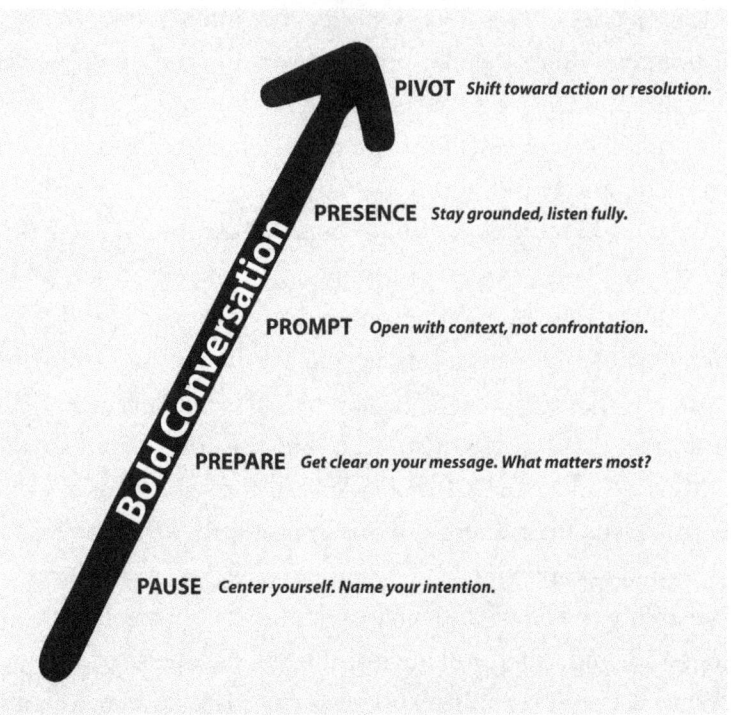

Figure 7.1 The 5P's of a Bold Conversation

When Silence Was No Longer an Option

She had been dreading the conversation for eight months.

The tension between her and her co-founder had become more than uncomfortable, it was affecting the team. Meetings were clipped. Strategic decisions stalled. Team members started coming to her separately, looking for clarity she was too exhausted to give.

The relationship had once been built on mutual respect. But now? It was silence, resentment, and the slow unraveling of something that used to feel aligned.

Every time she thought about bringing it up, she felt nauseous. What if it blew up? What if it damaged the brand? What if the conversation confirmed what she feared, that the partnership was already broken?

But one day, after a string of passive-aggressive exchanges and another missed deadline, she opened her laptop, blocked off her calendar, and typed this sentence into an email:

"We need to talk, not as co-founders, but as people who care about what we're building. Can we carve out 90 minutes, no distractions?"

That conversation did not fix everything. But it shifted the course of the company. It surfaced misaligned priorities, unspoken assumptions, and long-held fears. But more importantly, it reminded them both why they started in the first place.

It led to a realignment of responsibilities, a shared leadership reset, and a renewed agreement: we will not avoid the hard conversations anymore.

The culture began to change within a month.

People noticed.

They followed the lead.

What that leader learned is what I see again and again: bold cultures are not built by avoiding discomfort. They are built through repeated, courageous conversations that create alignment, build trust, and make it safe to speak the truth.

Potential Discomfort

Bold conversations typically create emotional tension for one or more participants. This discomfort might involve vulnerability, conflict, fear of rejection, concern about hurt feelings, or anxiety about repercussions. Neuroimaging research shows that social discomfort activates the same brain regions as physical pain. This biological reality helps explain why we avoid difficult conversations, our brains literally register them as threats to our safety.

Values Activation

Bold conversations engage core values. They're moments where what matters most becomes suddenly clear and present. When you feel your heart rate increase before a conversation, it's often because something you deeply value is at stake. When conversations activate our core values, we experience both psychological and physiological responses that can either enhance or inhibit our communication effectiveness.

Growth Catalyst

Bold conversations create inflection points, opportunities for accelerated development that aren't available through other means. The conversation itself becomes a doorway to new possibilities.

Challenging conversations can create what they call developmental heat, conditions that catalyze significant personal growth and transformation of mental models. Understanding these elements helps you recognize when bold conversations are needed and approach them with appropriate intention and care.

The Bold Conversation Framework: Five Elements for Impact

Every bold conversation requires five elements to create maximum positive impact. This framework provides structure without creating rigidity, helping you navigate complex interactions with both courage and skill.

Element #1: Clear Purpose

Before initiating any bold conversation, clarify your purpose—what specific outcome you hope to achieve. The clearer your purpose, the more effectively you can navigate the inevitable complexities that arise (see Figure 7.2).

Conversation Clarity

What I Want to Say:

This project is not working.

What I Really Mean:

We need to pivot our approach.

What They Might Hear:

You messed up.

What I Want Them to Understand:

We need to collaborate differently to succeed.

Break down your message into four essential parts: what you want to say, what you actually mean, what the other person might hear, and what you want them to understand. It is a powerful exercise in empathy, precision, and leadership maturity.

Figure 7.2 Conversation Clarity

Strong purposes focus on mutual benefit rather than self-protection. They are about moving forward together rather than proving points or allocating blame. When your purpose centers on shared success, both parties feel safer engaging in difficult topics because they sense you genuinely care about their interests too.

Examples of clear purposes include understanding someone's perspective so you can find a solution that works for both of you, sharing concerns about project timelines while identifying adjustments you can make together, or addressing conflict between departments to rebuild collaborative momentum. Notice how each example emphasizes partnership and shared problem-solving.

Weak purposes create weak conversations. If your purpose is to vent, prove someone wrong, or make yourself look good, the conversation will likely fail regardless of your technique. These self-serving motivations are usually transparent to the other person and immediately create defensiveness rather than openness.

Before entering any challenging conversation, ask yourself: "What outcome would benefit both of us?" This simple question transforms your mindset from adversarial to collaborative, setting the foundation for breakthrough dialogue.

Element #2: Psychological Safety

In bold conversations, creating this safety isn't optional, it's foundational. A comprehensive meta-analysis strongly predicts knowledge sharing, engagement, and performance, all critical outcomes of bold conversations. You can establish safety in a variety of ways for your conversation to be effective and heard.

- **Mutual Purpose:** Clearly communicate that you care about the other person's goals and concerns, not just your own. This isn't manipulation but genuine commitment to finding solutions that address everyone's needs.

- **Mutual Respect:** Demonstrate through words and actions that you respect the other person regardless of your disagreement. When people sense contempt or dismissal, productive conversation becomes impossible.

- **Curiosity Signals:** Show authentic interest in understanding the other person's perspective through open-ended questions, attentive listening, and verbal and non-verbal cues that indicate you value their input.

Safety doesn't mean avoiding difficult topics, it means creating conditions where difficult topics can be discussed productively.

Element #3: Balanced Candor and Care

Bold conversations require both truth and compassion. Either without the other creates problems, candor without care feels like aggression, while care without candor feels like avoidance.

This balance involves:

Direct Language: Use clear, specific language about what you've observed, think, and feel. Avoid vague generalizations, hints, or sugar-coating that obscures your message.

Empathetic Framing: Deliver your message with awareness of how it might impact the other person. Consider their perspective, needs, and potential reactions.

Invitation to Dialogue: Present your views as your perspective rather than absolute truth, creating space for the other person's equally valid perspective.

Leaders who combine directness with empathy create what she calls brave spaces, environments where difficult truths can be shared without destroying trust. Psychological safety and accountability aren't opposing forces but complementary dimensions of high-performing teams. The highest performing teams have both, creating environments where people feel safe to speak up and are also held to high standards.

Element #4: Constructive Engagement

How you engage during the conversation itself largely determines its outcome. Constructive engagement involves specific practices that maintain connection while addressing difficult topics, ensuring the conversation moves forward productively rather than spiraling into defensiveness or withdrawal.

Present-moment attention forms the foundation of constructive engagement. Stay fully focused on the interaction rather than rehearsing your next point or getting lost in internal reactions. Mindful presence allows you to detect subtle cues that might otherwise be missed, a slight change in tone, a hesitation before answering, or body language that signals discomfort. Research shows that engagement quality, measured through factors like energy, turn-taking, and attention patterns, predicts team performance better than any other factor, including individual intelligence, personality, and skill.

Perspective flexibility is equally critical. Remain open to adjusting your understanding as new information emerges. The most productive conversations happen when both parties feel heard and understood, which requires genuine willingness to shift your viewpoint based on what you learn. This does not mean abandoning your position, but rather holding it lightly enough that it can evolve through dialogue.

Finally, take responsibility for pattern interruption when conversations slide into unproductive patterns like defensiveness, withdrawal, or aggression. You can shift the dynamic through thoughtful questions, genuine acknowledgment of their concerns, or even suggesting a brief break to reset. The key is recognizing these patterns early and taking proactive steps to redirect the conversation toward mutual understanding and forward progress.

Restarting a Stalled Conversation

Even the best-planned bold conversations can sometimes stall. Here's how you can reset and refocus effectively:

Pause briefly and acknowledge openly:

"It feels like we're a bit stuck. I want to make sure we're understanding each other clearly."

Ask a clarifying question:

"Can you help me understand what's most important to you right now?"

Refocus on mutual purpose:

"Let's step back a moment. Our goal is [shared goal]. Can we look at this again from that perspective?"

Suggest a short break:

"Maybe it would help us both to take a quick break and return in a few minutes with fresh eyes?"

These simple interventions can help realign the conversation and get you both back on a productive track.

Element #5: Forward Movement

The ultimate measure of a bold conversation is whether it creates movement, progress toward understanding, resolution, or aligned action. Forward movement requires several elements for success.

Actionable Insight: Focus on generating insights that inform clear next steps rather than endless analysis or abstract discussion.

Specific Agreements: Create explicit agreements about who will do what by when, especially when addressing complex issues that require multiple conversations.

Follow-Up Plans: Establish how and when you'll check in on progress, creating accountability without micromanagement.

The Bold Conversation Preparation Tool

Before your next difficult conversation, take 10 minutes to prepare using these prompts:

Purpose & Clarity

What specific outcome would make this conversation successful?

For me: _____

For them: _____

For our relationship/organization: _____

Safety Preparation

How might they feel threatened by this conversation?

Competence concerns: _____

Autonomy concerns: _____

Belonging/status concerns: _____

What specific words will I use to establish mutual purpose and respect?

Balanced Approach

What direct truth needs to be spoken? (Be specific and behavioral)

How can I frame this with genuine care for the other person?

Engagement Readiness

What might trigger me during this conversation?

What will I do if I notice myself getting triggered?

Forward Focus

What specific agreements or next steps do I hope will result?

How will we know if those steps are working?

Complete this preparation, then take three deep breaths before initiating the conversation. Better preparation leads to better outcomes.

Reflection Practice: After significant conversations, take time to extract learning about both the content discussed and the conversation process itself.

Research on team performance found that teams who regularly review both task outcomes and process effectiveness demonstrate exponentially faster improvement than those who focus only on results.

A few years ago, I faced one of the most challenging conversations in my career. A key leader in my organization was consistently missing deadlines and underdelivering on critical projects. It wasn't just affecting outcomes, it was eroding trust within our team. I felt the weight of responsibility: the stakes were high, discomfort was inevitable, and our shared values of integrity and accountability were deeply involved. Before initiating the conversation, I took a moment to clarify my purpose. It wasn't to assign blame or vent frustration, it was to genuinely understand what was happening and collaboratively identify a solution. This clarity became my anchor, especially as anxiety crept in.

I intentionally began by emphasizing our mutual goals, underscoring that I genuinely valued this leader's contributions. I explicitly communicated respect and sought their perspective openly, creating psychological safety. Though my heart rate increased, I reminded myself this tension was proof that something meaningful was at stake.

Balancing candor and care, I specifically described what I had observed without judgment: missed deadlines, incomplete work, and noticeable team frustration. I shared the impact of these patterns, ensuring my language remained behavior-focused rather than personal. Throughout the discussion, I actively engaged, carefully listening to their explanations and perspectives, and adapting my understanding in real-time.

By the conversation's end, we reached clear, actionable next steps with shared accountability. We scheduled regular check-ins to monitor progress, reinforcing our mutual commitment. The impact was immediate, not only did performance improve, but trust deepened significantly, affirming the power of approaching difficult conversations with courage, clarity, and compassion.

Bold Conversation Types

While the framework above applies broadly, specific types of bold conversations benefit from tailored approaches. Let's explore four conversation types that disproportionately impact leadership effectiveness.

Performance Conversations Addressing Gaps and Growth

Performance conversations are powerful opportunities to close the gap between current outcomes and desired standards, directly influencing individual growth, team effectiveness, and organizational accountability. Recent research confirms that the effectiveness of these conversations depends far more on their frequency and the quality of the interaction than on formal structures. Organizations are increasingly moving away from traditional annual performance reviews, recognizing their limitations and shifting instead toward frequent, development-focused check-ins. When initiating meaningful performance conversations, always start by establishing clear alignment, ensuring both parties share a mutual understanding of expectations, many performance gaps are rooted in misalignment rather than skill or motivation deficits. It's also crucial to focus on patterns of behavior rather than isolated incidents, as patterns reveal underlying issues and reduce defensiveness by avoiding the impression of nitpicking.

Connect improvement clearly to the individual's personal aspirations and values, not merely organizational objectives. Highlight that personal relevance significantly increases motivation and sustained effort. For sensitive or difficult discussions, utilize contrast statements to clarify intent and maintain trust, for instance, clearly stating, I'm not questioning your commitment; I'm concerned about the impact missed deadlines are having on our team. Finally, involve the individual in co-creating solutions, as people are more committed to plans they actively help shape, leading to greater accountability and long-term improvement.

Conflict Conversations Transforming Tension into Alignment

Conflict conversations address tension between individuals or groups with different perspectives, priorities, or approaches. These conversations transform potentially destructive energy into constructive outcomes. The latest research on conflict management emphasizes the distinction between relationship conflict (personal friction) and task conflict (disagreement about ideas or approaches). Studies show that while relationship conflict nearly always harms performance, moderate task conflict can enhance innovation and decision quality when managed effectively.

When navigating conflict conversations, addressing issues early significantly increases the likelihood of a positive resolution, research indicates conflicts handled within the first 24–48 hours are about 80% more likely to be resolved effectively compared to those left unaddressed. Begin each conversation by highlighting areas of mutual agreement before delving into differences; this approach creates psychological safety and emphasizes common ground, reducing defensiveness.

Avoid attributing negative motives or intentions. Instead, focus objectively on behaviors and their impacts. Demonstrate genuine understanding through active listening techniques such as paraphrasing and summarizing; studies consistently show that when people feel understood, their defensiveness diminishes even if disagreements remain. Finally, if discussions stall due to opposing positions, shift the conversation toward the shared values and underlying interests behind each perspective. This values-driven approach often reveals common goals, making resolution more achievable.

Change Conversations Building Buy-In for Transformation

Change conversations focus on building understanding, commitment, and momentum for organizational transitions. They're crucial for moving from announced change to embraced change. How change is communicated dramatically influences success rates.

When leading conversations around change, clarity and authenticity are essential. Start by connecting clearly to purpose, helping your team understand not just what is changing, but why it matters deeply and personally to each of them. Anchoring change to meaningful purpose generates significantly stronger buy-in and engagement. Equally important is your willingness to acknowledge the discomfort and loss often associated with change, whether it's the loss of status, familiar routines, or certainty about the future.

Being open about these realities builds trust, reduces resistance, and makes room for genuine dialogue. Rather than announcing change as a top-down directive, invite ongoing conversations that allow everyone to voice concerns, ask questions, and participate actively. As you guide these discussions, make the change relevant by clearly articulating how it will personally impact day-to-day roles and responsibilities, general statements rarely inspire specific actions. Finally, proactively celebrate early wins and visible progress to reinforce that change isn't merely possible, it's already underway, creating tangible momentum that motivates your team forward.

Ethical Challenge Conversations

Ethical challenge conversations address situations where actions or decisions conflict with values, integrity, or organizational standards. These are often the most difficult but impactful conversations leaders navigate. Fear of retaliation remains the primary barrier to speaking up on ethical concerns. When initiating conversations around ethical concerns, your approach significantly influences whether the dialogue becomes productive or defensive.

Always consider the context carefully, certain ethical issues are best addressed privately, while others benefit from broader team discussions. Finally, recognize when an issue cannot be resolved through initial dialogue, and understand how and when to escalate the matter appropriately through established organizational channels. This balanced and strategic approach to ethical conversations ensures integrity, promotes trust, and preserves organizational alignment.

The ability to navigate these specific conversation types with skill and courage differentiates exceptional leaders from merely effective ones. Each conversation type creates inflection points where your leadership impact expands or contracts based on your willingness to engage boldly.

> "The conversations you avoid are the conversations that define you as a leader."

Overcoming Conversation Barriers

Despite understanding the importance of bold conversations, most leaders still find themselves avoiding them. Research shows that 85% of executives identify holding difficult conversations as a top development need understanding and addressing the specific barriers that prevent these conversations is essential for leadership growth (see Figure 7.3).

Working with Fear and Productive Discomfort

Fear remains the primary reason leaders avoid necessary conversations. This fear takes several forms, including:

- **Relationship Damage:** Concern that the conversation will harm important relationships.
- **Emotional Discomfort:** Anticipation of feeling anxious, embarrassed, or rejected.

- **Uncertainty:** Worry about unpredictable responses or outcomes.

- **Competence Concerns:** Doubt about having the right language or approach.

Difficult conversations activate the brain's threat detection system, triggering the call social pain neural responses almost identical to physical pain. This key shift involves transforming how you relate to conversation discomfort. Instead of viewing discomfort as a signal to avoid the conversation, recognize it as verification that the conversation matters. Leaders who make this reframe consistently report breakthrough results in their communication effectiveness (see Figure 7.4).

When working through fear, especially around difficult conversations, practical and intentional strategies can help you stay grounded and effective. Start by clearly acknowledging your fears rather than suppressing them. Naming our emotions helps lessen their intensity and supports clearer thinking and decision-making.

Bold Conversation

Bold conversations rarely begin with the right words, they begin with the right preparation. These questions are designed to help you step into courageous dialogue with clarity, accountability, and intention.

1. What's the bold outcome I want from this conversation?

2. What am I assuming or making up about the other person?

3. What am I willing to own or take responsibility for?

4. What is the impact if I don't have this conversation?

5. What support, script, or grounding do I need to feel ready?

Figure 7.3 Questions to Prepare for a Bold Conversation

The BOLD Leader

Rate Your Confidence

Every bold conversation begins with self-awareness. This self-check tool is designed to help you assess where you currently stand before stepping into your next bold coversation.

1. Avoiding

I'm delaying or dodging the conversation.

2. Tentative

I might bring it up, but not clearly.

3. Neutral

I'll say it, but I'll play it safe.

4. Anchored

I know what I want to say and why.

5. Bold

I'm ready to lead the conversation with clarity and care.

Figure 7.4   Bold Conversation Confidence Scale

Next, actively distinguish between your worst-case scenarios and realistic potential outcomes, remembering that most bold conversations are far less damaging than you might imagine. Connecting the conversation directly to your core purpose is another powerful way to sustain your courage. Actions aligned with our deeper purpose are more likely to persist, even when they feel uncomfortable. Finally, consider building your courage gradually by starting with moderately challenging conversations and moving progressively toward more complex and sensitive interactions. This incremental exposure builds your comfort level and skill set over time, enabling you to navigate fear productively and confidently.

Timing Intelligence: When to Engage, When to Wait

Not every bold conversation needs to occur immediately, and understanding timing is crucial for their effectiveness. Several factors influence the optimal timing of difficult discussions (see Figure 7.5). Emotional readiness is especially important, as conversations initiated when emotions are running high typically lead to poorer outcomes. Context also significantly impacts effectiveness, addressing private matters in public settings, or attempting to tackle complex issues without adequate preparation or time, consistently leads to frustration or misunderstanding.

Additionally, resource availability plays a critical role, initiating challenging conversations when you're rushed, exhausted, or unfocused often results in lower-quality interactions and reduced outcomes.

Grounded Conversations

Intention   What is the reason I'm having this conversation?

Ownership   What am I responsible for in this situation?

Outcome   What do I want the other person to understand?

Figure 7.5   Bold Conversation Anchors

The BOLD Leader

Recognizing conversational patterns is another essential consideration, as addressing issues early, before negative patterns become entrenched, makes resolution simpler and more productive. Effective timing requires carefully balancing urgency with wisdom. Ask yourself honestly, am I delaying this conversation because of discomfort, or am I genuinely waiting for more favorable conditions? This reflective question helps ensure you're acting strategically rather than avoidantly, leading to more impactful and productive bold conversations.

Finding Words for Difficult Messages

Many leaders avoid bold conversations because they struggle to find appropriate language. The right words don't just communicate content, they create safety, demonstrate respect, and invite dialogue even around challenging topics (see Figure 7.6). The

Bold Conversation Reframe Tool

Thought		Bold Reframe
They are being difficult.	------>	This is going to create clarity.
This is going to be uncomfortable.	------>	They are trying to protect something important.
I don't want to be misunderstood.	------>	I want to be intentional and clear.
They might get defensive.	------>	They might be surprised, but I will stay grounded.
I'm not good at hard conversations.	------>	I'm learning to lead with courage.

Our internal dialogue often determines how we show up to a conversation.
This tool offers intentional reframes that help shift your mindset from fear, avoidance, or self-doubt into clarity, empathy, and courage.

Figure 7.6 Examples of Bold Conversation Reframe

Bold Conversations

language you choose significantly influences the outcome of your conversations. One critical distinction involves using "I" statements rather than "you" statements. Beginning sentences with "I" expresses your perspective without assigning judgment, reducing defensiveness and facilitating more open dialogue. Another key pattern is emphasizing specific behaviors instead of character traits. Addressing concrete actions, such as errors in recent reports, fosters clarity and openness, while labeling someone personally ("You're careless") tends to escalate resistance and conflict. Additionally, it's essential to clearly distinguish between direct observations and subjective inferences.

Directly stating what you've observed ("I noticed you've missed the last two team meetings") helps maintain neutrality and reduces defensiveness compared to subjective interpretations like "You don't seem committed." Finally, employing tentative rather than absolute language encourages engagement by acknowledging your perspective's provisional nature.

Phrases like "I'm wondering if…" or "From my perspective…" invite dialogue and signal openness to alternative viewpoints, whereas definitive statements can prematurely close discussions. Mindfully using these language strategies creates stronger connections, improves conversational effectiveness, and enhances mutual understanding.

Developing your language capacity isn't about manipulative word tricks but about finding authentic expressions that honor both truth and relationship. The more precisely you can articulate difficult messages while maintaining respect, the more effective your bold conversations become.

Bold Conversation Starters

The way you start a challenging conversation significantly influences the outcome. When initiating discussions about performance, clearly state the specific situation and reinforce the importance of mutual success and shared accountability. For conflicts, directly acknowledge the tension and express genuine interest in understanding the other person's perspective, signaling your intent to resolve the issue together rather than assigning blame.

In conversations about organizational changes, openly invite team members to share their thoughts, questions, or concerns to demonstrate your commitment to inclusive, collaborative solutions (see Figure 7.7). Similarly, when facing ethical dilemmas, approach the dialogue with curiosity and a desire to understand the underlying reasoning behind decisions, rather than immediately passing judgment.

Bold Conversation Planning

My intention for this conversation is...
(Clarifies your "why" and ensures the purpose of the conversation stays centered.)

I will take responsibility for...
(Establishes personal accountability and emotional maturity.)

The most important point I need to communicate is...
(Helps you cut through the noise and zero in on what truly matters.)

What I need to listen for is...
(Reminds you that communication is two-way, and that insight often lives in what's said.)

I will anchor myself by remembering...
(Grounds you in a calming truth, value, or purpose to steady your energy in real time.)

Figure 7.7 Bold Conversations Planning Template

Effective opening statements always clearly address the specific issue at hand, emphasize mutual purpose and collaboration, foster open dialogue, and center around shared success. Practicing this intentional approach sets the stage for more productive, impactful, and authentically bold conversations.

Quick Scripts for Common Bold Conversations

- When someone isn't meeting performance expectations:

  "I want to discuss our current timeline because I've noticed several key deadlines being missed. I genuinely want to understand what might be causing these challenges so we can address them together."

- When addressing an ethical concern:

  "I've been reflecting on our recent decision regarding [specific situation], and I'm trying to understand how it aligns with our shared values. Can we talk through this together to make sure we're staying true to what we stand for?"

- When resolving interpersonal conflict:

  "I've sensed some tension between us around [specific issue]. I really value our relationship and collaboration, and I'd love to understand your perspective better so we can move forward positively."

- When navigating resistance to change:

  "I know this change involves uncertainty, and that can feel difficult. Can we talk openly about any concerns you might have, and see how we can address them together?"

Bold Conversation Practices

Understanding the principles behind bold conversations is essential, but transforming that understanding into real-world skill requires deliberate, purposeful practice. One particularly effective approach is mental rehearsal, intentionally visualizing and mentally preparing for a conversation before it occurs. Mental rehearsal engages many of the same neural pathways activated during actual practice, significantly improving your outcomes and reducing anxiety. Effective mental rehearsal involves anticipating multiple scenarios rather than sticking rigidly to a predetermined script.

Preparing emotionally is critical. Practicing specific language and critical phrases in advance can also enhance conversational clarity and confidence. Finally, imagining a positive outcome can strengthen your mental blueprint for success, reinforcing confidence and preparedness. Ultimately, mental rehearsal isn't about memorizing exact words, it's about cultivating presence, adaptability, and responsiveness for impactful conversations.

Soliciting specific feedback about your conversation approach accelerates development far beyond what self-assessment alone can accomplish. Targeted feedback creates the fastest improvement in complex capabilities. To consistently elevate your bold conversation skills, create ongoing opportunities for meaningful feedback. Instead of asking vague questions, clearly request observations on specific aspects of your approach, such as, "How did my opening affect your comfort in speaking openly?" or "Did my framing help us move forward constructively?" Seek insights from multiple angles, including your team, peers, mentors, and communication experts. Approach these conversations with a genuine focus on growth rather than evaluation, "I'm actively working to improve how I handle conflict conversations; what could I do to be more effective?" After receiving feedback, visibly demonstrate how you're applying it, reinforcing your commitment and encouraging others to continue sharing honestly. Leaders who intentionally and regularly seek targeted feedback typically build their skills and confidence at a much faster rate, transforming vulnerability into lasting boldness.

Leaders who systematically gather conversation feedback typically develop skills at 3–5 times the rate of those who rely solely on self-assessment. The temporary vulnerability of asking for feedback creates long-term conversation capability that transforms your leadership impact.

The Bold Conversation System

Individual bold conversations matter, but creating a comprehensive system for effective communication transforms your overall leadership impact. This system (see Figure 7.8) integrates preparation, execution, learning, and development into a continuous cycle.

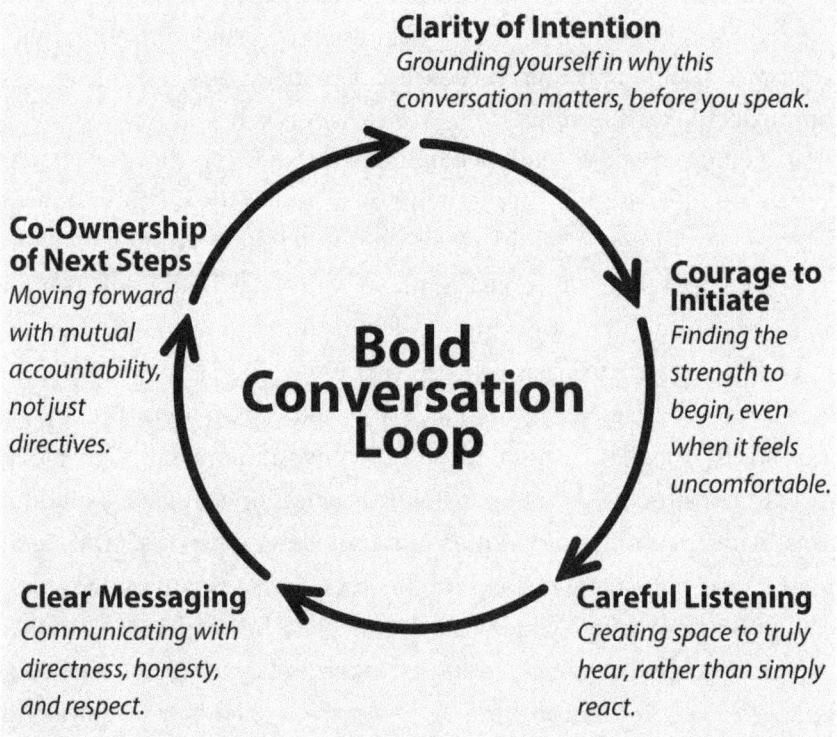

Figure 7.8 The Bold Conversation Loop

Start by mapping the bold conversations currently needed in your leadership context. This landscape reveals patterns, priorities, and development opportunities that might otherwise remain hidden.

Complete this inventory by identifying the following three key ingredients to your bold conversation map.

1. **Pending Conversations**

   Which specific bold conversations have you been delaying or avoiding? List the person, topic, and desired outcome for each.

2. **Recurring Challenges**

   Which conversation types consistently create difficulty for you? Performance feedback? Conflict resolution? Change management?

3. **Development Priorities**

   Based on your leadership context, which conversation capabilities would most significantly enhance your impact if strengthened?

This mapping process transforms vague communication concerns into specific action priorities. It also reveals underlying patterns, if you consistently avoid certain conversation types or struggle with specific individuals, these patterns indicate development needs.

Conversation Portfolio Management: Balancing Your Approach

Just as financial investors manage a portfolio of assets, effective leaders manage a portfolio of conversation approaches. Different situations require different styles, and leadership flexibility comes from having multiple approaches available.

Versatile communicators, those who can adapt their approach to different contexts, consistently outperform those with a single preferred style, regardless of how effective that preferred style might be.

"Your conversation culture becomes your organization's invisible operating system, determining what's possible regardless of your formal strategies and structures."

An effective conversation portfolio equips you with the flexibility to lead skillfully through diverse and challenging situations. Rather than relying solely on your preferred style, you develop the capacity for directive communication, delivering clear messages that prompt immediate action when necessary. You also build comfort with collaborative dialogue, creating space to genuinely explore diverse perspectives and navigate complex issues. Mastering coaching conversations helps you focus on developing others' capabilities, fostering ongoing growth rather than merely directing tasks. At times, confrontational clarity is required, empowering you to address critical issues directly and decisively before they escalate. Equally important is your ability to engage in relationship repair, thoughtfully restoring connections that have been strained. By intentionally strengthening communication styles outside your comfort zone, you become a leader capable of responding confidently and effectively, no matter the context.

Conversation Culture

Your personal ability to have bold conversations creates an immediate impact, but shaping a courageous conversation culture throughout your organization generates deeper, lasting transformation. A teams' conversational norms directly influence overall performance, creativity, and innovation. To actively shape this culture, begin by openly modeling the conversations you want to encourage, embrace feedback openly, discuss difficult topics, and demonstrate vulnerability to set a powerful example.

Equip your team through consistent skill-building, offering training and resources that support effective communication and courageous dialogue. Intentionally recognize and celebrate moments when team members speak uncomfortable truths, reinforcing that honest conversations are both valued and expected. Create dedicated spaces and times for bold conversations, structuring forums that make challenging discussions more approachable and productive. Finally, consistently monitor and assess your organization's conversational health through regular surveys, interviews, or observation treating communication culture as strategically as any other core priority.

What You Have Learned

You have now learned that the difficult conversations you're tempted to avoid are precisely the ones essential to your effectiveness as a leader. Bold conversations, whether they're about performance gaps, conflict resolution, change management, or ethical challenges, set transformative leaders apart by proactively addressing critical issues before they escalate into crises. You've explored the importance of clear purpose, psychological safety, balanced candor and care, constructive engagement, and forward movement in navigating these impactful interactions. This chapter highlighted the necessity of mastering different conversation styles, actively overcoming barriers like fear and discomfort, and building the flexibility to adapt your approach to diverse situations. Ultimately, you've discovered that bold conversations aren't just about improving individual interactions; they're about shaping an organizational culture where trust, openness, and courageous dialogue drive lasting impact and growth.

Bold Truth

The conversations you choose to avoid shape your leadership just as significantly as the conversations you bravely engage in perhaps even more so. The extent of your leadership impact is directly tied to your willingness to step beyond conversational comfort zones into necessary, challenging discussions. While some leaders naturally navigate these interactions with ease, the truth is that anyone can develop strong conversational skills through intentional practice and commitment.

Your Bold Move

Transform your conversation impact through deliberate action.

1. Identify the one bold conversation you've been avoiding that would create the greatest positive impact if addressed effectively. Use the Bold Conversation Preparation Tool to plan your approach.

2. Have that conversation within the next 72 hours. The window between preparation and action should be narrow enough to maintain momentum but wide enough for thoughtful planning.

3. Conduct a thorough debrief after the conversation. What worked? What didn't? What would you do differently next time? Document these insights to accelerate your learning.

4. Share your experience with a trusted colleague. Describing what you tried, what happened, and what you learned reinforces your development while potentially influencing others.

These steps create immediate impact while establishing patterns that transform your long-term leadership effectiveness. The most influential leaders aren't necessarily those with the most charisma or the highest positions, they're those willing to initiate and navigate the conversations that truly matter.

As you reflect on your next bold conversation, remember this: Every difficult interaction you bravely initiate isn't just about the immediate outcome, it's about shaping who you are as a leader. It's about choosing clarity over avoidance, courage over silence, and integrity over comfort. Right now, commit to making your next conversation one that deepens trust, strengthens connection, and models bold leadership for everyone around you. What bold conversation have you been avoiding, and how might your leadership, and your life, change by choosing to engage courageously?

Bold Metrics

Percentage of critical conversations proactively initiated versus avoided.

Specifically, track how often you proactively initiate challenging conversations rather than avoiding or postponing them. Measuring this consistently will reflect your growing boldness, willingness, and capability to handle important conversations that directly impact leadership effectiveness and organizational performance.

Setting the Stage for What Comes Next

Bold conversations don't just transform individual moments, they ignite lasting momentum. You've now strengthened your ability to lead powerful, courageous conversations that break barriers and drive clarity. But true bold leadership extends far beyond individual interactions. You do not need to say it perfectly. You just need to say it. Bold leadership starts with bold language and the willingness to use your voice for what matters most. In the next chapter, you will learn how bold leaders trust their instincts, even when the path ahead is unclear.

In Chapter 8, you will take your boldness even further, discovering how to embed it deeply into the DNA of your organization. You will explore practical, proven strategies for cultivating a culture where psychological safety thrives, healthy challenge sparks innovation, and continuous growth becomes the standard rather than the exception. Bold leadership is more than personal courage it's about fostering an environment where courage becomes contagious, multiplying impact across your teams, shaping your organization's identity, and defining your leadership legacy. Individual acts of courage. It is about creating conditions where courage multiplies, where boldness is woven into the fabric of your team, your organization, and your legacy.

Chapter 8

Bold Data, Instinct, and Courage

You have done the work. You have believed in yourself, owned your truth, and learned from every part of your journey. Now comes the moment some leaders avoid, taking clear, bold action. This is the inflection point. Not tomorrow. Not someday. This is your moment. In today's complex world, the most consequential decisions arrive with incomplete data, competing priorities, and significant stakes. Leaders who wait for perfect information rarely get the chance to lead at all. This chapter explores how to act boldly by integrating three essential elements: data-driven insight, intuitive judgment, and the courage to move forward despite uncertainty.

Because analysis has value. Instinct has wisdom. But only courage converts them into impact. In the space between what the data tells you and what your instinct knows lies the territory of bold leadership. Bold leaders break free from these patterns by integrating data, instinct, and courage into unified action.

> "Analysis has value. Instinct has wisdom. But only courage converts them into impact."

The Decision Dilemma

In today's data-rich environment, many leaders find themselves paradoxically paralyzed by the very information meant to empower them. Decision hesitation creates substantial organizational costs.

Several factors commonly contribute to decision paralysis among leaders. One significant factor is analysis paralysis, where leaders believe that accumulating more data will yield certainty, leading them into endless cycles of information gathering that stall decisive action without meaningfully reducing risk. Another critical factor involves the suppression of instinct. Many organizational cultures emphasize data-driven decisions so heavily that leaders undervalue or overlook the importance of intuitive insights gained through experience, which are often crucial for effective decision-making. Additionally, false precision can create dangerous illusions of certainty; detailed spreadsheets and sophisticated analyses may give leaders artificial confidence about inherently unpredictable future outcomes, leading to unexpected setbacks and failures. Finally, accountability avoidance often plays a hidden yet pivotal role, leaders sometimes delay decisions not because of insufficient information, but due to a reluctance to accept responsibility for potential negative consequences. Recognizing and addressing these patterns enables leaders to break free from paralysis and step boldly into decisive, effective action.

Consider a marketing vice president confronted with contradictory signals about a major campaign launch. The data analytics team projects positive ROI based on market research and historical patterns. Yet the VP senses something is off, perhaps in the messaging tone, the market timing, or the competitive landscape. The easiest path is to follow the data, which provides both conventional validation and shared accountability if things go wrong. But what if the instinct reflects pattern recognition from years of experience that hasn't been captured in the models? What if those subtle misgivings represent valuable insight that could prevent a costly mistake?

Bold leaders develop approaches to navigate this territory, integrating data and instinct rather than choosing between them, and finding the courage to act with conviction even amid ambiguity.

The Bold Decision Triad

Effective decision-making requires integrating data, instinct, and courage in a unified approach that honors both empirical evidence and human judgment. Rather than viewing these elements as conflicting forces, the Bold Decision Triad treats them as complementary, each reinforcing the others and contributing to balanced, confident leadership.

The first essential component of the Bold Decision Triad is *data literacy,* a capability that goes beyond merely collecting information to transforming it into genuine insights. Bold leaders leverage data differently from their hesitant counterparts; instead of simply confirming existing beliefs or justifying indecision, they use data actively to challenge assumptions and identify new opportunities. Organizations with robust data-driven decision-making practices are, on average, 5% more productive and 6% more profitable compared to their competitors. The critical difference, however, isn't the sheer volume of data but the leaders' ability to interpret it effectively.

Successful leaders train themselves in pattern recognition to separate meaningful trends from statistical noise, carefully identify critical constraints in data sets without letting limitations become reasons for inaction, actively seek out data that contradicts established assumptions, and exercise judgment to discern between data that's simply interesting and data genuinely critical to decision-making. Data literacy isn't about mastering statistics; it's about cultivating the discernment needed to extract maximum strategic value from information.

Complementing data literacy, *intuitive intelligence* plays an indispensable role, especially in complex environments where uncertainty persists.

Intuition in leaders is a sophisticated form of pattern recognition honed by extensive experience and deliberate reflection. Bold leaders actively cultivate this informed intuition, grounding their gut feelings in structured experience rather than random impressions. This cultivation

Bold Data, Instinct, and Courage

involves intentionally reviewing past decisions to identify underlying patterns that inform future choices. Leaders also proactively seek diverse experiences and viewpoints, broadening their mental models and preventing narrow, limited judgments. They create accelerated feedback loops, rapidly connecting decisions to outcomes to refine intuition continuously. Furthermore, bold leaders engage in cognitive debiasing techniques, such as conducting pre-mortems, imagining a future scenario where a decision has failed, to identify and counter cognitive biases before they distort intuitive judgment. Data and instinct thus become powerful partners; data provides a solid foundation for informed intuition, and intuition contextualizes and interprets data in meaningful ways, bridging gaps where information remains incomplete.

The third crucial element, *decisive courage*, directly addresses the common gap between decision-making and action, a gap that frequently undermines otherwise sound decisions. Nearly half of organizational decisions fail, not due to poor analysis or inadequate planning, but because of delayed or insufficient implementation. Bold leaders bridge this implementation gap by demonstrating decisive courage. They understand that calculated risk-taking involves carefully weighing both the explicit risks of action and the less visible, but equally dangerous, risks of inaction and delay.

Example of Making a Bold Call

One leader had been circling the same misaligned strategy for months, paralyzed by the pressure to get it right. By applying the D90 Method, she made the bold choice to sunset a product line, focus on a neglected strength, and completely redesign her team's rhythm. Within three months, not only did revenue increase by 20%, but employee engagement scores hit a new high. She didn't just change her to-do list, she changed her trajectory.

Bold leaders also recognize *decision velocity*, differentiating between decisions that are easily reversible and can thus be made rapidly, and those that carry significant, irreversible consequences that require deeper deliberation, yet still demand timely, decisive action. They communicate decisions clearly and confidently, articulating their rationale in ways that inspire commitment and mobilize others even amid uncertainty. This communication is not about projecting false certainty but rather authentic, confident clarity. Additionally, bold leaders practice adaptive persistence, remaining firmly committed to their decisions while staying responsive to new information that might necessitate strategic adjustments.

Ultimately, the Bold Decision Triad embodies a dynamic interplay of analytical rigor, intuitive wisdom, and courageous action, empowering leaders to confidently navigate complexity and uncertainty. In integrating data literacy, intuitive intelligence, and decisive courage, bold leaders create conditions for consistently effective decisions, decisions that are neither paralyzed by analysis nor diminished by reckless impulsivity but strengthened by thoughtful synthesis and confident implementation.

> "The greatest risk isn't making an imperfect decision, it's perfect analysis followed by imperfect execution."

The Bold Decision Process

The Bold Decision Framework, Figure 8.1, provides powerful guidance across a variety of situations, yet specific decision types often require distinct strategies to ensure effectiveness. One critical category is strategic decisions, which fundamentally shape the future direction of an organization, determining where to compete, how to differentiate, and what capabilities to build. These decisions

Bold Data, Instinct, and Courage

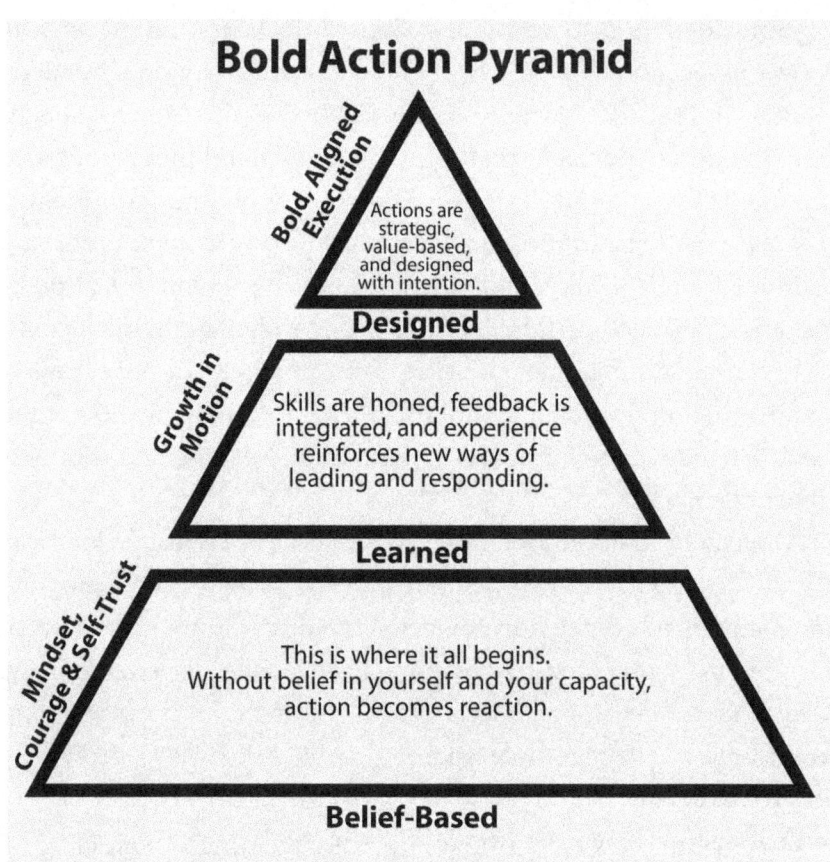

Figure 8.1 The Bold Action Pyramid

"Navigating strategic decisions successfully requires an intentional expansion of the time horizon, moving beyond short-term thinking to envision implications several years ahead."

inherently involve high stakes, considerable uncertainty, and substantial long-term consequences.

Leaders who explicitly broaden their strategic perspective to encompass longer-term impacts consistently make more innovative and impactful choices compared to those constrained by near-term pressures.

Effective strategic decisions also involve rigorously testing the underlying strategic logic rather than relying solely on data-driven projections, which inevitably lose accuracy over longer periods. Strategic failures frequently arise from flawed underlying assumptions rather than poor execution. To safeguard against this, bold leaders carefully scrutinize the critical "if-then" assumptions that underpin their strategies. Furthermore, because the future is inherently uncertain, successful strategic decision-making often involves developing multiple plausible scenarios rather than banking on a single predicted outcome.

Finally, proactive risk assessment is vital before committing to a strategic direction. This powerful exercise surfaces hidden risks and assumptions, significantly enhancing strategic rigor. Ultimately, strategic decisions demand thoughtful, reflective processes paired with decisive commitment once the direction is chosen. Bold leaders excel by achieving the delicate balance between deep analysis and clear, confident action.

The Bold Decision Checklist

When facing a consequential decision, use this checklist to ensure you're integrating data, instinct, and courage effectively:

Data Literacy

☐ Have we gathered relevant data rather than just available data?
☐ Have we examined the data from multiple perspectives?
☐ Have we identified the limitations and blind spots in our analysis?
☐ Have we distinguished between correlation and causation?

Intuitive Intelligence

☐ Have I created space for reflection beyond analytical thinking?
☐ Have I sought intuitive input from diverse perspectives?

(continued)

Bold Data, Instinct, and Courage

(continued)

☐ Have I distinguished between informed intuition and casual impressions?

☐ Have I surfaced and examined any emotional responses to the options?

Decisive Courage

☐ Have I considered both the risks of action and the costs of inaction?

☐ Have I distinguished between reversible and irreversible aspects of this decision?

☐ Have I established clear accountability for implementation?

☐ Am I prepared to communicate with appropriate conviction?

Process Integrity

☐ Did we frame the question effectively before gathering information?

☐ Have we established decision criteria before evaluating specific options?

☐ Have we assigned appropriate decision rights to the right people?

☐ Have we created a clear timeline for moving from analysis to action?

Complete this checklist before finalizing significant decisions to ensure balanced integration of all three elements of the Bold Decision Triad.

Different Challenges, Different Approaches

While the Bold Decision Framework provides a strong foundation applicable to many leadership contexts, certain types of decisions require distinct, tailored approaches. Leaders frequently encounter specific categories of decisions that call for customized strategies and insights. Understanding the nuances of each type can significantly enhance decision quality, execution effectiveness, and organizational success. Let's explore four of the most common decision categories, strategic, operational, crisis-driven, and people-centered decisions, and examine how bold leaders can adapt and refine their approach for each unique challenge.

Strategic decisions shape the very heart of an organization, guiding essential choices about where to compete, how to stand apart from competitors, and which capabilities to develop. By their nature, these decisions carry significant consequences, considerable uncertainty, and implications that stretch far beyond immediate outcomes (see Figure 8.2). Bold leaders recognize the importance of extending their vision beyond short-term pressures, actively imagining how their choices today will play out years down the road. Leaders who explicitly adopt longer time horizons consistently make more innovative and fundamentally different strategic decisions than those who focus on immediate or near-term goals.

In addition to extending their perspective, effective leaders understand that strategic decisions rely heavily on sound logic and tested assumptions, rather than purely numerical projections. Strategies more commonly falter due to faulty logic than due to poor

"People decisions compound over time, shaping organizational culture, innovation, and long-term success."

implementation. To mitigate this risk, bold leaders methodically examine and test the core "if-then" statements underpinning their strategies, ensuring each assumption holds firm and aligns clearly with organizational realities. This disciplined testing approach enhances strategic clarity and reduces hidden vulnerabilities.

Bold Data, Instinct, and Courage

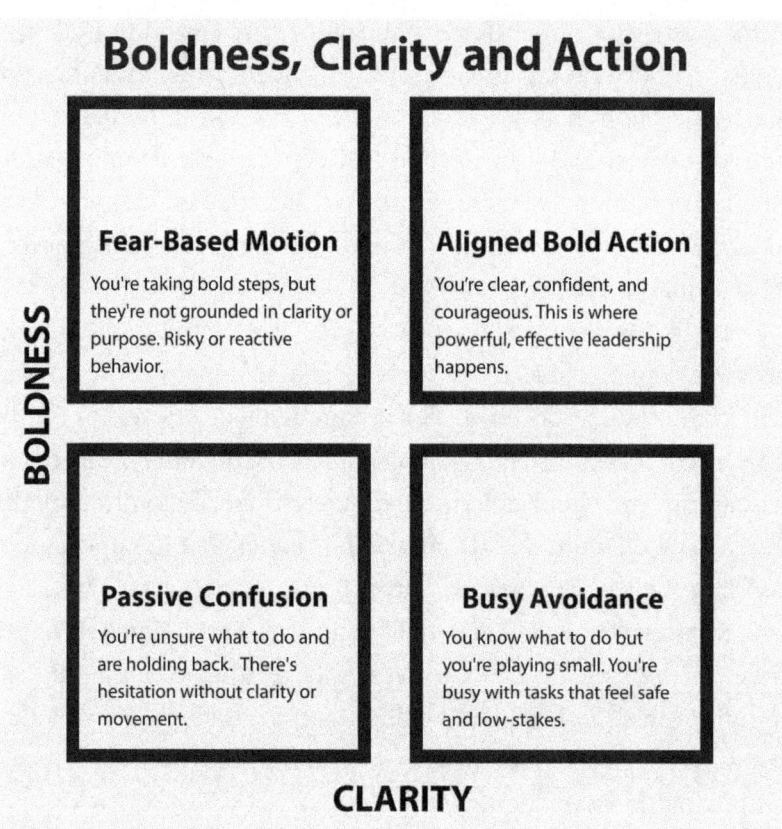

Boldness, Clarity and Action

BOLDNESS

Fear-Based Motion
You're taking bold steps, but they're not grounded in clarity or purpose. Risky or reactive behavior.

Aligned Bold Action
You're clear, confident, and courageous. This is where powerful, effective leadership happens.

Passive Confusion
You're unsure what to do and are holding back. There's hesitation without clarity or movement.

Busy Avoidance
You know what to do but you're playing small. You're busy with tasks that feel safe and low-stakes.

CLARITY

Figure 8.2 Bold Action Grid

Since the future is inherently uncertain, bold leaders also embrace scenario planning as a critical strategic practice. Instead of committing to a single forecasted outcome, they thoughtfully develop several plausible scenarios, each based on varied assumptions and potential developments. By evaluating strategies across these different future contexts, leaders gain flexibility and resilience, reducing their vulnerability to unexpected disruptions. Shell's well-known scenario-planning approach offers a strong example of this technique, demonstrating how considering multiple futures can uncover robust strategic options.

Finally, anticipating potential pitfalls before finalizing decisions greatly strengthens strategic outcomes. Strategic decisions demand careful and thoughtful deliberation, coupled with the courage to commit decisively once a path forward is clear. Bold leaders excel precisely by achieving this careful balance, taking ample time for reflection and testing, while also maintaining readiness and conviction to move forward confidently and decisively.

People-related decisions, including hiring, promoting, assembling teams, and managing performance, can yield outsized impacts, often far greater than the time typically invested in making them would suggest. Despite their profound influence, these decisions are frequently approached with less structure and discipline than financial or strategic choices. To maximize effectiveness, bold leaders recognize that selecting and developing talent demands the same careful attention, intentionality, and rigor applied to other critical business decisions.

> "Selecting talent is more than finding skill, it's choosing character, curiosity, and emotional intelligence."

Effective people decisions require leaders to carefully balance competence and character. Hiring choices based solely on technical skills regularly fall short compared to selections that carefully assess both functional expertise and deeper character attributes, such as adaptability, curiosity, resilience, and emotional intelligence. Leaders who explicitly integrate both skill-based competence and broader personal qualities ensure stronger alignment with organizational values and long-term success.

One significant challenge leaders face in people decisions is the tendency toward pattern matching, the instinctive preference for candidates who remind us of ourselves or previously successful hires. This unconscious bias significantly narrows candidate pools, reduces diversity, and limits organizational innovation. To counteract

Bold Data, Instinct, and Courage

this tendency, bold leaders establish explicit, diverse criteria for candidate selection before beginning the review process. This intentional strategy helps mitigate unconscious biases and fosters teams that are both more inclusive and more innovative.

Consistency in evaluation processes is also crucial. Rather than relying solely on general impressions or gut feelings, effective leaders utilize structured interview techniques and clearly defined assessment criteria. Structured interviews significantly outperform unstructured methods in predicting candidate performance, reducing both subjective biases and overlooked critical qualities. This disciplined approach helps leaders more accurately identify talent that aligns with organizational needs and culture.

However, experienced leaders should not discount the value of intuition entirely. Intuitive judgments are particularly reliable when they emerge from extensive experience and expertise. Thus, seasoned leaders with deep domain experience can trust their intuitive impressions, but these instincts should always be verified through structured interviews, careful reference checks, and consistent evaluation frameworks. By carefully blending structured assessments with experience-informed intuition, bold leaders maximize decision accuracy and organizational alignment.

Ultimately, bold leaders appreciate that people decisions compound significantly over time, shaping organizational culture, performance, and innovation. Recognizing this long-term influence, they apply thoughtful rigor and balanced judgment to selecting, developing, and managing talent, ensuring their organization continually thrives through exceptional teams and outstanding individuals.

Responding Under Pressure

Innovation decisions uniquely challenge leaders because they involve venturing into unknown territory and creating value in markets that can't be reliably predicted. These decisions require distinct approaches that intentionally blend data, instinct, and courage, helping leaders navigate uncertainty, Figure 8.2, without stalling progress. One effective method to approach innovation strategically is known as discovery-driven planning. Unlike traditional business planning, which tends to extrapolate current knowledge into the future, discovery-driven planning focuses explicitly on surfacing, clarifying, and systematically testing key assumptions. By proactively identifying and addressing uncertainties, leaders can significantly improve their chances of successfully bringing new ideas to market.

Another powerful practice for managing innovation effectively is to establish balanced innovation portfolios. Instead of betting all resources and efforts on a single, high-stakes idea, bold leaders strategically create portfolios that blend initiatives with varying risk profiles and potential rewards. The most consistently successful innovators maintain a diversified mix of core incremental improvements, adjacent moderate-risk opportunities, and transformational high-risk, breakthrough ideas projects. This portfolio approach helps leaders spread risk, leverage opportunities across multiple horizons, and sustain long-term growth.

Innovation thrives in environments that foster rapid experimentation and continuous learning. Fast-cycle learning approaches, such as the lean startup methodology, help teams efficiently validate their ideas, quickly learn from real-world feedback, and adjust their direction as needed. By developing minimum viable products (MVPs) and rapidly iterating based on user responses, bold leaders minimize investment risks while maximizing learning, ensuring that innovation remains responsive to actual market needs and realities.

> "Innovation isn't about predicting the future, it's about systematically discovering it through bold exploration and rapid learning."

Bold Data, Instinct, and Courage

Because innovation inherently involves uncertainty, the process necessarily includes occasional setbacks and learning from failures. Ultimately, effective innovation decisions are not binary choices or simple go/no-go checkpoints. Instead, they represent structured learning journeys where uncertainty is progressively reduced, assumptions continuously tested, and insights rapidly integrated. Bold leaders embrace innovation as a disciplined, courageous exploration that consistently creates meaningful, sustainable value.

Key Practices for Bold Innovation

- **Discovery-Driven Planning:** Clearly articulate and systematically test your key assumptions.

- **Balanced Portfolios:** Maintain diverse innovation initiatives across core, adjacent, and transformational areas.

- **Fast-Cycle Learning:** Rapidly test ideas with minimal investment and adjust based on real-world feedback.

- **Psychological Safety:** Encourage openness, experimentation, and transparency to learn from both successes and setbacks.

Navigating the Data-Instinct Strategically

> "Effective decision-making often demands a careful synthesis of these two powerful yet sometimes contradictory sources of insight."

Navigating the intersection between data-driven analysis and intuitive judgment represents one of the most nuanced and challenging aspects of bold leadership.

Successful leaders don't rely exclusively on one or the other, instead they employ specific strategies to thoughtfully blend data and instinct, recognizing both their strengths and limitations.

One critical element of successfully integrating data and intuition is developing a clear awareness of data's inherent constraints. Data is essential but inevitably carries certain limitations that bold leaders must keep in mind. Historical bias, for instance, means data often represents past realities rather than future possibilities. This backward-looking nature can prove particularly problematic in rapidly evolving markets, where relying exclusively on historical trends may provide misleading guidance. Finally, because data doesn't interpret itself, bold leaders acknowledge interpretation variance. Different stakeholders can draw dramatically different conclusions from the same data set based on their distinct mental models and assumptions.

> "Bold decisions aren't about choosing data over intuition or vice versa, they're about skillfully blending both to illuminate the clearest path forward."

Strengthening intuitive judgment also plays a vital role in effective decision-making, but leaders must distinguish between informed intuition and casual impressions influenced by biases or limited experience. Effective intuition emerges from deliberate reflection on extensive, relevant experience rather than random gut feelings. To enhance intuitive reliability, bold leaders deliberately cultivate deep domain expertise, recognizing that intuition thrives best where substantial knowledge and deliberate practice intersect.

> "Bold leaders proactively create accelerated feedback loops, systematically linking intuitive judgments to actual outcomes, allowing them to quickly refine their instincts based on real-world evidence."

Moreover, they actively diversify their input sources, seeking intuitive insights from multiple knowledgeable perspectives rather than relying solely on their own impressions. Regular reflection on past decisions,

217

carefully noting where intuition proved accurate or misleading, also reinforces meta-awareness of personal intuitive strengths and limitations.

When data and intuition appear to conflict, bold leaders employ targeted strategies to resolve these apparent tensions. Often, perceived conflicts originate from differing underlying assumptions. By explicitly identifying and examining these assumptions, leaders frequently reveal the root cause of the disagreement and find viable paths forward. Another powerful approach involves seeking additional perspectives from diverse experts, which often highlights previously unnoticed blind spots or biases present in either the analytical or intuitive viewpoint. Furthermore, conducting small-scale experiments or tests enables leaders to validate hypotheses without committing entirely to either direction prematurely. Leaders might also adjust the scope of their decisions, making smaller, reversible choices initially while collecting further insights to inform subsequent, larger-scale commitments. Finally, when a leader possesses deep domain expertise and strong intuitive capabilities, their instincts deserve considerable weight, even when in apparent conflict with data, provided they carefully explore the reasons for this divergence rather than simply disregarding analytical insights.

How to Navigate Data-Instinct Conflicts

1. **Surface Assumptions:** Explicitly identify underlying assumptions driving data interpretation and intuitive judgments.

2. **Seek Diverse Inputs:** Gather insights from various experts to reduce biases and illuminate blind spots.

3. **Experiment Small:** Use limited, controlled experiments to quickly validate assumptions without high risks.

4. **Scale Decisions Appropriately:** Make smaller, reversible decisions first to maintain flexibility while building confidence.

5. **Trust Proven Intuition:** When expertise is deep, trust intuition significantly, but verify through rigorous analysis.

A Personal Example: When Data and Instinct Collided

Three years ago, I faced a decision that perfectly illustrates the Bold Decision Triad in action. We were considering launching our first major online program. The data looked promising, market research showed strong demand, our pilot sessions had excellent feedback scores, and the financial projections were solid. But something felt off. My instinct was telling me the timing was wrong. The online learning space was becoming saturated, and I sensed our audience was experiencing webinar fatigue. The data said "go," but my gut said "wait."

Instead of choosing between them, I used the Bold Decision Triad. First, I dug deeper into the data, specifically looking for what might contradict our assumptions. I discovered that while interest was high, actual completion rates for similar programs were dropping. The data had gaps.

Next, I explored my instinct. Where was this feeling coming from? I realized it was pattern recognition from years of watching learning trends. I had seen this enthusiasm-to-execution gap before.

Finally, I exercised decisive courage. Instead of a full launch, we created a smaller pilot with built-in learning loops. We could test our assumptions quickly and adjust based on real results.

The result? The pilot revealed exactly what my instinct had sensed, people wanted the content but in a different format. We pivoted to a cohort-based model that became our most successful program launch ever.

This decision taught me that bold leadership is not about choosing data over instinct or vice versa. It is about skillfully blending both to illuminate the clearest path forward.

The 4-Step Bold Decision Process ACTIVITY

When facing your next significant decision, use this simple process:

Step 1: Frame the Decision (5 minutes)

What exactly are we deciding?

By when do we need to decide?

Who is accountable for the outcome?

Step 2: Gather Intelligence (Time-boxed)

What does the data tell us? What is it missing?

What does our experience suggest?

What would we do if we had to decide right now?

Step 3: Integrate and Decide (15 minutes)

Where do data and instinct align? Where do they conflict?

What are the risks of action versus inaction?

What is our decision and our rationale?

Step 4: Communicate and Act (Immediate)

How will we communicate this decision with conviction?

What are our immediate next steps?

When will we review progress and adjust if needed?

This process takes the concepts from theory to practice, ensuring you integrate data, instinct, and courage every time you face a consequential decision.

Courage Can Be Built

Courage often appears more mysterious and less attainable than analytical skills or intuition, yet research consistently demonstrates that it can indeed be cultivated through deliberate, targeted practices.

One powerful practice for building courage involves reframing the way we perceive fear. Rather than interpreting physiological responses, such as an increased heart rate, heightened alertness, and nervous energy, as signs of threat, effective leaders actively reinterpret these sensations as preparation for an important challenge. Our behavioral outcomes significantly depend on how we cognitively label these physical reactions. When perceived as threatening, these sensations tend to inhibit performance and decision-making. Conversely, when reframed as energizing for an important challenge, these same physical responses actually enhance performance and decision-making capabilities. Bold leaders therefore deliberately practice recognizing and accepting these physiological cues without judgment, Figure 8.3, consciously labeling them as indicators of challenge activation rather than threat response. By shifting this interpretation, leaders can channel nervous energy productively into active preparation and confident execution, transforming fear from a barrier into an empowering resource.

"Bold leaders recognize courage not as an innate trait, but as a capability they can systematically build and refine."

Another essential practice for developing courage is normalizing failure as a natural and necessary component of growth. Fear of failure often fuels hesitation and delay, hindering decisive action. Leaders who openly share their own experiences of failure and the lessons they've learned encourage psychological safety within their teams. This openness not only reduces stigma around setbacks but also enhances trust and credibility. Leaders and organizations benefit significantly by developing explicit recovery rituals, structured practices that enable reflection on setbacks, the extraction of meaningful insights, and effective re-engagement.

"Courage isn't the absence of fear, it's reframing fear as fuel for bold, meaningful action."

Bold Data, Instinct, and Courage

The 5-Minute Bold Move Checklist

☐ What decision or action am I avoiding right now?

☐ What would I do if I wasn't worried about failing or being judged?

☐ What's one small, bold step I could take in the next 5 minutes?

☐ Who could I share this with to increase my accountability?

☐ What would future me thank me for doing right now?

Post it. Bookmark it. Whatever you do, don't underestimate what one bold minute can set in motion. Because when you take action in alignment with who you are and what you want, confidence follows.

Figure 8.3 Bold Move Checklist

Practices to Cultivate Courage

Fear Reframing:

Notice physiological responses to fear without judgment.
Consciously label these feelings as energizing preparation rather than threats.
Direct nervous energy toward positive action rather than hesitation.

Failure Normalization:

Regularly review setbacks for insights rather than blame.
Share personal failures openly to foster trust and psychological safety.
Implement structured recovery rituals that build resilience and support effective re-engagement.

Ultimately, bold leadership demands courage that is consistently nurtured through reframing fear and normalizing productive failure. Leaders who commit to these practices build stronger resilience, higher performance, and more courageous decision-making throughout their organizations.

Decision Velocity: Matching Speed to Context

When it comes to decision-making, bold leaders know that it's not just about how you decide, it's about how fast you decide based on the

> "Speed is not the enemy of wisdom, indecision is."

situation in front of you. Velocity matters. But speed without strategy can be just as damaging as over-analysis that stalls progress. The key is knowing when to pause and when to move.

To activate Decision Velocity in your leadership practice:

- **Classify Before You Commit:** Train yourself and your team to quickly label decisions by type, reversible or not, high or low stakes, urgent or strategic. This alone can eliminate unnecessary meetings and analysis loops.

- **Check the Reversibility Meter:** Before stalling out over a "perfect" plan, ask: If this goes sideways, can we pivot? If the answer is yes, bold leaders act faster, iterate, and adjust.

- **Balance Speed with Quality:** Our brain's default under uncertainty is to delay. But research on decision-making effectiveness suggests that speed, even with incomplete information, can lead to better outcomes, if paired with feedback loops and adaptive learning.

- **Use Time as a Leadership Lever:** Decision deadlines aren't about pressure, they're about clarity. When a timeframe is clear, your brain focuses. Set the expectation: What do we need to decide by when? Then stick to it.

Bold Data, Instinct, and Courage

> "Bold leaders don't obsess over perfect decisions. They commit to making the right next move, faster."

Decision speed was a better predictor of organizational success than decision quality alone. It's not that quality doesn't matter, it does, but without timely execution, even the best ideas stall out.

The Neuroscience of Timed Decisions

Our brains crave certainty. Under stress or ambiguity, the prefrontal cortex can get overwhelmed, making it harder to assess options and act. But decision-making under time constraints can improve performance, especially when the brain is trained to view time limits as a focusing mechanism rather than a threat. Setting decision deadlines reduces activation in the amygdala (associated with fear) and increases engagement of executive function, helping leaders think clearly and act boldly under pressure.

Communicating with Confidence

One of the most powerful, and often misunderstood, courage practices in bold leadership is conviction. Not blind certainty. Not bravado. But the grounded confidence to commit to a direction, communicate it with clarity, and move forward, despite uncertainty. This is not about eliminating doubt; it's about choosing movement over paralysis and doing so with intention.

Conviction is cultivated, not inherited. And it becomes especially essential in what I call the post-decision moment, that window between choice and action where second-guessing often creeps in. Bold leaders develop the skill of decisional closure, a clear internal signal that the exploration phase is over and it's time to execute. Unless truly new, meaningful information arises, the door stays shut. This decisional discipline enhances both clarity and energy across teams.

From there, it's about language. Practicing confident uncertainty, communicating with grounded clarity like, "Based on what we know now, this is the right direction," signals assurance without pretending to know the unknowable. This style of communication, grounded in both research and experience, builds trust more effectively than either overconfidence or hesitance. Conviction, when paired with psychological safety, helps align prefrontal decision circuits with motivational drive, reducing the anxiety loop triggered by uncertainty.

"Conviction isn't about being certain. It's about being committed."

Bold leaders also develop a forward-focused posture. Once the decision is made, they deliberately shift the language from "what should we do?" to "how do we make this work?" This executional shift doesn't just redirect focus, it rewires team energy. And perhaps most critically, conviction must remain consistent across contexts. Mixed messages destroy trust and slow momentum. Conviction isn't loud. It's steady.

Bold Data, Instinct, and Courage

Conviction Development

In the realm of bold leadership, conviction is not about unwavering certainty but about the deliberate choice to move forward with confidence amid uncertainty. It's the capability to commit to a direction, communicate that commitment clearly, and maintain momentum, even when all variables aren't fully known.

Developing conviction involves several key practices:

- **Decisional Closure:** Establish a clear psychological boundary between the decision-making phase and the execution phase. Once a decision is made, avoid reopening deliberations unless new, significant information emerges.

- **Confident Uncertainty:** Communicate decisions with language that reflects commitment while acknowledging the inherent uncertainties.

- **Forward Focus:** Shift the team's attention from debating the decision to implementing it effectively. This transition from deliberation to action fosters engagement and progress.

- **Consistency Across Contexts:** Maintain a consistent message about the decision across all audiences and platforms. Inconsistencies can undermine trust and dilute the perceived commitment to the chosen path.

"The decisions that define your leadership aren't the easy, obvious ones, they are the choices you make when both the stakes and the uncertainties are highest."

These practices transform conviction from a personal trait into a strategic leadership capability. As discussed earlier in the book, courage in leadership is less about innate personality and more about deliberate, practiced behaviors that can be developed and refined.

Conviction Communication Tips

A practical guide to articulating and sustaining conviction.

Mental Shift

Signal the transition from decision-making to execution with clear markers, such as stating, "The decision is now finalized, we are moving to implementation."

Language Framing

Use statements that convey confidence and acknowledge uncertainty.

"Given our current understanding, this is the optimal path forward."

"We're committed to this direction and will adapt as we go."

Action Orientation

Encourage questions that focus on execution.

"What are our immediate next steps?"

"Who will lead each component of the implementation?"

Consistency Check

Regularly review communications across channels to ensure the message about the decision remains consistent and aligned. Implementing these strategies can enhance team alignment and drive effective execution of decisions.

What You Just Learned

- How bold leaders navigate the challenging terrain where data, instinct, and courage intersect.

- You've discovered how to rise above decision paralysis by integrating analytical rigor with intuitive insight, and most importantly, by exercising the courage to act decisively even amid uncertainty.

- You've learned that bold decisions aren't about eliminating risks, they're about thoughtfully managing them, balancing what the data reveals with what your instinct senses, and turning uncertainty into meaningful action.

- You've also seen that bold leadership isn't a static trait but an intentional capability that can be built, refined, and sustained over time.

- Boldness isn't defined by perfection, but by your commitment to courageous action. The true power of your leadership emerges not from having every answer, but from your ability to confidently navigate the unknown, inspiring others to do the same.

- The fear of disappointing others often leads leaders to overfill their plates. Every yes to someone else's agenda is a quiet no to your boldest work.

Bold Truth

Conviction doesn't eliminate uncertainty, it harnesses it. Boldness is the continual practice of committing confidently, even without perfect clarity.

Your Bold Move

Your bold move for this chapter is to put these principles into immediate action:

1. Identify a significant decision you've been delaying despite having sufficient information. Use the Bold Decision Checklist to evaluate whether you've integrated data, instinct, and courage effectively.

2. Commit to making this decision within the next week. Establish a specific deadline that creates healthy urgency while allowing appropriate preparation.

3. Document both your decision process and your reasoning. This documentation creates accountability while providing valuable reference for future reflection.

4. Communicate your decision with appropriate conviction to those responsible for implementation, focusing on moving from deliberation to action.

These steps create immediate impact while establishing patterns that transform your long-term leadership effectiveness. The most influential leaders aren't necessarily those with perfect foresight but those willing to make thoughtful commitments in the face of inevitable uncertainty.

Bold Metric

After your next three significant decisions, reflect briefly:

Data Check: Did I clearly understand and critically assess the available data?

Instinct Check: Did I thoughtfully consider my intuitive reactions, leveraging past experiences?

Courage Check: Did I act decisively and communicate my choice confidently, despite uncertainty?

Quickly note a yes or no for each. Aim to achieve a consistent yes in all three areas, signifying you're on track for well-rounded, bold decision-making.

Setting the Stage for What Comes Next

You've now equipped yourself with powerful tools to communicate confidently, make decisions swiftly, and act with courageous conviction, even amid uncertainty. Yet, as any bold leader knows, the real challenge isn't simply making one bold move. It's continuing to make bold moves, consistently, over the long haul.

As we step into Chapter 9, we'll take these foundational capabilities even further. You'll learn how to integrate bold leadership into your daily habits and team culture through the practical, actionable approach of the BOLD365 system. This method ensures your boldness doesn't become just another inspirational moment that fades into routine, but rather a sustainable, replicable practice.

Because bold leadership isn't defined by singular acts of courage, it's about creating a lasting impact, day after day, year after year. It becomes part of who you are, shaping how you lead, respond, and evolve, even when pressures mount and circumstances challenge you to retreat. Every bold leader leaves behind one of two things: a list of intentions or a life of impact. This chapter is your invitation to choose impact. Let's dive into how you can sustain your bold leadership, not just for today or tomorrow, but for every day moving forward.

Part IV

Bold Alignment

Bold leadership is not just about occasional victories, it is about sustained, courageous decision-making that defines who you are. This final part will guide you in embedding boldness into your daily habits, creating consistency that endures even when challenges arise. By aligning bold actions with your core values, you'll craft an inspiring leadership legacy that resonates deeply and lasts far beyond today.

Chapter 9

Bold On Repeat

You have come incredibly far. You now deeply understand the psychology behind bold action, you're actively using the BOLD Framework, and you're confidently leveraging the power of the D90 Method to execute your boldest initiatives. You've turned setbacks into breakthroughs, mastered the art of bold conversations, and honed your ability to make clear, courageous decisions that skillfully blend data, intuition, and conviction.

> "Boldness is not a moment of inspiration it's a discipline maintained through deliberate practice."

Yet, as every seasoned leader knows, the greatest test isn't making bold moves, it is sustaining them over the long haul. How do you keep courage alive when comfort calls you back? How do you ensure boldness remains a steady rhythm rather than an occasional burst?

In this chapter, you'll explore the answer through the practical and powerful BOLD365 system (see Figure 9.1), a way to integrate courage seamlessly into your everyday leadership. Because real impact isn't built on random acts of boldness, but on consistent, intentional practices that compound over time.

> "Boldness isn't a moment, it's a habit you build, practice, and protect every single day."

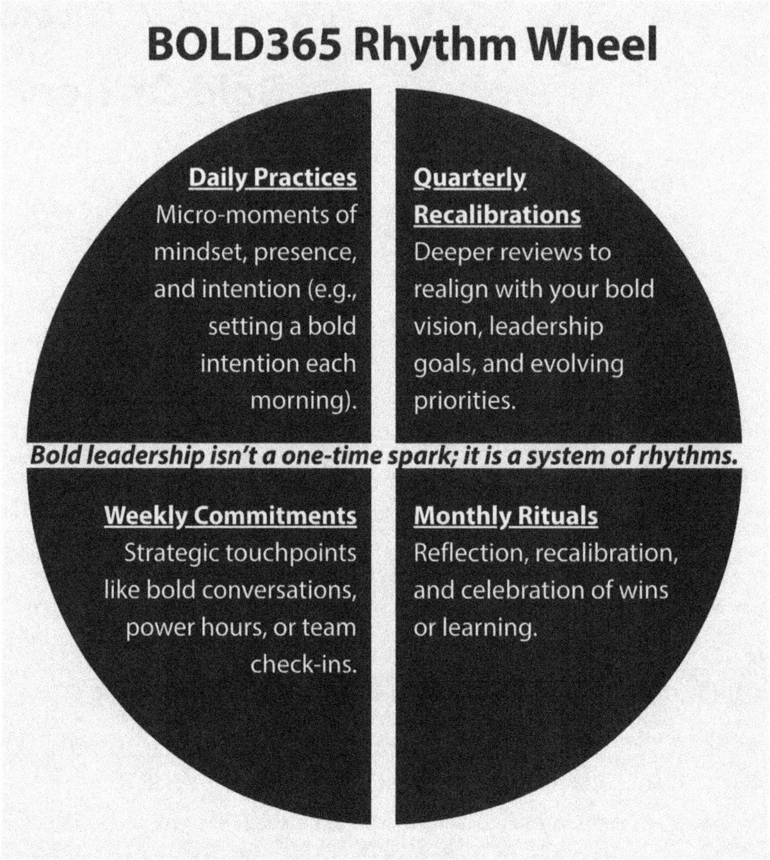

BOLD365 Rhythm Wheel

Daily Practices
Micro-moments of mindset, presence, and intention (e.g., setting a bold intention each morning).

Quarterly Recalibrations
Deeper reviews to realign with your bold vision, leadership goals, and evolving priorities.

Bold leadership isn't a one-time spark; it is a system of rhythms.

Weekly Commitments
Strategic touchpoints like bold conversations, power hours, or team check-ins.

Monthly Rituals
Reflection, recalibration, and celebration of wins or learning.

Figure 9.1 BOLD365 Rhythms of Work

The Sustainability Challenge

Bold leadership frequently follows a predictable pattern. Leaders experience an inspiring moment, commit to a courageous approach, implement it briefly, and then gradually drift back to previous patterns. This regression isn't a character flaw but a natural result of powerful forces that work against sustained boldness.

Several interrelated factors make sustaining bold leadership particularly challenging. One common obstacle is the urgency trap, where daily operational pressures consistently overshadow longer-term developmental goals. Leaders frequently find themselves caught in a cycle where urgent tasks continuously push aside strategic leadership priorities that are critically important but not immediately pressing, as prioritizing the urgent over the important.

"The greatest barrier to bold leadership isn't fear, it's the gravitational pull of daily routine."

Another significant barrier is having insight without effective integration. Leaders often experience transformative insights from training or coaching sessions, yet these insights alone rarely translate into lasting behavioral change. Knowledge by itself does not automatically alter behavior, sustainable change requires deliberate implementation systems, clear routines, and consistent reinforcement.

Feedback delays further complicate the sustainability of bold leadership practices. The rewards associated with courageous actions and innovative approaches typically unfold gradually and incrementally, whereas discomfort, uncertainty, and risks are immediate and tangible. This delayed reinforcement can create powerful disincentives for sustained bold behavior unless supported by structured feedback mechanisms and consistency.

Additionally, environmental resistance within organizations often subtly but persistently discourages ongoing bold leadership. Established organizational cultures, entrenched systems, and traditional expectations frequently exert pressure toward conformity, predictability, and risk aversion, quietly encouraging leaders to revert to safer, more familiar behaviors rather than persist in bold innovation.

Consider, for instance, a mid-level executive who recently completed an intensive leadership development program designed to encourage bold decision-making. Initially energized, she returned to her organization determined to practice courageous conversations, swift decision-making, and strategic risk-taking. She diligently applied these practices for two weeks. However, when faced with a critical project deadline, immediate pressures prompted her to fall back into familiar habits, avoiding uncomfortable conversations, delaying critical decisions in pursuit of certainty, and opting for consensus over decisive action.

Her regression did not reflect diminished personal commitment or lack of courage; rather, it resulted directly from the absence of robust organizational systems capable of sustaining bold behavior under ongoing pressure. This scenario illustrates a crucial insight: sustainable bold leadership requires not merely individual courage or episodic effort but intentional organizational systems, supportive structures, and continuous reinforcement that make bold action the norm rather than an exceptional occurrence.

The Bold Sustainability Principle

The central principle of sustainable bold leadership is deceptively simple, rhythms outperform resolutions. Research in behavior change shows that consistent, manageable practices integrated into existing routines create more lasting change than dramatic commitments that require constant willpower.

This principle contradicts how most leaders approach development. Rather than creating systems that make bold behaviors inevitable, they rely on motivation and determination, resources that inevitably fluctuate under pressure. The alternative approach focuses on embedding bold practices into existing rhythms, so they become the path of least resistance rather than requiring continuous effort.

Science of Sustainable Practice

Daily behaviors occur habitually in consistent contexts. These automatic patterns operate without requiring significant cognitive resources, making them remarkably resilient under pressure, precisely when bold leadership is needed but traditionally most vulnerable. By designing systems that embed bold practices into daily, weekly, and monthly rhythms, leaders create sustainability that motivation alone cannot achieve. The key distinction, bold leadership becomes something you do automatically rather than something you must continuously choose despite resistance.

The BOLD365 System for Sustainable Courage

Most leadership programs rely heavily on insight and inspiration but often miss the essential step of embedding those insights into everyday action. The BOLD365 system takes a different path, it ensures that boldness isn't just something you occasionally reach for, but something woven naturally into your daily rhythms. It's about building a reliable system of courage, one that's consistent, actionable, and integrated into the existing structure of your life (see Figure 9.2).

> "Boldness doesn't emerge from sporadic acts of courage but from everyday practices embedded in your routine."

Daily Bold Micro Steps

Consistent, manageable actions, which could also be called tiny habits or small steps, create momentum that gradually leads to transformative outcomes. The secret to lasting boldness, therefore, is not intensity but consistency. Picture starting each day with a quick mental rehearsal. As your coffee brews, you spend just two minutes visualizing yourself confidently navigating a challenging situation you anticipate later that day. Even brief visualization exercises activate the same neural pathways as actual practice, effectively priming your mind for courageous action.

Bold Momentum Maintenance

FUEL	FRICTION
The source of your fire.	**The resistance.**
This is what energizes and inspires your bold leadership: your purpose, your why, and the people who lift you up.	These are the internal or external blocks that slow your momentum, like overcommitment, fear, or unnecessary noise.
FOCUS	**FLOW**
The clarity.	**The consistency.**
Your top priorities and aligned intentions. When you know what matters most, your energy becomes powerful and precise.	This is the systems, habits, and boundaries you create to stay in motion, so boldness becomes part of your everyday rhythm.

Figure 9.2   Four Forces of Bold Leadership Momentum

Throughout your day, small practices reinforce boldness. Perhaps before your first meeting, you pause briefly, just sixty seconds, to identify a conversation or decision you're tempted to avoid. By deliberately scheduling it, you disrupt avoidance patterns before they take root. On your commute or between tasks, you intentionally question one assumption influencing your thinking. These micro-moments create a habit of courage and curiosity.

Each evening, a three-minute reflection on your boldness helps anchor learning. By acknowledging one moment when you acted courageously and another when you hesitated, you create gentle accountability that propels growth without pressure.

Daily Boldness in Action

Imagine Lisa, a senior project manager. Each morning, she visualizes confidently speaking up in meetings, a simple habit that significantly boosts her presence. Her daily discomfort check-in has transformed once-avoided conversations into routine, manageable tasks. Lisa's evening reflections remind her of progress made and highlight opportunities ahead. In a month, she notices a powerful shift, boldness has become her default.

Weekly Bold Rhythms

If daily practices build momentum, weekly practices deepen capability. Leadership growth isn't just about doing more. Each week, pick one meaningful conversation you've been avoiding and commit to having it. By regularly facing discomfort head-on you prevent minor challenges from becoming major issues. Similarly, identifying one significant delayed decision and actively pushing it forward prevents indecision from becoming your default mode.

Investing thirty to sixty minutes weekly in deliberate learning, whether it's reading about courageous leadership, practicing a new communication skill, or deepening your strategic thinking, accelerates your development exponentially. Deliberate practice consistently outperforms mere experience in enhancing skills.

> "Boldness requires a rhythm of intentional practice. Courage is strengthened week by week, not overnight."

Monthly Bold Rituals

To sustain boldness, you also need regular periods for deeper reflection. Monthly rituals provide the crucial space to pause and recalibrate amid daily demands. Structured monthly check-ins significantly accelerate growth compared to quarterly or yearly reviews. Imagine sitting monthly with a small circle of trusted colleagues, a bold leadership circle, where you openly discuss challenges and successes. Regular stakeholder feedback is also essential. Leaders often overestimate their boldness making external perspectives invaluable for accuracy and humility. By systematically seeking monthly feedback, you stay connected to reality, ensuring that your self-perception aligns with your actual impact.

Monthly strategy check-ins further protect boldness. Reviewing your strategic decisions ensures they're driven by courageous intentions, preventing gradual shifts toward safer, less impactful paths. Additionally, monthly reflection reconnects you with your core purpose, renewing emotional commitment to boldness. Regularly reconnecting to purpose enhances persistence through difficult times.

Quarterly Bold Recalibration

Even with daily, weekly, and monthly practices in place, occasional deeper resets are necessary. Quarterly intervals provide ideal checkpoints, long enough to assess significant progress but frequent enough to minimize drift. Quarterly bold immersions, such as half-day workshops or retreats, create the necessary space for deeper reflection, learning, and strategic realignment. These immersive experiences reinforce boldness more powerfully than shorter, routine activities can. Regular coaching sessions provide structured, personalized guidance, dramatically increasing sustainable behavioral change. Quarterly coaching sessions produce 60% greater leadership improvements compared to annual sessions alone. Additionally, assessing your broader organizational influence quarterly ensures your boldness positively shapes team culture. Exposure to varied perspectives significantly enhances adaptive and innovative capabilities.

Finally, conducting quarterly capability-gap analyses allows you to pinpoint precisely where your boldness thrives and where it falters, focusing future development strategically rather than reactively.

A Bold Quarterly Reset

Eric, an executive in financial technology, dedicates one full day each quarter to reflection. Guided by structured coaching, he evaluates his leadership impact, reassesses strategic alignment, and deliberately broadens his professional network. Eric credits these quarterly resets for transforming occasional bold acts into consistent bold leadership that shapes not only himself but his entire team's culture.

By integrating boldness into existing routines at multiple timeframes, daily microsteps, weekly practices, monthly rituals, and quarterly recalibrations, the BOLD 365 system provides a robust framework for sustained courageous leadership.

"Courage sustained isn't about moments of heroism. It's about reliable, repeatable practices embedded throughout your year."

ACTIVITY: The Bold Leadership Audit

Use this quarterly assessment to evaluate your bold leadership sustainability:

		1	2	3	4	5
Bold Conversations	I consistently initiate and navigate difficult conversations rather than avoiding them.	☐	☐	☐	☐	☐
Bold Decisions	I make decisions with appropriate speed, integrating data and instinct without unnecessary delay.	☐	☐	☐	☐	☐
Bold Vision	My strategic direction reflects genuine boldness rather than incremental safety.	☐	☐	☐	☐	☐
Bold Accountability	I hold myself and others accountable for commitments without unnecessary compromise.	☐	☐	☐	☐	☐
Bold Recovery	I transform setbacks into comebacks rather than allowing them to diminish my courage.	☐	☐	☐	☐	☐
Bold Development	I consistently invest in developing specific bold leadership capabilities.	☐	☐	☐	☐	☐

	1	2	3	4	5
Bold Culture Building I create an environment where others demonstrate greater courage because of my influence.	☐	☐	☐	☐	☐

For dimensions scoring below 4, identify specific BOLD365 practices to implement in the coming quarter.

Making Courage Your Default

While the BOLD365 system provides the framework for sustainable courage, specific strategies help implement this framework effectively across different leadership contexts.

Strategy 1 Environment Design for Default Boldness

Research in behavior design demonstrates that environmental factors influence behavior more powerfully than willpower or intention. Subtle environmental adjustments can dramatically shift behavior patterns without requiring conscious effort. Applied to bold leadership, this research suggests that creating environments that naturally elicit courage proves more effective than relying on determination alone. Practical applications include:

- **Visual Boldness Triggers:** Placing specific visual reminders of bold leadership commitments in your primary work environment. Visual cues significantly increase follow-through on intended behaviors.

- **Calendar Restructuring:** Redesigning your calendar to include specific time blocks for bold leadership practices rather than hoping to find time amid other priorities. Activities scheduled into specific time slots are 2 to 3 times more likely to be completed than those with general intentions.

- **Decision Environment Optimization:** Creating physical and digital environments that facilitate bold decision-making rather than encouraging delay. Simple adjustments like removing distractions, establishing clear decision criteria in advance, and creating dedicated decision spaces significantly influence decision quality and velocity.

- **Boldness Accountability Partners:** Establishing specific relationships focused on bold leadership development with regular check-ins and shared commitments. Commitment to another person increases behavior change success by 65% compared to solo commitments.

The key insight for bold leadership, rather than fighting against environments that subtly discourage boldness, create environments that naturally elicit courage through thoughtful design.

Strategy 2 Identity-Based Boldness

Identity-based approaches create more sustainable results than outcome-based approaches. Behaviors aligned with perceived identity persist far longer than those motivated by external rewards or pressure. Applied to bold leadership, this research suggests that developing a bold leader identity creates more sustainable courage than focusing primarily on bold actions. Practical applications include:

- **Bold Identity Affirmations:** Regularly articulating statements that reinforce your identity as a bold leader. Identity-congruent affirmations significantly influence behavior patterns when practiced consistently.

- **Bold Identity Narrative:** Developing and regularly reviewing stories that emphasize your history of courageous leadership. How we share our story and experiences shapes subsequent behavior more powerfully than the experiences themselves.

- **Bold Reference Points:** Identifying specific bold leaders who exemplify qualities you aspire to develop, using their examples as reference points for your own leadership. Specific, relevant exemplars significantly influence behavior development.

- **Public Identity Commitments:** Selectively sharing your bold leadership commitments with others, creating external expectations that reinforce internal identity development. Public commitments increase follow-through by creating identity consistency pressure. The key insight for bold leader, when bold leadership becomes part of how you see yourself rather than just something you occasionally do, sustainability increases dramatically because acting otherwise creates identity dissonance.

Strategy 3 Boldness Through Routinization

Routinization, transforming deliberate practices into automatic routines, creates remarkable sustainability. What distinguishes experts isn't just practice quantity but the development of automated routines that require minimal cognitive resources. Applied to bold leadership, this research suggests that transforming bold practices from conscious choices into automatic routines dramatically enhances sustainability. Practical applications include the following as examples:

- **Boldness Checklists:** Creating simple checklists for recurring bold leadership situations (difficult conversations, complex decisions, performance feedback) that make courage the default approach. Checklists significantly improve performance even for experts by reducing cognitive load and ensuring consistency.

- **Pre-Decision Routines:** Establishing specific routines you complete before making significant decisions, similar to an athlete's pre-performance routine. Consistent pre-performance routines enhance execution quality, particularly under pressure.

Bold On Repeat

- **Boldness Triggers:** Identifying specific triggers (times, locations, situations) that automatically prompt bold practices without requiring conscious initiation. Consistent context-behavior pairings eventually create automatic execution.

- **Recovery Protocols:** Developing standard responses to setbacks that automatically engage resilience practices rather than requiring new decisions during challenging moments. Pre-established recovery protocols significantly accelerate rebound from setbacks. The key insight for bold leadership, when bold practices become routinized, they persist even when motivation fluctuates or pressure increases because they require minimal cognitive resources to initiate and maintain.

Strategy 4 Momentum Through Measurement

Measurement significantly enhances sustainability. The simple act of monitoring progress increases goal achievement by creating awareness, accountability, and evidence of movement.

Applied to bold leadership, this research suggests that measuring bold behaviors creates momentum that sustains courage over time. Practical applications include:

- **Bold Behavior Tracking:** Maintaining simple records of specific bold leadership behaviors (conversations initiated, decisions accelerated, creative risks taken) to create visibility and momentum. The mere act of tracking behaviors increases their frequency by 30 to 50% through increased awareness.

- **Progress Visualization:** Creating visual representations of bold leadership development that make progress tangible and visible. Seeing evidence of progress significantly enhances persistence, particularly for long-term objectives.

- **Bold Leadership Metrics:** Establishing specific, measurable indicators of bold leadership impact beyond just activities.

These might include team psychological safety scores, decision velocity, innovation metrics, or feedback on courageous leadership behaviors. Outcome measurement creates stronger sustainable change than activity measurement alone.

- **Streak Maintenance:** Tracking consecutive days of bold practice completion to create psychological momentum. Maintaining unbroken streaks creates powerful motivation to continue, even when initial enthusiasm wanes. The key insight for bold leaders, measuring bold leadership systematically transforms abstract aspirations into concrete evidence of progress, creating momentum that sustains courage through challenging periods.

Sustainable Bold Leadership in Action

Recognizing the challenges and pressures that can occur across leaders in an organization, using the BOLD365 can support your leadership and reduce the impact of stress while keeping a focus on your priorities.

Daily Bold Practices

- A two-minute bold intention setting during your morning coffee.
- A midday courage check-in during your lunch break.
- A brief end-of-day reflection capturing bold moments and missed opportunities.

Weekly Bold Commitments

- Monday morning planning to identify one bold conversation to initiate that week.
- Wednesday decision acceleration for any pending decisions.
- Friday afternoon reflection on weekly bold leadership impact.

(continued)

Bold On Repeat

(continued)

Monthly Bold Development

- A monthly meeting with trusted colleagues specifically focused on bold leadership challenges.

- A structured bold leadership self-assessment at month-end.

- A dedicated learning session for specific bold leadership capabilities.

Environmental Redesign

- Create visual reminders of bold leadership commitments in your workspace.

- Restructure your calendar to include specific bold practice times.

- Establish an accountability partnership with a colleague working on similar development.

Measurement System

- A daily digital log of bold leadership moments.

- Weekly metrics on conversation timeliness and decision velocity.

- Monthly feedback from key stakeholders on your bold leadership impact.

The key insight for bold leaders, consistent, systematic bold practices integrated into existing rhythms created sustainable courage that sporadic bold moments never can achieve. By making boldness routine rather than exceptional, you can transform your leadership impact permanently rather than temporarily.

Navigating Common Obstacles

Even with the best systems, sustaining bold leadership can be challenging. There will inevitably be moments when your courage practices are disrupted, your growth plateaus, or you encounter resistance within your organization. Knowing how to anticipate and thoughtfully respond to these predictable challenges is crucial to your long-term success.

Facing the Inevitable Disruptions

Life rarely conforms neatly to our plans. Travel, emergencies, reorganizations, or personal setbacks can disrupt even the most robust routines. Contextual disruptions represent a leading cause for breaking established habits. Instead of viewing these interruptions as failures, bold leaders learn to navigate them strategically.

A key strategy is developing disruption protocols. These simplified or modified versions of your regular bold practices ensure consistency even in unpredictable circumstances. For example, when traveling or during busy weeks, you might shorten your daily reflection from ten minutes to three or identify a single, essential practice you maintain no matter how hectic things become.

Performing even small versions of your routines significantly increases the likelihood of fully restoring your habits afterward. Equally important are rituals for restarting your practices after a disruption, ensuring that temporary interruptions don't become permanent losses.

Each disruption also carries valuable insights. Noticing which practices you miss the most when disrupted reveals which elements of your boldness system have the highest impact, helping you refine your approach to emphasize what truly matters.

"Disruptions aren't setbacks, they're opportunities to clarify what matters most."

Practical Example of a Disruption Protocol

Anna, a senior marketing executive, often travels. Rather than abandoning her practices entirely when on the road, she created a streamlined version: two-minute visualization during her morning shower, a brief mental discomfort check-in before leaving her hotel, and a single-minute reflection note on her phone at night. By designing these simplified protocols, she sustains momentum even during demanding travel periods.

Overcoming the Bold Plateau

After initial excitement, it's common to reach a phase where progress feels stagnant, despite continued effort. Plateaus are natural, and temporary, stages rather than permanent limitations.

When you encounter a plateau, the key isn't to push harder on the same approaches but to strategically adapt your practices. Adjusting your methods to include fresh challenges can reignite growth. This process is called deliberate practice, which involves intentionally working at the edge of your current capabilities, continuously stretching yourself to progress further.

"Plateaus aren't endings, they're invitations to grow differently."

External perspectives can also help you see blind spots and growth opportunities that internal reflection alone might miss. Seeking feedback from mentors, coaches, or colleagues specifically about areas of stalled development can illuminate new paths forward. Additionally, focusing temporarily on complementary capabilities, such as improving emotional intelligence or analytical thinking, often unlocks progress in areas where boldness alone has plateaued.

Plateau Breakthrough Example

Carlos, a division director, felt stuck in his ability to make courageous decisions. After receiving external coaching feedback, he realized his plateau was tied to his discomfort with analytical ambiguity rather than a lack of courage. By temporarily shifting his focus to enhancing and learning more about how to improve his analytical skills, he broke through his plateau, reinvigorating his boldness from a new angle.

Navigating Environmental Resistance

Organizations naturally gravitate toward stability, predictability, and caution, often unintentionally discouraging bold behaviors.

Mapping resistance clearly, distinguishing between real barriers and perceived risks, can help you identify precisely where to strategically apply your boldness. Leaders often overestimate organizational resistance, mistaking discomfort, or perceived risk for genuine consequences. Clarifying this difference can empower you to act more boldly and confidently.

> "Environmental resistance isn't a stop sign, it's a roadmap guiding you toward strategic courage."

Aligning bold leadership practices explicitly with organizational priorities and core values can reduce resistance substantially. When colleagues see boldness clearly connected to achieving shared goals rather than contradicting them, they become less resistant and more collaborative. Demonstrating initial successes in areas of greater organizational openness builds momentum, gradually influencing more resistant contexts.

"Sustainable boldness isn't about maintaining constant intensity, it's about building systems that make courage your natural default rather than a special exception."

Building a coalition of supportive peers also strengthens your resilience. Developing strong peer support networks significantly improves your ability to maintain boldness, particularly in challenging environments. These relationships create a microculture that encourages courage even when the broader organizational environment does not.

Navigating Resistance in Action

Sarah, an HR executive, encountered significant resistance when advocating for more transparent and courageous performance conversations. Instead of forcing change everywhere at once, she began with a receptive department, demonstrating clear improvements. Building on this initial success, she created a coalition of influential colleagues who gradually expanded bold practices throughout the organization.

What You Just Learned

- Courage is sustainable when embedded in daily rhythms.
- Environment design beats willpower.
- Identity, not outcomes, sustains boldness.
- Measurement fuels momentum.

Bold Truth

Sustainable boldness is not fueled by motivation alone, it thrives on intentional systems, courageous identity, and visible growth.

Your Bold Move

Your bold move for this chapter is to implement the BOLD365 system in your leadership practice:

1. Three micro-habits tied to existing routines.
2. Two weekly practices scheduled for next month.
3. One monthly ritual calendared.
4. One environmental redesign (calendar, workspace, accountability partner).

These steps create the foundation for sustainable bold leadership, not through dramatic transformation but through systematic integration of courage into your regular leadership rhythm.

Bold Metric

Reflecting on your ability to maintain your focus on being a bold leader, quickly rate yourself (1–5) on each of the following dimensions:

- **Rhythms:** I've embedded bold practices into daily, weekly, monthly, and quarterly routines.
- **Environment:** I've intentionally structured my environment to support bold decisions.
- **Identity:** I consistently see and describe myself as a bold leader.
- **Measurement:** I regularly track and visibly celebrate my progress toward bold leadership goals.

Aim for an overall score of 4 or higher, signaling that you've built reliable systems to sustain your bold leadership over time.

Setting the Stage for What Comes Next

You have made incredible strides in embedding bold leadership into your daily life, creating systems and structures that sustain courage consistently. But as powerful as these techniques and habits are, they are not the full story. There is one essential truth that separates the leaders who act boldly from those who live boldly, no matter what comes their way.

In our final chapter, we will uncover that truth, the core commitment that bold leaders make deep within themselves. This is not about tips, tricks, or methods. It is about a fundamental decision: choosing courage as your default setting, not just when it's easy, but especially when it is hard.

You now have the systems to lead with sustainable courage. But bold leadership does not end with systems. In the final chapter, we explore the essential inner decision that separates those who act boldly from those who *live* boldly.

Because the secret of bold leadership is not just what you do, it is who you choose to be.

Chapter 10

The Bold Leader's Secret

You have come a long way. You have discovered how to turn fear into forward motion using the BOLD Framework, structured your boldest moves with the D90 Method, cultivated resilience through comebacks, and built consistency with the BOLD365 system.

> "The most profound secret of bold leadership is not a tactic or strategy, it is a foundational choice that precedes every other."

But here is what the boldest leaders eventually realize: bold leadership is not just a method. It is an identity. It is not something you turn on when the timing feels right, it is something you anchor into and return to, no matter the challenge.

This chapter is not about adding one more technique. It is about making one deep, internal decision: to stop waiting for permission to be bold and start living from the inside out, aligned with the truth of who you are.

These tools and frameworks are powerful, but the leaders who truly live boldly recognize something even deeper. It's not just about the practices, processes, or habits.

> "Boldness is not something you use, it is who you choose to be."

It is about a fundamental decision they have made deep within themselves: the choice to be bold, no matter the circumstances.

In this final chapter, we will uncover that decisive, inner commitment. You will discover how consistently bold leaders make courage an essential part of who they are, not something they do occasionally, but something they embody every single day. Make a decision now, right here, to become the kind of leader who chooses courage even when no one else understands it yet.

Let your leadership be a declaration of what matters.

Let the legacy you build be the one that gave others permission to live and lead differently.

The Leadership Choice

"Boldness is not something you try. It is someone you become."

Most people treat boldness like a behavior. Something you summon in specific moments, when the circumstances align or the consequences are manageable.

But bold leaders know something different.

They know boldness is not a situational skill. It is a decision you make in advance, before the stakes are high, before the path is clear, before you are fully ready. That decision becomes your operating system, the compass you trust even in uncertainty.

This is the shift from reacting to what others expect of you to creating your leadership from your own internal clarity and commitments. This is the secret of bold leadership. Not reacting.

"The boldest leaders aren't those who never feel fear, they are those who have made a decision to take action that transcends their fear."

This fundamental shift doesn't eliminate all the challenges we have discussed throughout previous chapters. Bold leaders still encounter fear, resistance, setbacks, and uncertainty. But the prior commitment to bold leadership transforms how these challenges are experienced, from potential barriers to courage into problems to be solved while maintaining courage.

Choosing Boldness First

Think about the difference between these two ways of leading:

A Circumstantial Orientation says:

"I will be bold when the time feels right, when I have more clarity, when the risks are low, when others will agree, or when my position seems safe."

A Foundational Orientation says:

"I've already decided to lead boldly, period. I'll figure out how courage can show up appropriately, no matter what the situation looks like, because boldness is central to who I am as a leader."

The difference might seem subtle, but it's transformative. Leaders who wait for ideal conditions will always find reasons to delay courageous action. But leaders who've chosen boldness as their baseline will consistently discover ways to express courage, even when challenges feel overwhelming.

We often think of boldness as a work concept, something we show in meetings or decisions. But the most powerful bold leaders have made boldness a way of being.

They are bold when the room is quiet.

"Courage is not reserved for peak moments. It is woven into your presence, your posture, and your principles."

They are bold when the outcome is uncertain.

They are bold even when no one sees it but them.

Leaders driven by internal commitment, rather than external circumstances, consistently show greater resilience, ethical clarity, and sustained effectiveness, regardless of their environment.

Here's the simple but powerful secret of bold leadership: The decision to lead boldly doesn't come after evaluating your circumstances, it precedes it.

The Anatomy of Your Choice

At its core, bold leadership is about making a foundational choice, a choice that shapes everything you do. And this choice operates on several meaningful levels. Let's first explore the deepest one, the decision to prioritize purpose over comfort.

You do not wait until you feel fully confident. You know you are ready when you realize that staying in misalignment is costing more than the risk of stepping forward.

This is your invitation to make boldness your default, not your exception. To stop treating courage as something you do, and start practicing it as your leadership baseline.

Bold leaders don't stumble upon courage by accident, they choose it deliberately, because they've decided purpose matters more than staying comfortable. When people focus on meaning and purpose, they build resilience capable of overcoming even the most challenging circumstances.

As a bold leader, this philosophical commitment shows up clearly in three important ways. First, you gain clarity of purpose, knowing exactly the impact you're aiming to create, independent of your current role, title, or situation. Second, you identify the core values that guide your actions, even and especially when following them brings temporary discomfort or resistance. And third, you consistently choose long-term impact over short-term comfort, accepting that meaningful leadership naturally involves tension and difficulty.

Leaders with a growth mindset approach challenges as opportunities, not threats. Instead of viewing discomfort as something to fear or

> "Bold leaders choose purpose over comfort, transforming discomfort into a compass pointing toward impact."

avoid, bold leaders transform discomfort into a valuable ally, a sign they're doing something that truly matters. A bold truth to share with you, choosing purpose doesn't remove discomfort. Instead, it fundamentally shifts your relationship with it, turning discomfort from an obstacle into evidence that you're courageously aligned with what matters most.

Agency over Circumstance

At the psychological level, bold leaders make a clear and conscious choice: they choose agency over circumstance. Instead of feeling limited by their environment or situation, they believe deeply that their actions and decisions matter, what psychologists describe as an internal locus of control. This powerful belief isn't simply optimism; it's a strategic mindset that fuels sustained boldness and effectiveness.

Leaders who adopt this internal locus of control consistently outperform those who don't, navigating organizational challenges with far greater resilience. How does this show up practically? Bold leaders focus intentionally on possibility rather than limitation. While acknowledging obstacles, they prioritize opportunities and solutions. They take full ownership of their responses, never blaming their approach solely on external pressures. And they consistently choose proactive initiative, taking meaningful action without waiting for ideal conditions or permission from circumstances.

Why does this psychological choice matter so much? People instinctively fear losses more intensely than they value equivalent gains, a phenomenon called loss aversion. This deeply rooted bias leads many leaders to default toward cautious decisions aimed at preserving the status quo rather than boldly seeking potential improvements.

Bold leaders, however, actively challenge this instinctive caution. They reorient their perspective, focusing not just on what might go wrong, but on what could go right. They strategically shift their psychological stance from protecting what they have to proactively pursuing what's possible.

The bold truth here is clear, courageous leadership isn't about ignoring risks. It's about refusing to let risk aversion dominate your decisions. By consciously choosing agency over circumstance, bold leaders maintain their ability to act decisively and courageously, even when facing uncertainty.

> "Boldness begins the moment you realize your actions shape your circumstances, not the other way around."

Practical Level

At the practical level, the boldest leaders make one fundamental decision: they prioritize courageous expression over flawless execution. Perfectionism is often the greatest enemy of bold leadership, keeping us stuck waiting for guarantees that never come. Boldness thrives when we're willing to act, even when our information isn't perfect and outcomes aren't guaranteed.

It's a subtle but powerful shift from thinking in terms of success or failure toward seeing every bold action as a meaningful step forward. It's about embracing a process of continual growth and refinement, knowing each courageous decision teaches something essential for future moves.

Bold leaders know that waiting for complete certainty means missing valuable opportunities. So, they develop a natural bias toward action, choosing momentum over hesitation when faced with imperfect information. They understand that courage

> "Bold leadership isn't about getting it perfect, it's about making progress and learning with every step."

inevitably involves setbacks, seeing these challenges as part of the journey, rather than evidence of failure. Bold leaders create these spaces intentionally, knowing that authentic courage often involves vulnerability and occasional missteps.

The truth here is clear for bold leaders, prioritizing expression over perfection isn't lowering your standards, it's redefining them. Bold leaders still pursue excellence fiercely. The difference is, they pursue excellence as a continuous, courageous process rather than as a prerequisite for action.

Prioritizing Impact over Recognition

At the relational level, bold leadership comes down to a simple but powerful decision: choosing lasting impact over short-term recognition or personal status. Exceptional lead-

> "Bold leaders don't chase applause, they build lasting impact."

ers understand this deeply. Truly transformative leaders pair quiet humility with relentless determination, always prioritizing meaningful outcomes for their organizations and communities rather than their own personal accolades. For bold leaders, success isn't measured by the spotlight or applause, it's measured by the genuine difference made in the lives of others. This focus on impact allows you to stay courageous even when recognition is delayed or absent, because your commitment isn't anchored in external approval but in meaningful

The Bold Leader's Secret

contribution. It gives you resilience, clarity, and authenticity when facing inevitable criticism or misunderstanding. Leaders who are motivated primarily by making a difference in the lives of others demonstrate greater endurance, adaptability, and courage, especially in the face of setbacks, compared to leaders driven primarily by personal ambition or external rewards. Choosing impact and service over status doesn't erase our human need for acknowledgment. But it clarifies your priorities. It creates a steadiness, ensuring that when the difficult choices arise, your decision is already clear, impact comes first.

Leading with Authentic Integration

At the deepest level, bold leadership isn't about what you do, it's about who you are. It's a commitment to authenticity, integrating courage into every part of your identity rather than compartmentalizing it into specific roles or moments. Truly effective leaders aren't those who create neatly separated professional and personal personas, but those who lead consistently from their genuine, integrated selves.

This means your core values aren't negotiable or situational; they're consistent across every context. It means you don't hide behind carefully managed facades; you lead transparently, bringing your full self to every interaction, even when that feels vulnerable. It also means you're genuinely open to growth, adapting and evolving without compromising who you fundamentally are.

Leaders who express authenticity and integration consistently demonstrate stronger resilience, ethical clarity, and trustworthiness, qualities that underpin truly bold leadership.

"Bold leadership isn't an act, it's your authentic self showing up courageously."

Choosing authenticity doesn't eliminate adaptability. It simply ensures that your adaptations are expressions of a consistent identity rather than reactions to external pressures. It's about letting your courage flow naturally from who you are, not something you muster up when the situation demands it.

Committing to Bold Leadership

Ultimately, bold leadership boils down to a single fundamental decision, a decision that clarifies and simplifies every choice you face afterward. Once you commit to leading boldly, every subsequent decision aligns more naturally, even when it isn't easy.

First, you anchor your boldness in a clear purpose: understanding exactly why you lead and the specific impact you're committed to achieving. Clarity of purpose sets transformative leaders apart from those who merely manage tasks or people. This clarity requires reflection on some powerful questions: What lasting difference am I committed to making? Which core values will I never compromise? What will make my leadership truly meaningful, regardless of recognition?

Answering these questions anchors your boldness deeply. It ensures your leadership purpose transcends any particular job, title, or circumstance, guiding you consistently through inevitable challenges.

Making a Bold Leadership Promise

Next, you articulate your bold leadership promise, clearly stating how you'll approach decisions, challenges, and opportunities, regardless of external pressure. Leaders who explicitly articulate their commitments significantly increase their follow-through and effectiveness.

Your bold leadership promise becomes a personal constitution. It clarifies how you'll act under pressure, what others can reliably expect from you, and which behaviors will always reflect your core values. This promise guides your decisions consistently, even when situations are complex or uncomfortable.

Creating Accountability

The power of your bold commitment multiplies when shared. Making commitments visible to others dramatically increases your follow-through. Share your bold leadership promise selectively with trusted colleagues who will encourage and challenge you. Document it in writing so you can revisit and reinforce your promise when your resolve naturally wavers. Regularly reviewing your commitment with others creates ongoing accountability, maintaining your boldness over time.

Designing Systems for Sustainability

"The secret of bold leadership isn't mysterious, it's the simple decision to choose courage every single day."

Finally, translate your bold commitment into lasting action by designing practical systems that reinforce your courage. Environments shape behaviors far more effectively than willpower alone. Create clear decision frameworks that explicitly incorporate your bold values. Establish regular rituals, weekly reflections, monthly check-ins, that sustain your courage and momentum. Adjust your environment, using visual reminders or practical cues, to keep boldness at the forefront of your everyday actions.

These intentional structures turn your courageous intentions into concrete actions, ensuring your bold leadership endures, even through distractions, stress, or shifting priorities.

The Bold Leader's Declaration

Use this template to craft your own bold leadership commitment:

My Leadership Purpose

The difference I'm committed to making through my leadership is:

My Non-Negotiable Values

The values that will guide my leadership regardless of circumstances are:

My Bold Promise

Others can expect that I will:

Even when it's difficult, I will:

I will never compromise on:

My Accountability System

The people who will hold me accountable to this commitment are:

I will review this commitment [Daily/Weekly/Monthly] by:

My Implementation Plan

The specific systems I'll create to sustain this commitment are:

When I face resistance, I will:

Sign and date this declaration, share it with your accountability partners, and review it regularly to maintain your bold leadership commitment.

When the Choice Wavers

Even when you've made the fundamental decision to lead boldly, there will inevitably be moments that challenge your commitment. Let's explore three common obstacles, moments when your status feels threatened, times of isolation, and periods of energy depletion, and discover practical ways to navigate each without compromising your courage.

Navigating Status Threat Moments

> "Your boldness isn't threatened by others' opinions, it's strengthened by your own clarity."

It's normal to feel defensive when your ideas or authority are challenged publicly, when you receive critical feedback, or when you're competing for recognition. Status threats trigger intense neurological responses, responses powerful enough to override rational thinking and potentially pull you away from bold leadership. But bold leaders intentionally reframe these moments. Instead of viewing challenges as threats, they choose to see them as opportunities to demonstrate secure, values-driven leadership. They broaden their perspective, intentionally considering alternative viewpoints rather than fixating on perceived attacks. When their status feels vulnerable, bold leaders deliberately reconnect with their deeper purpose, anchoring themselves to values far bigger than temporary discomfort or external validation.

Your Boldness Check-In

Quick Activity:

Pause right now and ask yourself:

- Am I currently leading boldly from conscious choice, intentional practice, or integrated identity?

- What's one simple step I can take today to move closer to fully integrated boldness?

Even a brief pause before responding, just a few intentional seconds, can dramatically change outcomes. This small delay helps reactive brain circuits quiet down, allowing the prefrontal cortex, responsible for perspective-taking and strategic decision-making, to regain control.

Handling Moments of Isolation

Choosing boldness sometimes places you at odds with the status quo. There will be moments when your courage puts you out of step with conventional thinking, leaving you feeling temporarily isolated, misunderstood and even sometimes, lonely. It will not last, but you do need to develop relationships with those that understand and support you. Bold leaders prepare themselves by proactively building supportive relationships. Connecting regularly with peers who share your bold orientation provides critical reinforcement during moments of doubt or isolation. Boldness requires conviction, a strength nurtured through consistent practice. Regularly revisiting why you chose bold leadership reinforces internal commitment, ensuring it remains strong enough to withstand external pressures. Additionally, cultivating identity and belonging beyond your immediate team or organization can significantly ease the discomfort of isolation. Leaders who maintain their courage even in isolation enhance overall team creativity and decision-making quality, transforming short-term discomfort into lasting impact.

> "Sometimes bold leadership means standing alone, temporarily, so others can see a better way forward."

Overcoming Energy Depletion

Leading boldly isn't easy, it requires significant emotional, mental, and physical resources. During busy or stressful periods, these resources naturally deplete, making courageous decisions increasingly difficult. Decision fatigue and energy depletion weaken our resolve, causing even committed leaders to default to easier, less courageous choices.

Bold leaders, therefore, manage their energy intentionally. They don't rely on willpower alone. Instead, they build consistent practices for restoring their energy, ensuring that their commitment remains strong even when their resources dip. Simple, predictable routines like short daily breaks, dedicated recovery rituals, or specific habits that recharge mental clarity are essential.

Identity in Action

Reflection Moment:

- Identify one leader you deeply admire whose boldness seems integrated into their identity.
- What specifically do they do that signals boldness as part of who they are, rather than what they do?

"Boldness is fueled by energy, not just intention, protect your resources so courage stays consistent."

Identifying the essential minimum viable boldness for energy-depleted periods is also key. You don't need to be at your peak every day, but you do need clarity about the core courageous actions you'll sustain even during tough moments. Designing your environment to minimize the energy required for bold decisions, using visual reminders or simplifying your routines, helps maintain your courage, even when you're running low. Systematic energy management is far more effective than sheer determination or willpower. Leaders who deliberately manage their energy consistently demonstrate greater resilience, effectiveness, and courage across diverse challenges.

Sustaining bold leadership doesn't mean avoiding challenges, it means intentionally preparing for them. By recognizing predictable tests, status threats, isolation, and energy depletion, and proactively designing strategies to navigate them, you'll find these challenges don't weaken your commitment, they reinforce it.

Evolution of Bold Leadership

The most powerful secret of bold leadership reveals itself fully when courage shifts from something you consciously do to something you naturally are. It's the moment when boldness stops being an occasional choice and becomes an integral part of your identity, a seamless expression of who you've become. Leaders form their identities as the transformation unfolds in stages, each building upon the previous one, guiding you toward genuine, integrated boldness.

Experimental Boldness: Courage as Discovery

Initially, boldness feels like an experiment, occasional acts of courage in moments when the stakes feel manageable or motivation is high. Perhaps you speak up when you'd usually stay silent, or you

> "Boldness starts with small, brave experiments that redefine your sense of what's possible."

make a tough decision despite some uncertainty. These early experiments aren't small or trivial, each step is a crucial step. They show you, often for the first time, that boldness isn't reserved for others, it's within your reach.

In this exploratory stage, you discover that you're capable of being courageous, challenging any old beliefs that boldness simply isn't part of your makeup. You start experiencing firsthand the positive impacts of bold choices, realizing that courage creates value far beyond theory. Gradually, you learn to recognize when boldness is appropriate in your environment and when courage can genuinely create meaningful impact.

Yet, at this stage, boldness remains something you consciously decide to do. It can feel fragile, easily disrupted by busy schedules, distractions, or low energy.

Intentional Boldness

As you continue intentionally choosing boldness, your courage becomes less occasional and more habitual. Instead of random bursts, you begin recognizing opportunities for courageous action consistently, guided by clear commitments and supported by practical routines.

In this stage, you build specific frameworks for courageous decision-making. You become skilled at spotting opportunities to lead boldly and acting on them reliably. The initial uncertainty around courage decreases because you've developed clarity about when and how to express boldness effectively. When setbacks inevitably occur, you're quicker to recover, more resilient to discouragement, and better able to sustain your bold trajectory.

> "Intentional boldness transforms courageous moments into courageous habits."

Courage Calibration

Quick Check:

- In your current role, which bold practice (Experimental, Intentional, Integrated) feels most familiar to you? Why?
- What might shift if you advanced to the next stage?

Though you still need conscious attention to maintain bold practices, these habits now feel less like isolated acts and more like part of your leadership rhythm, supported by systems that reinforce your courage day-to-day.

Courage as Identity

Eventually, your boldness no longer relies heavily on conscious choice or special circumstances. It simply becomes how you lead, naturally, authentically, and without extra effort. At this deepest level, courage moves beyond something you do and becomes who you fundamentally are.

Behaviors that initially require conscious effort or external reinforcement can, through consistent, values-driven practice, become a natural and integrated part of your identity.

Values Alignment Activity

- List your top three core values as a leader.
- For each, write down one concrete way you'll demonstrate that value courageously in the next week.

At this stage, bold leadership flows spontaneously and effortlessly in appropriate moments. Courage becomes your default setting, appearing naturally without conscious deliberation. Your internal self-talk and external communication reflect boldness as a core part

"The ultimate evolution of bold leadership is when courage stops being what you do, and simply becomes who you are."

The Bold Leader's Secret

of your identity, not an aspiration or occasional achievement. Every courageous act aligns seamlessly with your deepest values, creating a sense of integrity that's both powerful and authentic.

While supportive routines and systems remain valuable, boldness at this stage doesn't rely solely upon them. You no longer have to push yourself toward courage because courage is now a natural extension of your true self.

The Legacy of Bold Leadership

Ultimately, the greatest measure of your bold leadership isn't in awards, titles, or temporary achievements. It's found in the lasting imprint you leave behind, in the legacy that remains long after your official role or immediate influence fades. Bold leaders know this deeply. Their true success shows itself in the enduring impact on people, culture, and possibilities they leave in their wake.

Growing Capabilities in Others

> "Bold leadership isn't about growing followers. It's about growing leaders who multiply courage."

The hallmark of genuinely bold leaders is how effectively they multiply capability in the people around them. Leaders who consistently demonstrate courage significantly boost the independent thinking, resilience, and initiative within their teams. Bold leaders also empower others through thoughtfully designed stretch opportunities, projects that encourage growth and push beyond current abilities, balanced with supportive mentorship. Importantly, bold leaders help people reframe failure not as personal inadequacy but as an essential step toward improvement. These practices create ripple effects long after the leader's direct involvement, embedding courage as a sustainable trait within the next generation of leaders.

Transforming Organizational Culture

The legacy of bold leadership also manifests in the transformation of organizational culture itself. Leaders who consistently display courage gradually shift entire organizational belief systems, values, and habits, not just individual behaviors. How does this cultural shift happen? Bold leaders become living models of courageous action, visibly demonstrating exactly what boldness looks like in practice. They tell compelling stories that illustrate how courage creates meaningful impact, shaping a collective narrative that embeds boldness into organizational identity. Beyond modeling and storytelling, they reshape organizational structures, processes, and incentives to reward boldness rather than inhibit it.

Over time, these intentional actions create a culture that naturally encourages courage. This transformed culture becomes your legacy, reaching far beyond those you personally mentor or lead, influencing countless individuals who follow, long after your direct involvement ends.

> "Bold leaders don't just lead organizations; they reshape cultures where courage becomes contagious."

Expanding the Boundaries of Possibility

Perhaps the most profound legacy of bold leadership is expanding what others believe is possible. Your bold actions become reference points, vivid examples of what can be accomplished, breaking down previously accepted limitations and inspiring new horizons of possibility.

By taking courageous action, you don't just demonstrate what's achievable; you actively carve new paths through territories others assumed were impassable. Each time you defy conventional limits, you clear a trail for others to follow more confidently. Bold leaders don't just improve outcomes, they elevate collective visions, moving aspirations from incremental steps toward genuinely transformative achievements.

The Bold Leader's Secret

> "Bold leaders redefine possibility, lighting a path for those they'll never meet."

The power of this legacy isn't just in the immediate victories you achieve, but in the expanded opportunities and possibilities you leave behind. Your courage sparks belief in others, including people you might never personally encounter, inspiring them to imagine greater possibilities for themselves and their teams.

Ultimately, the legacy of your bold leadership is measured in how courage continues long after your direct influence ends. It's about multiplying capability, transforming cultures, and expanding possibilities, not simply achieving results during your tenure. Your true legacy becomes evident as boldness moves beyond what you do

> "The bold leader's secret creates a legacy that extends far beyond your position, transforming capabilities, cultures, and possibilities in ways that continue long after your direct influence ends."

and becomes embedded in the people, cultures, and beliefs that carry your courage forward.

Because in the end, bold leadership isn't just about your personal impact. It's about empowering others to step into their own courage, ensuring that your bold choice echoes far beyond your own moment in leadership.

What You Just Learned

- Leadership always comes down to choice, not circumstance. Bold leaders recognize that the decision to lead courageously isn't tied to titles, roles, or perfect conditions, it's a choice you can always make, no matter where you stand.

- Bold leadership begins as something you deliberately choose, but over time it becomes who you genuinely are.

- The greatest obstacles to boldness are rarely external, they're internal. Yes, organizational hurdles and cultural pressures exist. But the most significant barriers to courageous leadership are almost always the fears, assumptions, and limiting beliefs we carry inside ourselves.

- Your lasting legacy isn't built through occasional heroic gestures, it emerges from consistent, everyday courage. The deepest impact comes from reliably showing up boldly, day after day, choice after choice, steadily reshaping the lives, cultures, and opportunities around you.

Bold Truth

The most sustainable form of courage is identity-based. When boldness becomes who you are, not just what you do, everything changes.

Your Bold Move

Your bold move for this chapter, and for your entire bold leadership journey, is to make the fundamental choice to choose you, choose your path, choose to lead boldly.

1. Complete the Bold Leader's Declaration, creating explicit clarity about your leadership purpose, values, promise, and implementation approach.

2. Share your declaration with 3 to 5 trusted colleagues who will both support and challenge you in maintaining this commitment.

3. Create a specific daily practice that reinforces your bold leadership commitment, integrating it into an existing routine to ensure sustainability.

4. Schedule quarterly reviews for the next year where you'll evaluate your leadership choices against your bold commitment, creating ongoing awareness rather than sporadic attention.

Bold Metric

Your Legacy Statement

Take a few moments to craft your personal Bold Leadership Legacy Statement.

- What lasting impact do you want your leadership to have beyond your immediate role?
- How do you want people to describe your leadership long after you've moved on?
- What courageous choices will you consistently commit to in order to make this legacy real?

Once you write it down, keep it somewhere visible. Regularly check your choices against this statement, ensuring your bold leadership isn't just something you aspire to, but something you're actively building every day.

Taking Your Next Bold Step

As we come to the end of this chapter, I want you to remember something essential: The bold leader's secret isn't just an idea to grasp or a theory to understand. It's a powerful truth meant to be lived. Every insight you've discovered, every courageous practice you've embraced, every system you've implemented is preparing you for what's next, stepping boldly into the authentic leader you were always meant to be.

The courage you seek isn't outside of you, it's already there, ready and waiting. It simply requires your intentional decision, your steady commitment, and your willingness to express it in all that you do. From this point forward, your leadership isn't defined by occasional acts of bravery, but by a consistent expression of who you truly are, a bold leader committed to making a lasting difference.

So, make that decision. Embrace that commitment. Step confidently into your bold leadership identity. Because the world needs bold leaders like you, leaders who won't wait for perfect conditions but will courageously shape them. Leaders who understand that the greatest impact comes not from heroic gestures alone, but from daily acts of intentional boldness.

You are ready. The time is now.

> "Bold leadership isn't something you find, it's something you choose. Choose courage and let your boldness change the world."

Conclusion

Bold leadership is far more than a role you step into or a title you earn, it's the choice you consciously make, over and over, day after day. It's waking up each morning and deciding to lead with intention, clarity, and unwavering courage, even when the path ahead feels uncertain or intimidating.

As we conclude our journey together, I want to remind you of something deeply important; your boldness doesn't come from a place of perfect confidence or the absence of fear. Boldness lives precisely in those moments when you feel the tug of hesitation, uncertainty, or discomfort, yet you choose to step forward anyway. It's in your everyday decisions, your interactions, and how you respond to life's inevitable setbacks.

Throughout this book, we've navigated the complexities of fear and reframed it from something to avoid into an essential guide pointing toward what truly matters. We've explored how comfort, while enticing, often quietly holds you back from reaching your fullest potential. We've learned how to build momentum intentionally rather than waiting for it to magically appear. And perhaps most importantly, we've discovered the strength found within setbacks, transforming them into powerful catalysts for growth and resilience.

You've embraced the art of courageous conversations, finding your voice even when it feels vulnerable. You've practiced decisive action, moving forward despite imperfect information or uncertain outcomes. You've leveraged the structured power of alignment, ensuring your bold visions translate into meaningful and measurable results.

These insights and practices aren't merely lessons learned; they're now woven into the fabric of who you are as a leader. Each experience, reflection, and decision you've encountered throughout this journey has prepared you to step fully and confidently into your own authentic style of bold leadership.

Your true legacy, the lasting mark of your bold leadership, will not be defined by singular moments, but by the many small yet courageous choices you consistently make. It's in your quiet resolve to remain aligned with your core values, your willingness to speak truth even when your voice shakes, and your commitment to rise again every time you stumble.

As we reach this important milestone, pause and deeply reflect and ask yourself, "What bold legacy do I truly wish to create? How will my leadership impact those around me, long after my immediate influence has passed?"

Take a moment to define this vision clearly. Write it down in your own words, words that resonate deeply with your heart. Share it with someone who genuinely matters to you, someone who can hold you accountable with both honesty and kindness.

Commit wholeheartedly, not simply as a one-time act but as a daily practice and a lifelong dedication. Let this commitment guide you, ground you, and inspire you, even on your toughest days. Your bold legacy is built not by grand gestures alone, but by consistently showing up as your authentic, courageous self.

Remember, your boldness is not something to achieve and put aside. It's a continuous choice, a promise to yourself and those you lead that courage will always guide your way. You are ready for what comes next. This is not the end, it is truly just the beginning.

Step boldly forward, one courageous choice at a time.

I am honored to have been part of your journey.

Afterword

"Wait, you work with your mom?" I get asked this question a lot, usually accompanied by raised eyebrows and curious smiles. And every time, I answer: "Yes, and it's the boldest decision I ever made."

Growing up, I never fully grasped the depth of what bold leadership meant. I just knew my mom was different. She made decisions others hesitated on, tackled tough conversations head-on, and moved forward even when she didn't have all the answers. Her boldness wasn't loud or showy; it was steady, consistent, and full of courage. Watching her taught me firsthand that leadership isn't about playing it safe. It's about living aligned with what you value, need, and want.

Co-founding Bold Industries Group together has been one of the most challenging and rewarding experiences of my life. We have grown so much together and as individuals. We complement each other even in how we approach a new task or idea. I bring the detail-oriented practicality, while Leigh brings the creative vision. But we share the same core belief: leadership isn't about having perfect answers. It's about asking the right questions, making the tough calls, and owning every decision with integrity and grace.

In the years since we started the company, I have made bold moves that I never would have imagined: launching initiatives with uncertain outcomes, having difficult conversations with team members twice my age, traveling across the country to share our bold message and build community, taking responsibility for results that seemed beyond my experience level. Along the way, I've learned how hope coupled with action can turn into real change and how boldness is truly a continuum, from the earliest whispers of something new to taking a large leap into the unknown.

We are living in a world of constant change and uncertainty, but the fundamentals of bold leadership remain the same: clarity about what matters, courage to act on it, and commitment to keep growing even when it is uncomfortable.

We need leaders who can navigate uncertainty without losing their center. Who can build trust and make decisions quickly without sacrificing their humanity, creating a culture where innovation thrives and people are valued. That requires boldness. Not the kind that breaks things for the sake of disruption, but the kind that builds bridges toward a better future.

My mom never explicitly taught me how to be bold; instead, she showed me through example. Working alongside her, I've learned to trust my voice, stand confidently in my decisions, and build something meaningful. She taught me that being bold isn't about fearlessness, but that it's about feeling the fear and moving forward anyway, because you trust yourself, your vision, and your values.

When I think about the legacy we are creating together at Bold Industries Group, it is not just about the leaders we coach or the organizations we transform. It is about demonstrating that bold leadership can be taught, learned, and lived at any age, in any role, in any industry.

The world needs bold leaders. The world needs you. Now go lead boldly.

—Mayah Burgess

Bibliography

Chapter 1

Barrett, L.F. (2023). *Seven and a Half Lessons About the Brain*. Boston: Houghton Mifflin Harcourt.

Dajani, D.R. and Uddin, L.Q. (2015). Demystifying Cognitive Flexibility: Implications for Clinical and Developmental Neuroscience. *Trends in Neurosciences* 38 (9): 571–578.

Doidge, N. (2007). *The Brain That Changes Itself: Stories of Personal Triumph from the Frontiers of Brain Science*. New York: Viking.

Edmondson, A.C. (2011). *Teaming: How Organizations Learn, Innovate, and Compete in the Knowledge Economy*. San Francisco: Jossey-Bass.

Edmondson, A.C. (2023). *Right Kind of Wrong: The Science of Failing Well*. New York: Atria Books.

Eisenhardt, K.M. (1989). Making Fast Strategic Decisions in High-Velocity Environments. *Academy of Management Journal* 32 (3): 543–576.

Gärtner, A. and Singer, T. (2022). The Trainable Brain: How Contemplative Mental Training Reshapes the Structure and Function of the Social Brain. *Current Opinion in Psychology* 45: 101308.

Kahneman, D. (2011). *Thinking, Fast and Slow*. New York: Farrar, Straus and Giroux.

Kahneman, D. and Tversky, A. (1979). Prospect Theory: An Analysis of Decision under Risk. *Econometrica* 47 (2): 263–291.

Kashdan, T.B. and Rottenberg, J. (2010). Psychological Flexibility as a Fundamental Aspect of Health. *Clinical Psychology Review* 30 (7): 865–878.

Lieberman, M.D., Eisenberger, N.I., Crockett, M. et al. (2007). Putting Feelings into Words: Affect Labeling Disrupts Amygdala Activity. *Psychological Science* 18 (5): 421–428.

McKinsey & Company. "The Five Trademarks of Agile Organizations." 2019. https://www.mckinsey.com/business-functions/organization/our-insights/the-five-trademarks-of-agile-organizations (accessed 30 June 2025).

Samuelson, W. and Zeckhauser, R. (1988). Status Quo Bias in Decision Making. *Journal of Risk and Uncertainty* 1 (1): 7–59.

Schweizer, S. and Holmes, E.A. (2023). Harnessing Neuroplasticity to Build Psychological Resilience: From Basic Neuroscience to Clinical Application. *Nature Reviews Neuroscience* 24 (2): 77–91.

Shackman, A.J. and Gee, D.G. (2023). Salience Processing and Fear Learning: An Integrative Review and Emerging Framework. *Nature Reviews Neuroscience* 24 (5): 319–334.

Vohs, K.D., Baumeister, R.F., Schmeichel, B.J. et al. (2008). Making Choices Impairs Subsequent Self-Control: A Limited-Resource Account of Decision Making, Self-Regulation, and Active Initiative. *Journal of Personality and Social Psychology* 94 (5): 883–898.

Zeelenberg, M. (1999). Anticipated Regret, Expected Feedback and Behavioral Decision Making. *Journal of Behavioral Decision Making* 12 (2): 93–106.

Zenger, J. and Folkman, J. (2014). *The Inspiring Leader: Unlocking the Secrets of How Extraordinary Leaders Motivate*. New York: McGraw-Hill Education.

Chapter 2

Andrews-Hanna, J.R., Spreng, R.N., Dixon, J.R. et al. (2014). The Default Network and Self-Generated Thought: Component Processes, Dynamic Control, and Clinical Relevance. *Annals of the New York Academy of Sciences* 1316 (1): 29–52.

Barrett, L.F. (2023). *Seven and a Half Lessons About the Brain*. Boston: Houghton Mifflin Harcourt.

Christensen, C.M., Raynor, M.E., and McDonald, R. (2015). What Is Disruptive Innovation? *Harvard Business Review* 93 (12): 44–53.

Duhigg, C. (2012). *The Power of Habit: Why We Do What We Do in Life and Business*. New York: Random House.

Edmondson, A.C. (2023). *Right Kind of Wrong: The Science of Failing Well*. New York: Atria Books.

Friston, K. (2010). The Free-Energy Principle: A Unified Brain Theory? *Nature Reviews Neuroscience* 11 (2): 127–138.

Gallup. "State of the Global Workplace 2022 Report." 2022. https://www .gallup.com/workplace/349484/state-of-the-global-workplace-2022-report.aspx (accessed 30 June 2025).

Gino, F. and Staats, B.R. (2023). *Why Organizations Don't Learn*. Boston: Harvard Business School Publishing.

Kahn, W.A. (1990). Psychological Conditions of Personal Engagement and Disengagement at Work. *Academy of Management Journal* 33 (4): 692–724.

Levitt, B. and March, J.G. (1988). Organizational Learning. *Annual Review of Sociology* 14 (1): 319–340.

March, J.G. (1991). Exploration and Exploitation in Organizational Learning. *Organization Science* 2 (1): 71–87.

McEwen, B.S. and Morrison, J.H. (2013). The Brain on Stress: Vulnerability and Plasticity of the Prefrontal Cortex over the Life Course. *Neuron* 79 (1): 16–29.

Schwabe, L., Wiersma, M., and Wolf, O.T. (2022). Stress and Decision Making: A Critical Review. *Current Opinion in Behavioral Sciences* 45: 101149.

Chapter 3

Bourgoin, A., Wright, S.L., Harvey, J.-F., and Kouamé, S. (2024). "CEOs Often Feel Lonely. Here's How They Can Cope." *Harvard Business Review* (December 2024).

Beaty, R.E., Benedek, M., Barry Kaufman, S., and Silvia, P.J. (2015). "Default and Executive Network Coupling Supports Creative Idea Production." *Scientific Reports* 5 (1): 10964.

Caruso, C. "How the Brain Balances Risk and Reward in Making Decisions." *Harvard Medical School News*, February 19, 2025.

Cisek, P. and Kalaska, J.F. (2010). Neural Mechanisms for Interacting with a World Full of Action Choices. *Annual Review of Neuroscience* 33: 269–298.

Guitart-Masip, M., Dayan, P., Huys, Q.J.M., and Dolan, R.J. (2012). Go and No-Go Learning in Reward and Punishment: Interactions Between Affect and Effect. *NeuroImage* 62 (1): 154–166.

Howard, C. (2022). "Strategic Agility in Uncertain Times." *Harvard Business Review*.

Raisch, S. and Birkinshaw, J. (2008). Organizational Ambidexterity: Antecedents, Outcomes, and Moderators. *Journal of Management* 34 (3): 375–409.

Schweizer, S. and Holmes, E.A. (2023). Neuroplasticity and Resilience: New Insights for Psychological Science. *Psychological Science in the Public Interest* 24 (1): 1–42.

Seeley, W.W., Menon, V., Schatzberg, A.F. et al. (2007). Dissociable Intrinsic Connectivity Networks for Salience Processing and Executive Control. *Journal of Neuroscience* 27 (9): 2349–2356.

Shackman, A.J. and Gee, D.G. (2022). Salience Processing and Fear Learning: An Integrative Review and Emerging Framework. *Nature Reviews Neuroscience* 23 (5): 319–334.

Kauffman, S. (1993). *The Origins of Order: Self-Organization and Selection in Evolution*. Oxford: Oxford University Press.

Kauffman, S. (1995). *At Home in the Universe: The Search for the Laws of Self-Organization and Complexity*. New York: Oxford University Press.

McKinsey & Company. "The State of Organizations 2023: Ten Shifts Transforming Organizations." 2023. https://www.mckinsey.com/capabilities/people-and-organizational-performance/our-insights/the-state-of-organizations-2023 (accessed 30 June 2025).

Urban Land Institute. "The Power of Bold and Visionary Leadership." Accessed April 27, 2025. https://americas.uli.org/power-bold-visionary-leadership/ (accessed 30 June 2025).

Chapter 4

Bandura, A. (1997). *Self-Efficacy: The Exercise of Control*. New York: W. H. Freeman and Company.

Barrett, L.F. (2023). *Seven and a Half Lessons About the Brain*. Boston: Houghton Mifflin Harcourt.

Beaty, R.E., Seli, P., and Schacter, D.L. (2019). Cognitive Neuroscience of Creativity: A Critical Review. *NeuroImage* 190: 22–37.

Caruso, C. (2025). "How the Brain Balances Risk and Reward in Decision-Making." *Harvard Medical School News*, February 19, 2025.

Cisek, P. and Kalaska, J.F. (2010). Neural Mechanisms for Interacting with a World Full of Action Choices. *Annual Review of Neuroscience* 33: 269–298.

Doidge, N. (2007). *The Brain That Changes Itself: Stories of Personal Triumph from the Frontiers of Brain Science*. New York: Viking.

Edmondson, A.C. (2023). *Right Kind of Wrong: The Science of Failing Well*. New York: Atria Books.

Fast, N.J., Sivanathan, N., and Galinsky, A.D. (2012). Power and Overconfident Decision-Making. *Organizational Behavior and Human Decision Processes* 117 (2): 249–260.

Furby, L. (1991). Understanding the Psychology of Possession and Ownership: A Personal Memoir and an Appraisal of Our Progress. *Journal of Social Behavior and Personality* 6 (6): 457–463.

Gino, F. (2020). "Self-Efficacy and Adaptive Leadership." *Harvard Business Review*, May 2020.

Guitart-Masip, M., Dayan, P., Huys, Q.J.M., and Dolan, R.J. (2012). Go and No-Go Learning in Reward and Punishment: Interactions Between Affect and Effect. *NeuroImage* 62 (1): 154–166.

Kahneman, D. (2011). *Thinking, Fast and Slow*. New York: Farrar, Straus and Giroux.

Nickerson, R.S. (1998). Confirmation Bias: A Ubiquitous Phenomenon in Many Guises. *Review of General Psychology* 2 (2): 175–220.

Pierce, J.L., Kostova, T., and Dirks, K.T. (2001). Toward a Theory of Psychological Ownership in Organizations. *Academy of Management Review* 26 (2): 298–310.

Rotter, J.B. (1966). Generalized Expectancies for Internal Versus External Control of Reinforcement. *Psychological Monographs: General and Applied* 80 (1): 1–28.

Schwabe, L. and Wolf, O.T. (2013). Stress and Multiple Memory Systems: From 'Thinking' to 'Doing'. *Trends in Cognitive Sciences* 17 (2): 60–68.

Schwabe, L., Wiersma, M., and Wolf, O.T. (2022). Stress and Decision Making: A Critical Review. *Current Opinion in Behavioral Sciences* 45: 101149.

Schweizer, S. and Holmes, E.A. (2023). Harnessing Neuroplasticity to Build Psychological Resilience: From Basic Neuroscience to Clinical Application. *Nature Reviews Neuroscience* 24 (2): 77–91.

Sevgi, M., Molter, A.E.M., Vatinno, I.R. et al. (2020). Behavioral and Neural Correlates of Cognitive Control Over Social Decision-Making. *Social Cognitive and Affective Neuroscience* 15 (4): 417–427.

Chapter 5

O'Doherty, J.P., Hampton, A., and Kim, H. (2017). Model-Based fMRI and Its Application to Reward Learning and Decision-Making. *Annals of the New York Academy of Sciences* 1104 (1): 35–53.

Rock, D. and Schwartz, J. (2006). The Neuroscience of Leadership. *Strategy+Business* 43: 1–10.

Schwartz, J.M. and Begley, S. (2006). *The Mind and the Brain: Neuroplasticity and the Power of Mental Force*. New York: HarperCollins.

Steel, P. and König, C.J. (2006). Integrating Theories of Motivation. *Academy of Management Review* 31 (4): 889–913.

Chapter 6

Baumeister, R.F., Bratslavsky, E., Finkenauer, C., and Vohs, K.D. (2001). Bad Is Stronger Than Good. *Review of General Psychology* 5 (4): 323–370.

Brown, B. (2012). *Daring Greatly: How the Courage to Be Vulnerable Transforms the Way We Live, Love, Parent, and Lead*. New York: Gotham Books.

David, S. (2016). *Emotional Agility: Get Unstuck, Embrace Change, and Thrive in Work and Life*. New York: Avery.

Edmondson, A. (1999). Psychological Safety and Learning Behavior in Work Teams. *Administrative Science Quarterly* 44 (2): 350–383.

Emmons, R.A. and McCullough, M.E. (2003). Counting Blessings Versus Burdens: An Experimental Investigation of Gratitude and Subjective Well-Being in Daily Life. *Journal of Personality and Social Psychology* 84 (2): 377–389.

George, B. and Sims, P. (2007). *True North: Discover Your Authentic Leadership*. San Francisco: Jossey-Bass.

Heifetz, R.A. and Linsky, M. (2002). *Leadership on the Line: Staying Alive through the Dangers of Leading*. Boston: Harvard Business School Press.

Hoffman, B.G. and Icon, A. (2012). *Alan Mulally and the Fight to Save Ford Motor Company*. New York: Crown Business.

Isaacson, W. (2011). *Steve Jobs*. New York: Simon & Schuster.

Neff, K. (2011). *Self-Compassion: The Proven Power of Being Kind to Yourself*. New York: William Morrow.

Schultz, H. and Gordon, J. (2011). *Onward: How Starbucks Fought for Its Life without Losing Its Soul*. New York: Rodale.

Southwick, S.M. and Charney, D.S. (2012). *Resilience: The Science of Mastering Life's Greatest Challenges*. Cambridge: Cambridge University Press.

Stone, D. and Heen, S. (2014). *Thanks for the Feedback: The Science and Art of Receiving Feedback Well*. New York: Viking.

Tedeschi, R.G. and Calhoun, L.G. (2004). Posttraumatic Growth: Conceptual Foundations and Empirical Evidence. *Psychological Inquiry* 15 (1): 1–18.

Chapter 7

Amabile, T. and Kramer, S. (2011). *The Progress Principle: Using Small Wins to Ignite Joy, Engagement, and Creativity at Work*. Boston: Harvard Business Review Press.

Battilana, J. and Casciaro, T. (2020). The Catalyst Effect: The Impact of Transactional and Transformational Leadership on Innovation in Higher-Performance Organizational Cultures. *Journal of Management Studies* 57 (1): 1–27.

Behfar, K., Peterson, R., and Greer, L.L. (2019). How to Manage Relationship Conflict. *MIT Sloan Management Review* 61 (1): 47–52.

Bravely. (2023). *Workplace Health Index 2023*. Bravely Inc.

Brown, B. (2018). *Dare to Lead: Brave Work. Tough Conversations. Whole Hearts*. New York: Random House.

Bruneau, E.G. and Saxe, R. (2012). The Power of Being Heard: The Benefits of 'Perspective-Giving' in the Context of Intergroup Conflict. *Journal of Experimental Social Psychology* 48 (4): 855–866.

Buckingham, M. and Goodall, A. (2019). The Feedback Fallacy. *Harvard Business Review* 97 (2): 92–101.

Dreu, D. and Carsten, K.W. (2021). When Too Little or Too Much Hurts: Evidence for a Curvilinear Relationship Between Task Conflict and Innovation in Teams. *Journal of Management* 47 (7): 1964–1995.

Edmondson, A.C. (2019). *The Fearless Organization: Creating Psychological Safety in the Workplace for Learning, Innovation, and Growth*. Hoboken, NJ: John Wiley & Sons.

Eisenberger, N.I. and Lieberman, M.D. (2004). Why Rejection Hurts: A Common Neural Alarm System for Physical and Social Pain. *Trends in Cognitive Sciences* 8 (7): 294–300.

Kross, E. and Ayduk, Ö. (2017). Self-Distancing: Theory, Research, and Current Directions. *Advances in Experimental Social Psychology* 55: 81–136.

Stone, D. and Heen, S. (2014). *Thanks for the Feedback: The Science and Art of Receiving Feedback Well*. New York: Viking.

Weinberg, R.S. and Gould, D. (2007). *Foundations of Sport and Exercise Psychology*, 4e. Champaign, IL: Human Kinetics.

Chapter 8

Blenko, M.W., Mankins, M.C., and Rogers, P. (2010). The Decision-Driven Organization. *Harvard Business Review* 88 (6): 54–62.

Boin, A., Hart, P.'t., Stern, E., and Sundelius, B. (2016). *The Politics of Crisis Management: Public Leadership Under Pressure.* Cambridge: Cambridge University Press.

Bradley, C., Hirt, M., and Smit, S. (2018). *Strategy Beyond the Hockey Stick: People, Probabilities, and Big Moves to Beat the Odds.* Hoboken, NJ: Wiley.

Bryar, C. and Carr, B. (2021). *Working Backwards: Insights, Stories, and Secrets from Inside Amazon.* New York: St. Martin's Press.

Brynjolfsson, E., Hitt, L. and Kim, H. (2011). Strength in Numbers: How Does Data-Driven Decisionmaking Affect Firm Performance? *SSRN Electronic Journal.*

Dijksterhuis, A. and Nordgren, L.F. (2006). A Theory of Unconscious Thought. *Perspectives on Psychological Science* 1 (2): 95–109.

Edmondson, A.C. (2019). *The Fearless Organization: Creating Psychological Safety in the Workplace for Learning, Innovation, and Growth.* Hoboken, NJ: Wiley.

Ericsson, K.A. and Pool, R. (2016). *Peak: Secrets from the New Science of Expertise.* Boston: Houghton Mifflin Harcourt.

Fernández-Aráoz, C. (2014). 21st-Century Talent Spotting. *Harvard Business Review* 92 (6): 46–56.

Garton, E. and Mankins, M.C. (2017). *Time, Talent, Energy: Overcome Organizational Drag and Unleash Your Team's Productive Power.* Boston: Harvard Business Review Press.

Jamieson, J.P., Mendes, W.B., and Nock, M.K. (2013). Improving Acute Stress Responses: The Power of Reappraisal. *Current Directions in Psychological Science* 22 (1): 51–56.

Kahneman, D. and Klein, G. (2009). Conditions for Intuitive Expertise: A Failure to Disagree. *American Psychologist* 64 (6): 515–526.

Kahneman, D., Sibony, O., and Sunstein, C.R. (2021). *Noise: A Flaw in Human Judgment.* New York: Little, Brown Spark.

Keating, G. (2012). *Netflixed: The Epic Battle for America's Eyeballs.* New York: Portfolio.

Kim, W.C. and Mauborgne, R. (2015). *Blue Ocean Strategy: How to Create Uncontested Market Space and Make the Competition Irrelevant,* Expandede. Boston: Harvard Business Review Press.

Klein, G. (2007). *Sources of Power: How People Make Decisions*. Cambridge, MA: MIT Press.

Klein, G. (2013). *Seeing What Others Don't: The Remarkable Ways We Gain Insights*. New York: PublicAffairs.

Kuncel, N.R., Klieger, D.M., Connelly, B.S., and Ones, D.S. (2013). Mechanical versus Clinical Data Combination in Selection and Admissions Decisions: A Meta-Analysis. *Journal of Applied Psychology* 98 (6): 1060–1072.

McGrath, R.G. and MacMillan, I.C. (2009). *Discovery-Driven Growth: A Breakthrough Process to Reduce Risk and Seize Opportunity*. Boston: Harvard Business Review Press.

Nagji, B. and Tuff, G. (2012). Managing Your Innovation Portfolio. *Harvard Business Review* 90 (5): 66–74.

Nutt, P.C. (2002). *Why Decisions Fail: Avoiding the Blunders and Traps That Lead to Debacles*. San Francisco, CA: Berrett-Koehler Publishers.

Ries, E. (2011). *The Lean Startup: How Today's Entrepreneurs Use Continuous Innovation to Create Radically Successful Businesses*. New York: Crown Business.

Rivera, L.A. (2012). Hiring as Cultural Matching: The Case of Elite Professional Service Firms. *American Sociological Review* 77 (6): 999–1022.

Wilkinson, A. and Kupers, R. (2013). Living in the Futures: How Shell's Scenario Planning Approach Helps Leaders Navigate Uncertainty. *Harvard Business Review* 91 (5): 118–127.

Chapter 9

Amabile, T. and Kramer, S. (2011). *The Progress Principle: Using Small Wins to Ignite Joy, Engagement, and Creativity at Work*. Boston: Harvard Business Review Press.

ASTD (American Society for Training and Development) (2010). *The Power of Accountability*. ASTD Research Report. Alexandria, VA: American Society for Training and Development.

CCL (Center for Creative Leadership) (2018). *Leadership Development Impact Study*. Greensboro, NC: Center for Creative Leadership.

Cialdini, R.B. (2006). *Influence: The Psychology of Persuasion*. New York: Harper Business.

Clear, J. (2018). *Atomic Habits: An Easy & Proven Way to Build Good Habits & Break Bad Ones*. New York: Avery.

Cotterill, S. (2010). Pre-performance Routines in Sport: Current Understanding and Future Directions. *International Review of Sport and Exercise Psychology* 3 (2): 132–153.

Deci, E.L. and Ryan, R.M. (2012). Self-determination Theory. In *Handbook of Theories of Social Psychology*, edited by Paul A.M. Van Lange, Arie W. Kruglanski, and E. Tory Higgins, 416–437. Thousand Oaks, CA: Sage Publications.

Duhigg, C. (2012). *The Power of Habit: Why We Do What We Do in Life and Business*. New York: Random House.

Dweck, C.S. (2016). *Mindset: The New Psychology of Success*. New York: Ballantine Books.

Edmondson, A.C. (2019). *The Fearless Organization: Creating Psychological Safety in the Workplace for Learning, Innovation, and Growth*. Hoboken, NJ: John Wiley & Sons.

Ericsson, K.A. and Pool, R. (2016). *Peak: Secrets from the New Science of Expertise*. Boston: Houghton Mifflin Harcourt.

Fogg, B.J. (2020). *Tiny Habits: The Small Changes That Change Everything*. Boston: Houghton Mifflin Harcourt.

Gawande, A. (2009). *The Checklist Manifesto: How to Get Things Right*. New York: Metropolitan Books.

Gollwitzer, P.M. (1999). Implementation Intentions: Strong Effects of Simple Plans. *American Psychologist* 54 (7): 493–503.

Grant, Adam. "The Psychology of Your Future Self." Paper presented at TED2014, Vancouver, Canada, March 2014.

Harkin, B., Webb, T.L., Chang, B.P.I. et al. (2016). Does Monitoring Goal Progress Promote Goal Attainment? A Meta-analysis of the Experimental Evidence. *Psychological Bulletin* 142 (2): 198–229.

Heath, C. and Heath, D. (2010). *Switch: How to Change Things When Change Is Hard*. New York: Broadway Books.

Ibarra, H. (2019). *Act Like a Leader, Think Like a Leader*. Boston: Harvard Business Review Press.

Kaplan, R.E. and Kaiser, R.B. (2003). Developing Versatile Leadership. *MIT Sloan Management Review* 44 (4): 19–26.

295

Kegan, R. and Lahey, L.L. (2009). *Immunity to Change: How to Overcome It and Unlock the Potential in Yourself and Your Organization*. Boston: Harvard Business Press.

Kotter, J.P. (2014). *Accelerate: Building Strategic Agility for a Faster-Moving World*. Boston: Harvard Business Review Press.

McAdams, D.P. and McLean, K.C. (2013). Narrative Identity. *Current Directions in Psychological Science* 22 (3): 233–238.

Milkman, K.L., Beshears, J., Choi, J.J., et al. (2012). Following Through on Good Intentions: The Power of Planning Prompts. NBER Working Paper No. 17995. National Bureau of Economic Research, 2012.

Morgenroth, T., Ryan, M.K., and Peters, K. (2015). The Motivational Theory of Role Modeling: How Role Models Influence Role Aspirants' Goals. *Review of General Psychology* 19 (4): 465–483.

Mueller, J.S. (2017). *Creative Change: Why We Resist It. . . How We Can Embrace It*. Boston: Houghton Mifflin Harcourt.

Norcross, J.C. and Vangarelli, D.J. (1988). The Resolution Solution: Longitudinal Examination of New Year's Change Attempts. *Journal of Substance Abuse* 1 (2): 127–134.

Parker, P., Hall, D.T., and Kram, K.E. (2008). Peer Coaching: A Relational Process for Accelerating Career Learning. *Academy of Management Learning & Education* 7 (4): 487–503.

Sherman, D.K., Hartson, K.A., Binning, K.R. et al. (2013). Deflecting the Trajectory and Changing the Narrative: How Self-Affirmation Affects Academic Performance and Motivation Under Identity Threat. *Journal of Personality and Social Psychology* 104 (4): 591–618.

Chapter 10

Asch, S.E. (1956). Studies of Independence and Conformity: I. A Minority of One Against a Unanimous Majority. *Psychological Monographs: General and Applied* 70 (9): 1–70.

Avolio, B.J., Walumbwa, F.O., and Weber, T.J. (2009). Leadership: Current Theories, Research, and Future Directions. *Annual Review of Psychology* 60: 421–449.

Bandura, A. (1997). *Self-Efficacy: The Exercise of Control*. New York: W.H. Freeman and Company.

Baumeister, R.F., Vohs, K.D., and Tice, D.M. (2007). The Strength Model of Self-Control. *Current Directions in Psychological Science* 16 (6): 351–355.

Brown, B. (2018). *Dare to Lead: Brave Work. Tough Conversations. Whole Hearts*. New York: Random House.

Cialdini, R.B. (2006). *Influence: The Psychology of Persuasion*. New York: Harper Business.

Collins, J. (2001). *Good to Great: Why Some Companies Make the Leap. . . and Others Don't*. New York: HarperBusiness.

Dvir, T., Eden, D., Avolio, B.J., and Shamir, B. (2002). Impact of Transformational Leadership on Follower Development and Performance: A Field Experiment. *Academy of Management Journal* 45 (4): 735–744.

Dweck, C.S. (2016). *Mindset: The New Psychology of Success*. New York: Ballantine Books.

Edmondson, A.C. (2019). *The Fearless Organization: Creating Psychological Safety in the Workplace for Learning, Innovation, and Growth*. Hoboken, NJ: John Wiley & Sons.

Frankl, V.E. (1985). *Man's Search for Meaning*. New York: Washington Square Press.

Grant, A.M. (2013). Leading with Meaning: Beneficiary Contact, Prosocial Impact, and the Performance Effects of Transformational Leadership. *Academy of Management Journal* 55 (2): 458–476.

Ibarra, H. (2015). The Authenticity Paradox. *Harvard Business Review* 93 (1/2): 52–59.

Judge, T.A., Erez, A., Bono, J.E., and Thoresen, C.J. (2002). Are Measures of Self-Esteem, Neuroticism, Locus of Control, and Generalized Self-Efficacy Indicators of a Common Core Construct? *Journal of Personality and Social Psychology* 83 (3): 693–710.

Kahneman, D. and Tversky, A. (1979). Prospect Theory: An Analysis of Decision Under Risk. *Econometrica* 47 (2): 263–291.

Kegan, R. and Lahey, L.L. (2009). *Immunity to Change: How to Overcome It and Unlock the Potential in Yourself and Your Organization*. Boston: Harvard Business Press.

297

Bibliography

Kernis, M.H. and Goldman, B.M. (2006). A Multicomponent Conceptualization of Authenticity: Theory and Research. *Advances in Experimental Social Psychology* 38: 283–357.

Kotter, J.P. (2001). What Leaders Really Do. *Harvard Business Review* 79 (11): 85–96.

Kouzes, J.M. and Posner, B.Z. (2016). *Learning Leadership: The Five Fundamentals of Becoming an Exemplary Leader.* San Francisco: The Leadership Challenge.

Lieberman, M.D. (2009). The Brain's Braking System (and How to 'Use Your Words' to Tap Into It). *NeuroLeadership Journal* 2: 9–14.

Loehr, J. and Schwartz, T. (2003). *The Power of Full Engagement: Managing Energy, Not Time, Is the Key to High Performance and Personal Renewal.* New York: Free Press.

Nemeth, C.J. and Goncalo, J.A. (2004). Creative Collaborations From Afar: The Benefits of Independent Authors. *Creativity Research Journal* 16 (1): 1–8.

Rock, D. (2008). SCARF: A Brain-Based Model for Collaborating with and Influencing Others. *NeuroLeadership Journal* 1 (1): 44–52.

Ryan, R.M. and Deci, E.L. (2000). Self-Determination Theory and the Facilitation of Intrinsic Motivation, Social Development, and Well-Being. *American Psychologist* 55 (1): 68–78.

Schein, E.H. (2016). *Organizational Culture and Leadership,* 5e. Hoboken, NJ: Wiley.

Thaler, R.H. and Sunstein, C.R. (2008). *Nudge: Improving Decisions About Health, Wealth, and Happiness.* New Haven, CT: Yale University Press.

Walumbwa, F.O., Avolio, B.J., Gardner, W.L. et al. (2008). Authentic Leadership: Development and Validation of a Theory-Based Measure. *Journal of Management* 34 (1): 89–126.

Acknowledgments

Writing *The BOLD Leader* was another powerful journey of growth, reflection, and gratitude and it would have never been possible alone.

My deepest thanks goes to my incredible family, my mom, dad, sisters, and brother, whose unwavering support continues to give me strength, joy, and the courage to keep making bold moves.

To my daughter, thank you for believing fiercely in our vision and walking boldly alongside me every single day. Your strength, kindness, love, and heart make everything we create together extraordinary. I am endlessly proud and grateful to share this bold journey with you.

To my husband, whose love, patience, and unwavering belief in me has supported every bold step I've taken since we met. Your love, encouragement, and kindness inspire me daily and I would not be who I am without you. You make every adventure better and every challenge easier.

And to our four living and goofy dogs, thank you for your daily reminders to stay present and grounded. Your unconditional love and playful chaos have made the journey filled with fun.

I owe heartfelt gratitude to an original bold leader and mentor in my life, Julie Hanser, whose wisdom and generosity profoundly shaped my leadership from my days as a graduate student at Xavier University and administrative fellow at Mercy Healthcare Partners.

Although Julie is no longer with us, her bold spirit and compassionate guidance remain a lasting influence in my life and her bold legacy lives on.

To all the inspiring leaders I worked with at Duke University, especially Dr. Christopher Willett, Carolyn Carpenter, and Tracy Gosselin, thank you for challenging me, sharpening my perspective, and teaching me what it truly means to lead boldly. Your mentorship and friendship has been instrumental in shaping my approach to growth and my evolution as a leader, and I'm forever appreciative.

To the incredible Bold Leaders Collective and the community of women leaders that I have the privilege to be with every day, your resilience, vulnerability, and fierce commitment to being bold have profoundly impacted this book and my life.

To Cassandra Worthy for writing the powerful Foreword to this book. Cassandra, your energy, insight, and authenticity deeply inspire me, and I'm honored to have your bold voice introduce these pages.

To my Wiley publishing and editorial team, thank you for your dedication and thoughtful insight. Your belief in this book pushed me to deepen my thinking and sharpen my voice. This work is stronger because of your partnership.

Finally, to every reader who has picked up this book and chosen boldness, I'm honored to share this journey with you. Your courage inspires me daily, and your commitment to growth and authenticity reminds me why this work matters.

Thank you for being part of this bold adventure. May you continue to step forward boldly, always.

About the Author

Leigh Burgess is a visionary leader, dynamic connector, and catalyst for change, dedicated to empowering others to step into their boldness and see all the possibilities in life through the lens of self-belief. After over 20 years in the corporate world, she launched Bold Industries Group, a platform that's redefining what it means to live and lead with purpose.

Through her Bold events, the Bold Leaders Collective community, the Bold Lounge Podcast and her impactful speaking and coaching, Leigh inspires changemakers to elevate, lead, and live their boldest and best life. Her signature B.O.L.D. Framework, Believe–Own–Learn–Design, combines mindset, strategy, and wellness into a powerful guide for living boldly.

Along with this book, her national best-selling first book, *Be BOLD Today: Unleash Your Potential, Master Your Mindset and Achieve Success*, is your go-to guide through the framework to unlock your potential, strengthen your mindset, and take intentional steps toward your biggest dreams.

Leigh contributes regularly to Forbes, Fast Company, and Entrepreneur. She was also honored as a one of SUCCESS Magazine's 50 Women of Influence and one of their Top 25 Changemakers.

You can learn more and connect with Leigh at leighburgess.com.

Index

Page numbers followed by *f* and *t* refer to figures and tables, respectively.

experiencing, 3–6
hidden, 1
metrics for, 45
as your ally, 8–10
Fear vs. Discomfort Matrix,
52–54, 53f
Federal Express
(FedEx), 5, 32–33
Feedback, 15, 36, 106
helpful vs. unhelpful, 157–158
loops, 72
and sustainability, 235
Feedback Resistance, 133
Financial commitment, 135
First leadership frontier, 19–21
Follow-up plans, 179
Forward focus, 224
Forward motion, 23–25, 179–181
Foundational orientation,
circumstantial
vs., 257–258
Frame It (in Fuel
Formula), 25, 29
Framing, empathetic, 177
Fuel Formula, 23–30, 25f,
33–34, 39–40, 54
Fuel It (in Fuel Formula), 28–29

Gaps, performance
conversations
addressing, 182–183

Goals, 118, 123
Growth:
in Bold Leadership Triangle,
75–77
conversations as catalyst
of, 174
performance conversations
addressing, 182–183
Growth mindset, 17, 18

Habit loops, 47, 55
Hard talks, 15
Hesitation, 23, 36
cost of, 21–23
voice, 99
Hidden fears, 1
High-leverage actions,
identifying, 122
Hiring decisions, 210–212

Ideas, bold, 16
Identity, courage as, 271–272
Identity affirmations, bold,
244–245
Identity-based boldness, 244–245
Identity commitment, 135
Identity narratives, bold, 244
Identity Reinforcement, 128
Impact and Integration (Phase 3
of D90 Method), 130–131
Indecision, 33, 37–39

309

Index

310

311

Index

313